THE EUROPEAN CURRENCY CRISIS

THE EUROPEAN CURRENCY CRISIS

What Chance Now for a Single European Currency?

Paul Temperton, Editor
The Independent Economic Research Company (TIER)

Probus Publishing Company

Cambridge, England
Chicago, Illinois

First published in 1993 by
Probus Europe, Sheraton House, Castle Park, Cambridge CB3 0AX, England

This publication is designed to provide accurate and authoritative information in regard to the subject matter covered. It is sold with the understanding that the publisher is not engaged in rendering legal, accounting or other professional service.

Designed, illustrated and typeset by Nick Battley, London, England

ISBN 1 55738 560 2

Produced in association with Book Production Consultants Plc
25–27 High Street, Chesterton, Cambridge CB1 2LE, England

Printed in the United Kingdom by
St Edmundsbury Press Ltd, Bury St Edmunds,

For Emily

Contents

PART III: Central bank independence and a single currency — necessity, hindrance, or alternative?

Part IV: Perspectives on the crisis — ERM member countries

PART V: Perspectives on the crisis — European countries with floating-exchange rates

APPENDIX 1

APPENDIX 2

Preface

In book publishing, as in plans for European monetary union, fixed timetables create problems. The original deadline for contributions to this book was the end of June 1993, a deadline with which most contributors happily complied. The events of late-July and early-August, however, when Europe was plunged into yet another currency crisis — or, more accurately, a new intensification of the currency crisis which had continued since the summer of 1992 — meant that completion of the book had to be delayed in order to give all contributors a chance of amending their chapters. Despite this, the book is still being published, as intended, on the first anniversary of Black Wednesday, 16 September 1992, when sterling and the lira were forced to leave the ERM. It remains to be seen whether the events of July/August 1993 will leave the timetable for Emu intact — but that is the very subject matter of the book.

The original idea for the book came from the indefatigable honorary life member of the EFFAS-European Bond Commission, Stuart McLean. The Commission published the fifth edition of its highly-popular book — *The European Bond Markets* — as the ERM crisis started to break, and it was Stuart's idea to have a companion book which focused on the turbulence in the currency markets.

One important theme which runs through the book is the conflict between central banks and the market: indeed, 'Central Banks vs. the Markets' was, at one time, considered as a title. The conflict has manifested itself most publicly in the frustrated attempts by central banks, with limited foreign exchange reserves, to act against massive international capital flows. The resolve and determination of some central banks has been harder to beat than that of others, but all — with the exception of the Dutch central bank — have finally succumbed to the force of the market.

As this book goes to print, this triumph of the free market is being widely celebrated. The 'temporary' move to wider ERM bands, it is claimed, will not prove to be temporary at all, but instead will mark the move to floating-exchange rates. This will permit significantly lower interest rates in countries which are no longer constrained by the Bundesbank, economic growth will be boosted, unemployment will fall, and this will all happen without a rise in inflation. Such events may come to pass, but three notes of caution are warranted. First, even with wider bands, most countries do not seem set on cutting interest rates sharply, and are still aiming to maintain a close exchange rate, and interest rate, link with Germany; second, fiscal policy remains tight across Europe, hampering any recovery; third, there remain serious structural impediments to growth and employment creation which (if the single market is jeopardized) could be exacerbated by the demise of the ERM.

Many thanks must go to all the contributors to the book who, as mentioned above, met the original deadline as well as finding time to update their chapters at a late stage to reflect the events of late-July and early-August 1993. It is regretted that the Banque de France could not provide a contribution which reflected the recent change in circumstances.

London, 11 August 1993   *Paul Temperton*

PART I

*The European exchange rate mechanism
— dead or alive?*

Chapter 1

Introduction

Paul Temperton, Editor
The Independent Economic Research Company

The European currency crisis has now continued, with varying intensity, for over a year. The events of September 1992 — when the UK, Italy and Finland were forced to float their currencies and Spain to devalue the peseta — proved to be the antecedents to a series of currency devaluations and flotations. Most recently, all ERM currencies apart from the Dutch guilder have adopted wider bands of fluctuation, a move which is officially described as 'temporary'. Many, however, see it as little short of a generalized floating-exchange rate system. Given that the move to European monetary union (Emu) set out in the Maastricht Treaty was based on ever-closer exchange rate linkages between European currencies, plans for a European single currency by the end of the century have been dealt a severe — some might say a fatal — blow.

It is difficult to make sense of the kaleidoscope of events that make up the crisis when they are viewed in purely chronological terms. It is, therefore, the aim of this introductory chapter to draw out the key themes which run through the recent problems and assess the extent to which they still remain a cause for concern. We highlight problems which are specific to Europe, but the discussion raises much broader issues: the relationship between central banks (and governments) and markets in an increasingly liberated financial world; the suitability of Europe for a fixed-exchange rate system and a single currency; the uneasy balance between political priorities and economic forces; and the extent to which the current European recession and the high level of unemployment have been exacerbated by the policies which have been pursued.

Before turning to these broader issues, we start by discussing the economic and policy background to the European currency crisis, highlighting four issues:

- the effects of German reunification;

- the use of exchange rate linkages as economic virility symbols. This manifested itself both in the growing number of countries forging links to the Deutschemark or the Ecu, as well as an increased unwillingness to change exchange rate parities;

- the growing tension between the needs of a country's domestic economy and those dictated by exchange rate policy; and

- the aberrant operation of the ERM — the 'Walters critique' — which has led to inappropriate economic policies being pursued in some countries.

Superimposed on this background, from mid-1992 onwards, was growing uncertainty about the viability of the Maastricht Treaty. There were recurrent doubts about whether it would be ratified; more fundamentally, about whether it made sense for Europe to enter into greater economic, monetary and political union; and, if it did, whether the Maastricht Treaty provided an appropriate blueprint for such a move.

The proximate cause of each of the changes in the ERM since September 1992, however, has been the sheer scale of international capital flows which have resulted once confidence in the ability of a country to maintain its exchange rate parity was lost. We discuss this issue before returning to an assessment of whether the fundamental economic problems behind the crisis remain a cause for concern and, finally, assessing some of the broader issues which have been raised.

Throughout this first chapter generous cross-referencing to the other contributions is made in order to provide something of a road map for the rest of the book.

The effects of German reunification

The rumblings of the ERM crisis were first felt in 1990, when Europe faced the effects of German reunification. Following the fall of the Berlin Wall in November 1989, Chancellor Kohl pressed for quick monetary union between East and West Germany, which took place on 1 July 1990, just three months before the final dissolution of East Germany on Unification Day, 3 October 1990. German reunification certainly falls into the category of events which economists refer to as 'shocks': a major external event, which could be expected to destabilize the ERM.

The ERM had been hit by shocks before. Indeed, it was launched in the midst of the second oil shock in 1979. At that time the sharp rise in oil prices produced differing inflationary effects throughout the ERM member countries and frequent realignments were used to offset the loss of price competitiveness which would have resulted from sticking with unchanged exchange rate parities. The initial few years of the ERM's life were particularly turbulent: between 1979 and 1983 there was a realignment of the ERM, on average, once every eight months.

Initially, however, German reunification seemed to pose no threat of such a shock to the ERM. Certainly the event was a *political* shock, the first case of planned economy being absorbed into a capitalist economy, but the economic effects, at least initially, were unclear. Chancellor Kohl and his finance minister, Waigel, expected the costs of reunification to be relatively easily absorbed and during 1990 they repeatedly asserted that no tax increases would be needed to pay for reunification (Marsh, 1992). Reunification, they argued, would boost west German growth, hence raising government tax revenues, and would, therefore, be 'self-financing'. This boost to German growth was not expected to be inflationary as the east German economy was expected to provide a cheap source of labour — simultaneously reducing capacity constraints in west German industry and putting downward pressure on west German wages.

Events developed in a rather different manner. The terms of the monetary union between east and west Germany — when a (limited number) of east German marks were converted into Deutschemarks at a 1:1 exchange rate and the average exchange rate amounted to 1.8 east German marks per Deutschemark — meant that east Germany was immediately put at a wage cost disadvantage. At such an exchange rate east German wages were almost one half the level of west German wages; but the level of productivity in east Germany was one quarter the west German level[1]. The loss of competitiveness which resulted could have been corrected if east German wages had fallen but in fact quite the opposite happened, with west German unions pushing for substantial wage increases in the east. Comments by Chancellor Kohl, to the effect that east Germans could quickly attain the same living standards as their west German counterparts, fuelled the push for wage equality. In Margaret Thatcher style, east German workers priced themselves out of work and unemployment rose sharply. By 1991, almost half of east German workers were either unemployed or on short-time working. Thus, far from being the cheap source of labour for west Ger-

---

[1] *In the third quarter of 1990, east German wages were 39 per cent of the west German level; productivity, as measured by GDP per employee, was 26 per cent of the west German level. By the first quarter of 1993, productivity in the east was 42 per cent of the west German level, but wages had risen to 70 per cent of the level in the west.*

many, east Germany quickly turned into a massive drain on German government finances. In 1991 and 1992, 16m east Germans were subsidized in
various ways by the west German government, costing around Dm 150bn
per year.

An initial boost to west German growth did occur (see Figure 1.1) —
particularly in the construction sector — but this did not provide enough of
a boost to tax revenues to compensate for the high transfer payments to the
east. The size of the government budget deficit rose alarmingly, despite the
tax increases which were announced in 1991 (see Figure 1.2).

Most damaging of all as far as the Bundesbank was concerned, the inflationary consequences were not, as hoped, benign. Inflationary pressures
were quick to emerge in certain sectors of the economy — most markedly
in housing, as the number of east Germans moving west added demand in
an economy already up against capacity constraints — and the overall inflation rate rose steadily from 3.1 per cent at the time the Berlin Wall fell to a
peak of 4.8 per cent in March 1992 (see Figure 1.3).

The Bundesbank reacted to the potent inflationary brew of strong economic growth, the surge in the government's budget deficit and the increase in monetary growth (see Figure 1.4), by continuing to increase the
level of German short-term interest rates (see Figure 1.5).

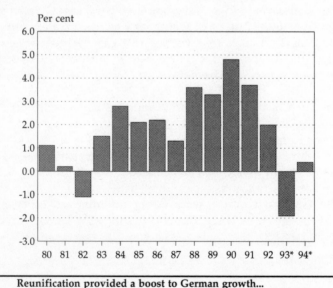

Figure 1.1   Reunification provided a boost to German growth...
* 93 & 94 figures are estimated by The Independent Economic Research Company (TIER)

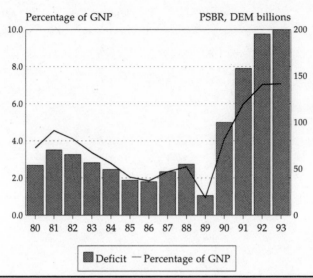

Figure 1.2   ...but this was not enough to prevent a sharp rise in the budget deficit

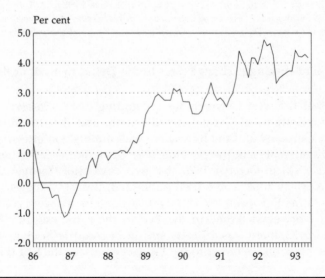

Figure 1.3   Reunification pressures led to a rise in German inflation...
Source: Datastream

	Target (%)	Outturn (%)	Target met?
1975	8	10	no
1976	8	9	no
1977	8	9	no
1978	8	11	no
1979	6-9	6	yes
1980	5-8	5	yes
1981	4-7	4	yes
1982	4-7	6	yes
1983	4-7	7	yes
1984	4-6	5	yes
1985	3-5	5	yes
1986	3.5-5.5	8	no
1987	3-6	8	no
1988	3-6	7	no
1989	about 5	5	yes
1990	4-6	6	yes
1991	3-5	5.2	no
1992	3-5	9	no
1993	4.5-6.5	7 (June)	no

Figure 1.4   ...and boosted German monetary growth

Note: Targets were for the central bank money stock up to 1988; from 1988, for M3. Target was set on a fourth quarter to fourth quarter basis for all years except 1975 (December to December) and for 1976-78 (average growth in the year). The 1992 target was originally set at 4-6%, but was reduced mid-year.

The fashion of linking exchange rates to the Deutschemark or the Ecu

To imply that the west Germans were deluding just themselves about the cost and implications of German reunification, and that the future consequences for Germany and the ERM were well understood elsewhere, would be to totally misrepresent the position. The UK took the important decision to enter the ERM in October 1990, just two days after German Unification Day; and Norway took a less well-publicized, but nevertheless important decision as far as European exchange rate arrangements were concerned, by linking the Norwegian krone to the Ecu in the same month[1]. From June 1989 to mid-1992, there was a steady stream of countries seeking to link the value of their currencies either to the Deutschemark or the Ecu (Figure 1.6).

---

[1] *See Chapters 20 and 22, respectively.*

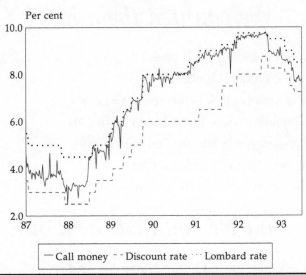

Figure 1.5   The Bundesbank reacted by ratcheting up interest rates
Source: Datastream

Even if developments in the German economy had been foreseen accurately, it is arguable that this move to pegging of exchange rates would still have taken place. German reunification came at the same time as plans for further monetary and political union in Europe were being hammered out. The Delors Report setting out a three stage move to European monetary union was published in June 1989; at the Rome summit in October 1990 all EC countries except the UK agreed to start the second stage — involving the establishment of the embryonic European Central Bank and ever tighter exchange rate links — in January 1994; and the Maastricht Treaty, building on those proposals, was agreed in December 1991.

Throughout the early-1990s, linking one's currency to the Deutschemark or the Ecu, either inside or outside the confines of the ERM, became one of the clearest ways of a country expressing its pro-Europe tendencies. To be sure, there was still an economic rationale — in that linking one's currency to that of a low-inflation country would act as a counter-inflationary discipline in restraining inflation — but this seemed secondary in most cases[1].

---

[1] *See, for example, the discussion in Chapters 19 and 20 on Finland and Norway.*

We counted them in...

- Spain joins the ERM in June 1989
- UK joins the ERM in October 1990
- Norway announces link to the Ecu in October 1990
- Sweden announces link to the Ecu in April 1991
- Finland announces link to the Ecu in June 1991
- Portugal joins the ERM in April 1992
- Cyprus announces link to the Ecu in June 1992

...and we counted them out.

- Finland devalues the markka in November 1991
- Finland floats the markka on 8 September 1992
- Italy devalues the lira on 13 September 1992
- UK withdraws from the ERM on 16 September 1992
- Italy suspends intervention agreement in the ERM on 16 September 1992
- Spain devalues the peseta by 5% on 16 September 1992
- Sweden floats the krona on 19 November 1992
- Spain and Portugal devalue by 6% on 22 November 1992
- Norway floats the krone on 10 December 1992
- Ireland devalues the punt by 10% on 30 January 1993
- Spain devalues the peseta by 8% on 13 May 1993
- Portugal devalues the escudo by 6.5% on 13 May 1993
- All ERM currencies move to fluctuation bands of +/- 15% around unchanged central rates. Separate bilateral agreement between Germany & Netherlands to maintain +/- 2 1/4% bands on 2 August 1993

Figure 1.6   We counted them in...and we counted them out

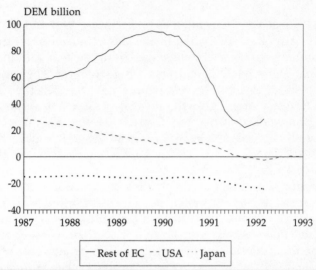

Figure 1.7   Germany's trade surplus shrank as a result of reunification
Source: Datastream

	Inflation from Q1 1987 to Q2 1992 based on:-					Implied revaluation (+) or devaluation (-) against the Ecu (%)
	CPI	WPI	Export prices	Unit wage costs	Average	
Deutschemark	15.0	11.0	4.8	15.4	11.5	1.7
Dutch guilder	12.3	5.0	10.1	2.7	7.5	5.7
Belgian franc	15.3	8.8	6.4	-1.1	7.3	5.9
French franc	18.2	8.0	12.9	9.2	12.1	1.2
Italian lira	35.0	22.6	33.2	31.8	30.7	-17.4
Danish krone	19.8	n/a	n/a	n/a	19.8	-6.6
Irish punt	18.2	n/a	n/a	n/a	18.2	-4.9
Spanish peseta[1]	17.6	2.6	5.1	10.2	8.9	-0.9
British pound[1]	6.6	3.7	5.4	3.1	4.7	-0.8

[1] *Inflation since ERM membership in each case with the implied revaluation based on the Ecu weighted average inflation since membership*

Figure 1.8   The outline of a realignment based on relative inflation trends

There was an increasing unwillingness to change existing ERM parities...

Furthermore, German reunification did not, during 1991 and the first half of 1992, lead to any great pressures in the ERM. Indeed, the Deutschemark was often amongst the weakest currencies in the system with the higher-interest-bearing, higher-yielding currencies the strongest. The rest of Europe, during this period, benefited in two main ways from developments in Germany. First, the still strong growth rate of west Germany sucked in imports from other European countries and diverted German resources to satisfying domestic demand. As a result, exports from other European countries to Germany rose sharply and Germany's trade surplus shrank (Figure 1.7). Second, interest rate differentials between the rest of Europe and Germany were narrowing. Credibility in the plan for European monetary union, both before and in the few months after the agreement of the Maastricht Treaty, was strong; there had been no ERM realignment since 1987; and liberalization of capital flows throughout Europe was progressing faster than laid down by the timetable for the move to monetary union. These factors, coupled with Germany's apparent problems, enabled other European countries to avoid following the full extent of the increase in German interest rates.

...although inflation differentials suggested the need for a lira devaluation...

ERM realignments, especially in the early years of the system, had been based to a large extent on inflation differentials. With lower and more convergent inflation rates in the late-1980s, however, the case for a realignment on this ground became less strong. Indeed, in the early-1990s such calculations gave no firm indication of the need for any country to realign, with the one exception of the Italian lira.

There is no uniquely correct inflation measure to use in such calculations: consumer prices (CPI) are important as a domestic indicator of inflationary pressures, but wholesale prices (WPI), export prices or unit wage costs all provide better indicators of the trend in industrial competitiveness. In Figure 1.8 the average of these four measures of inflation is calculated between January 1987 — the time of the last realignment of the ERM — until the second quarter of 1992. For each country their performance can then be measured against the average inflation rate based on the weights of currencies in the Ecu. This then gives the implied revaluation or devaluation of each currency against the Ecu which is needed to offset cumulative inflation.

As far as Italy was concerned, such calculations implied the need for a 17.4 per cent devaluation against the Ecu in order to restore lost price competitiveness. For the other countries, relatively small adjustments were indi-

	Italy	ERM average
1979-1983		
Average cumulated inflation differential (%) vs. Germany between devaluations	9.8	5.9
Average devaluation (%) vs. Deutschemark	6.3	5.3
Proportion of inflation differential offset by devaluation (%)	64.4	89.7
1984-1987		
Average cumulated inflation differential (%) vs. Germany between devaluations	9.3	7.3
Average devaluation (%) vs. Deutschemark	4.7	3.8
Proportion of inflation differential offset by devaluation (%)	50.7	52.1

Figure 1.9   Italy's history of offsetting inflation differentials with lira devaluation

cated. Even in Italy's case, however, there were two arguments indicating that a devaluation need not be so large.

First, the history of the ERM since inception is one of only partial adjustment for such inflation differentials. In Figure 1.9 we show that in the early years of the ERM, ERM members offset typically less than 90 per cent of the cumulative inflation differential when realignments took place. Italy offset rather less than that (64 per cent). In the mid-1980s, the proportions were typically 50 per cent. Such partial offsetting of cumulative inflation was, indeed, one of the main channels through which the ERM was supposed to bring lower inflation: it ensured that manufacturers' margins were squeezed, putting pressure on them to restrain domestic costs, mainly through wage restraint.

Second, Italy's trade balance was not, at least on the surface, cause for concern (Figure 1.10). The trade deficit had shown no trend deterioration since the 1987 realignment. Of course, with the boost to other countries' European exports as a result of German reunification, Italy should have been doing considerably better than that: France, for example, had moved into healthy trade surplus (Figure 1.11). The comparison between the trend in costs and prices in the two countries shows the extent to which Italy's loss of competitiveness was starting to tell (Figure 1.12).

If the two 'fundamental' economic arguments did not provide a strong case for a lira devaluation, the final factor in persuading the Italian authorities to hold the line and not devalue was that this would have undermined the credibility of counter-inflation policy. We return to this issue later.

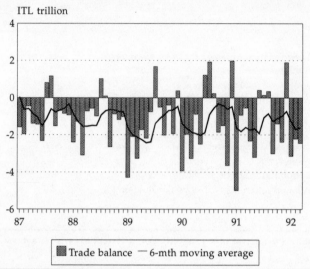

ITL trillion

Figure 1.10   Italy's trade balance
Source: Datastream

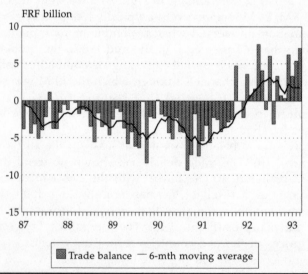

FRF billion

Figure 1.11   France's trade balance
Source: Datastream

Cumulative inflation differentials since the last realignment are a good guide to the necessary adjustment of a currency's parity if the question is merely one of offsetting an accumulated inflation differential. There is a more fundamental question of the extent to which the entry-level to the system was right in the first place, an issue which is all the more important for recent entrants. In the case of both the peseta and sterling there had been, since entry to the system, doubts about the suitability of their central rates.

...and work on equilibrium exchange rates suggested sterling had entered the ERM at the wrong rate

Perhaps the most influential estimate of sterling's appropriate rate was made by John Williamson (1991). He estimated that sterling's 'fundamental equilibrium exchange rate' (FEER) was Dm 2.24/£ (see Figure 1.13). The fundamental equilibrium exchange rate is that which is expected to generate a current account surplus or deficit equal to the underlying capital flow over the course of the economic cycle, given that the country is pursuing 'internal balance' — broadly defined as an acceptably low unemployment rate (see Williamson (1985)). Some explanation for the low estimate of sterling's FEER rate lies in the fact that the Deutschemark was estimated to have been overvalued against all currencies by around 10 per cent at the time the estimates were made (late 1991). Correcting for that, however, would still have suggested a rate of around Dm 2.50/£, well below sterling's Dm 2.95/£ central ERM rate.

The Bundesbank's criticism of sterling's exchange rate was more down to earth. They thought that any country which was running a substantial current account deficit in the midst of one of its worst post-war recessions must have an overvalued exchange rate. With the current account deficit at £12bn (2 per cent of GDP) in 1992, something was, they could argue, clearly wrong.

FEER estimates for the peseta are not available, although there was similar, quite widespread concern, about the level of the peseta. Dornbusch (1990) referred to the peseta as 'frivolously overvalued' in late-1990, with a real exchange rate index of 120 compared with 100 in 1980-82, and 77 in 1970.

Establishing or maintaining 'credibility' was policy makers' main reason for not realigning

Arguments for a realignment based on economic 'fundamentals' such as inflation differentials and trade performance had become progressively less important during the late-1980s and early-1990s. Establishing the 'credibil-

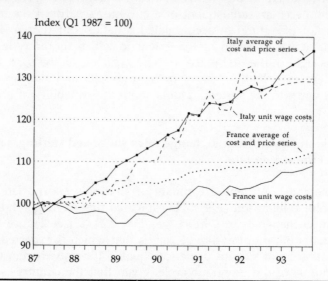

Figure 1.12   Italian & French cost and price measures

	Deutschemark	French franc	British pound
French franc *ERM central rate*	3.35		
FEER rate	3.98		
British pound *ERM central rate*	2.95	9.89	
FEER rate	2.24	8.92	
Italian lira *ERM central rate*	747	223	2207
FEER rate	902	227	2022

Figure 1.13   Estimates of Fundamental Equilibrium Exchange Rates (FEERs) and ERM central rates (pre-September 1992)
Source: Williamson (1991)

ity' of counter-inflationary policies became of utmost importance to European policy-makers. An unchanged exchange rate parity in the ERM was a vital element of establishing and maintaining that credibility, and France's *franc fort* policy was the shining example.

After the 1987 devaluation of the French franc in the ERM the 'cohabitation' government — then, as now, between the (Socialist) President Mitterrand and a (Conservative-controlled) National Assembly — embarked on a policy of not devaluing the franc against the Deutschemark. This became the main plank of economic — and indeed foreign — policy and the central exchange rate against the Deutschemark in the ERM has been unchanged since then at FFr 3.35/D-mark. When the policy was first introduced, French consumer price inflation was 3 per cent higher than in Germany, but the inflation differential fell steadily, with the rate falling below the German rate in June 1991. Short and long-term interest rate differentials with Germany also fell steadily from 1986 onwards but, as is discussed in detail later, failed to fall below the German level on a permanent basis. (The success of the *franc fort* policy is shown in Figures 1.14 to 1.17.).

Once the ERM had proved successful as a tool for reducing inflation...

For many other countries, apart from France, the main purpose of the ERM in the mid- to late-1980s was to help reduce inflation to the German level. Germany, with its history of low inflation acted as the 'anchor currency' for the system. Such policies enjoyed a marked degree of success and inflation rates in many ERM member countries were successfully reduced during this period. Of course, this could be just coincidence and have little to do with the ERM — the relatively slow growth in Europe during the period combined with the sharp fall in oil prices in 1986 could explain the improvement. The body of evidence, however, is against such a conclusion[1].

By the early-1990s the ERM was proving to be too successful in this counter-inflationary respect. The inflation rate in Denmark fell below that in Germany in July 1990; the Belgian rate dropped below in July 1991; the French rate fell below the German rate in June 1991; and the inflation rate in the Netherlands was consistently below the German rate for most of the late-1980s, a situation that was maintained (with the exception of 1991) during the 1990s. Moreover, this was not a transitory phenomenon: in general, inflation rates continued to fall further below the German rate in 1991-1993.

It was this success which led to the first problems in the ERM almost a year before the September 1992 crisis.

...conflicts between domestic requirements and those of the ERM were quick to surface

With the French inflation rate having fallen to below the German rate in June 1991, economic growth slowing as the boost from German reunification

---

[1] *The Bank of England in its review of the literature on the ERM concluded that "..empirical evidence that the ERM has stabilized bilateral exchange rates between members and that the system has contributed actively to the process of inflation convergence among ERM countries is relatively clear cut" (Bank of England 1991).*

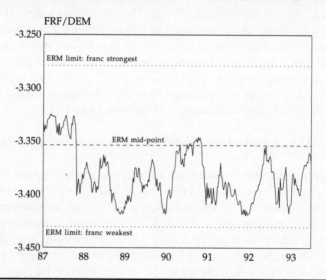

Figure 1.14   French franc / Deutschemark exchange rate and bands
Source: Datastream

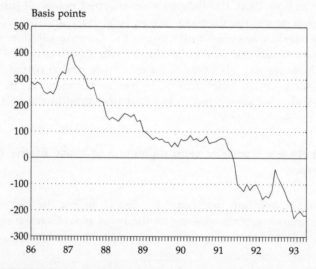

Figure 1.15   French–German inflation differential
Source: Datastream

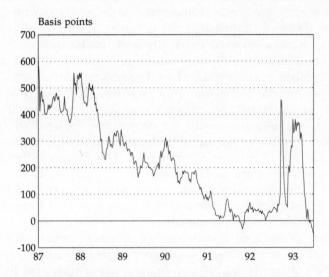

Figure 1.16   French-German three-month interest rate differential
Source: Datastream

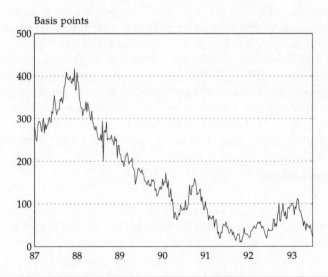

Figure 1.17   French-German ten-year bond yield differential
Source: Datastream

started to wear off and with the franc trading comfortably within its ERM bands, the French government attempted to bring its short-term interest rates below those of Germany in the autumn of 1991 — with disastrous results. The franc weakened markedly and the Banque de France was forced into two embarrassing increases in official interest rates, in November and December, in order to alleviate the pressure on the franc.

One uncomfortable fact about fixed-exchange rates had been forgotten, or ignored, by the French government: if an exchange rate is fixed, short-term interest rate equality results. Of course, the French franc/Deutschemark exchange rate was not perfectly fixed, there was some room for the franc to move within its exchange rate band. Unfortunately it did: it weakened. A lower interest rate in France than in Germany could be accepted in the market if the franc is generally expected to appreciate within its exchange rate band, but the autumn 1991 experiment acted instead to kindle fears about a French franc devaluation.

The failure of this 1991 French attempt to bring interest rates below the German level did not prevent the UK government discussing similar plans in early 1992[1] although the Bank of England never attempted to lower UK rates below the German level.

A second attempt by France to cut interest rates to below the German level was made in July 1993 after the new government had paved the way by announcing its intention of sharing the role of anchor currency in the ERM. A case for adopting this role could be made on the basis of the low French inflation rate, the state of French public sector finances, and the fact that the recession was less severe in France than in Germany.

The attempt, however, was seen as reflecting a growing conflict between domestic needs — although the recession was less marked than in Germany, unemployment was still very high — and the needs of maintaining currency stability in the ERM[2]. It remains to be seen whether the French will use the greater latitude given to them by wider fluctuation margins in the ERM to cut interest rates significantly below those in Germany.

The 'Walters critique'

From the late-1990s up until mid-1992, the ERM seemed still to be operating without problems for the countries with higher inflation and interest rates

---

[1] *See 'The Sunday Times', 10 May 1992.*

[2] *The theme of the tension between domestic and ERM needs is developed by Walters in Chapter 2 and Congdon in Chapter 4.*

— Spain and the UK, in particular. Inflation and interest rates in both coun-tries were falling and capital inflows were strong in order to take advantage of the attractive combination of a pegged-exchange rate and higher interest rates.

The surface calm, however, masked the fact that the ERM had operated (as with the UK in 1987-1990) or was operating (as with Spain since enter-ing the ERM in 1989) in a quite inappropriate manner. Consider the exam-ple of Spain and how economic policy is expected to adjust once the country joins the ERM.

The ERM is supposed to work in the way set out in Figure 1.18[1]. First, (the route on the left hand side of Figure 1.18) the peseta would be ex-pected to be under some pressure given the higher Spanish inflation rate, obliging the Bank of Spain to intervene in support of the peseta. To the extent that this intervention was not sterilized it would lead to a contraction in relative monetary growth. Second, Spain would be expected to have real interest rates higher than on average in the other ERM countries in order to maintain the pegged value of the peseta, augmenting the contractionary ef-fects of intervention. Both these 'monetary routes' would lead to relatively slower domestic demand in Spain and hence an improvement in relative inflation performance. Tight monetary policy would also be supplemented by tight fiscal policy to reduce domestic inflationary pressures.

Sir Alan Walters[2] argues that the adjustment process in the ERM may not operate along these lines at all, but rather in the way set out in Figure 1.19. He argues that with exchange rates pegged, capital will flow from countries with low interest rates to those with higher interest rates. This will lead to downward pressure on nominal and real interest rates and also require the government to intervene to keep down the value of the 'high inflation' currency. Thus the thrust of monetary policy would be in totally the wrong direction to that which is appropriate.

Such pressures were certainly evident in Spain. There was a marked convergence of short- and long-term interest rate differentials with Ger-many from 1989 to 1991 and the Bank of Spain's foreign exchange re-serves rose spectacularly: from $43.7bn in May 1989 to a peak of $72.4bn in June 1992.

If the monetary route to tightening domestic policy is thus not only ruled out but, indeed, leads to a looser monetary stance being adopted then it can be argued that more of the burden of adjustment in domestic policy has to

---

[1] *The mechanism involved is no different to that of all fixed-exchange rate systems — Bretton Woods, the gold standard etc.*
[2] *See Chapter 2.*

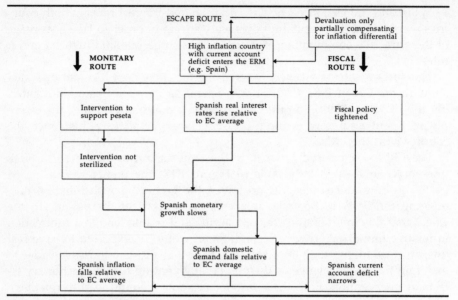

Figure 1.18   How the ERM is supposed to work...

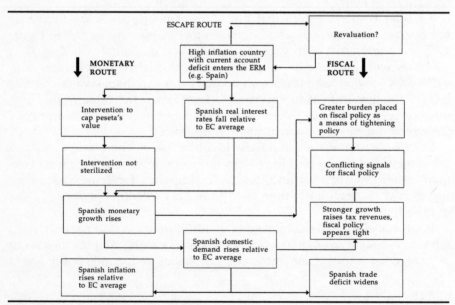

Figure 1.19   ...and how it has worked

be taken by fiscal policy[1]. One problem, however, is that strong growth, by raising tax revenues and reducing government expenditure will reduce the government's borrowing requirement and may give the impression that fiscal policy is tight, rendering the appropriate adjustment less likely. The UK experienced this problem during the 1987-88 period of 'capping' sterling's value (Temperton (1992)); and Spain, benefiting from continued fast economic growth after ERM entry in June 1989, failed to tighten fiscal policy significantly until the 1992 ERM crisis had already developed.

Examples of the Walters critique in operation are discussed in Chapter 2.

Maastricht uncertainty

The 'No' vote in the Danish referendum on the Maastricht Treaty on 2 June signalled the start of concern about prospects for the ERM. Under the three stage plan for the move to Emu set out in the Maastricht Treaty, the ERM is to be transformed into a system of ever more stable exchange rates with the intention that this will provide a glidepath for the move to eventual monetary union. Once the Maastricht plan was brought into question by doubts about its ratification, first the higher-yielding bond markets and then the exchange rates of the weaker currencies, came under pressure. Mounting concern about the Italian lira necessitated a sharp rise in Italian short-term interest rates during the summer of 1992 and heavy intervention was needed to support the lira[2].

As discussed above, cumulative inflation differentials indicated the need for a devaluation of the lira in the ERM and, indeed, the devaluation of 7 per cent which occurred on 13 September 1992 was close to the normal '50 per cent offset' of the cumulated inflation differential discussed above. At this early stage in the ERM crisis, it could be argued that the ERM was merely operating in the way in which it was designed. But the lira devaluation increased, rather than reduced, the turbulence in the ERM and the market was concerned that the French referendum on the Maastricht treaty on September 20 would also produce a 'No' vote. The combination of this uncertainty, coupled with the factors discussed above — the fact that the ERM was holding interest rates at a level that was too high for domestic purposes, concern about the parity at which sterling had entered the system, the problems of macroeconomic management under the 'excess credi-

---

[1] *See Holtham, Chapter 3, although Walters, Chapter 2, emphasizes that exchange controls are a more appropriate response.*
[2] *See Chapter 18.*

bility' of the ERM — were the fundamental factors behind the ERM crisis of 1992/93.

Fault lines? What fault lines?

These fundamental factors, which have now brought the very viability of the ERM into question, provided the backdrop to the crisis. But the immediate explanation of the withdrawal of the UK and Italy from the system, the abandonment of the Nordic currencies' Ecu links and the emergency move to wider bands in August 1993 was the scale of international capital flows that could be mobilized against a currency once confidence in it maintaining its parity had been lost. Such capital flows were far in excess of central banks' reserves and all the countries which broke their exchange rate links during the crisis seriously ran the risk of completely running out of foreign exchange reserves[1].

When the UK pulled out of the ERM in September 1992, they blamed the 'fault lines' in the ERM for sterling's departure from the system. The official inquiries by the EC central bank governors and the EC Monetary Committee [2] found no evidence of fault lines in the ERM itself. "We have looked at the system [the ERM] with a magnifying glass", said Wim Duisenberg, chairman of the Committee of Central Bank Governors, "but we have not found any fault lines".

A magnifying glass may not, of course, be the best instrument to use when searching for fault lines. Both the Group of Ten and the IMF (Dini 1993, IMF 1993) took a much broader view of the ERM problems in their assessments and came up with an interpretation of the problems which was more sympathetic to the UK government's view. They stressed the difficulties which central banks faced in operating in a world characterized by massive capital flows. The analysis is straightforward. In early 1992, before the ERM crisis erupted, central banks in Europe had, in total, around $275bn in foreign exchange reserves. This is small in relation to the size of the world's capital markets and the turnover on the foreign exchange market. Total turnover in the foreign exchange market is four times that amount — $1 trillion — *per day*. There are around $14 trillion of assets now under the control of global fund managers, and around $2.5 trillion (roughly evenly split between bonds and equities) invested cross-border.

---

[1] *Referring back to Figure 1.18, the ERM jolted back abruptly to operating in the way in which it was supposed to work.*

[2] *See Appendix 2.*

Key statistics (US$ billion)

Outstanding stock of publicly-traded debt and equity[1]:	24,000
Global institutional investment[2]:	14,000
Cross-border holdings of tradeable securities[1]:	2500
Global swaps market[3]:	4400
Foreign exchange turnover per day[1]:	1000
Foreign exchange reserves[4]:	
- USA	65
- Japan	83
- Europe	279

Data:

[1] *IMF (1993)*

[2] *United Nations' estimate, quoted by John Plender in the Financial Times, 9 July 1993*

[3] *Financial Times, 22 July 1993*

[4] *For May 1993, excluding gold*

Figure 1.20   Central banks versus the markets

About $300bn was invested by these fund managers in the higher-yielding ERM and Ecu-linked markets in the period immediately before the crisis.

The emancipation of capital markets — as Professor Dr. Jochimsen from the Bundesbank describes it in Chapter 13 — is a potentially huge problem facing central banks. As the IMF report (IMF 1993) put it: "the markets eventually decide on what are unsustainable [economic] situations and, when they do, their size alone, increasingly allows them to force adjustments".

The problem will get worse: the scale of international investment has grown quickly since the early-1980s and further fast growth is in prospect. There are still substantial restrictions on many pension funds from investing overseas, but these are likely to be eased over time, and those funds which do invest overseas are likely to increase that proportion further: the IMF (IMF 1993) estimates that the share of foreign currency-denominated assets in the world's 300 largest pension funds will increase from about 7 per cent at present to 12 per cent by the mid-1990s. Furthermore, this will be an increased share of a larger cake as the entire pool of institutional funds will grow further under the combined effects of a continued trend towards institutionalization of the pool of savings; an increase in the size of (particularly private sector) pension funds and insurance companies in the developed countries; and a rapid rise in the financial wealth of many newly-industrializing countries[1]. The imbalance between the size of the markets and official reserves is shown in Figure 1.20.

Concerns about the size of markets and the powerlessness of central banks are not new: the 'gnomes of Zurich', 'hot money' and the like, have troubled governments for many years. One period of great concern about the force of the market was 1984-85, when the markets were pushing the US dollar up to a level which was clearly not warranted by economic fundamentals; the perceived ineffectiveness of central banks perpetuated the market's excesses. The Plaza agreement of September 1985, whereby the Group of Five leading economies agreed to push the US dollar's value down — and use intervention as a way of doing so — marked a watershed in international attitudes to foreign exchange intervention (Funabashi 1989). Confidence on the part of central bankers and finance ministers in their ability to manage exchange rates remained strong throughout the subsequent Louvre Accord in February 1987 and, indeed, was still evident shortly before the September 1992 ERM crisis[2].

The Dini Report also highlighted one other disturbing feature of capital market developments: that there is a tendency to swing from periods of excessive optimism to excessive pessimism with regard to the prospects for individual currencies and markets. Indeed, the most worrisome aspect of the 1992/93 conflict between central banks and the markets is that it has been characterized, at times, by speculative attacks on currencies for which it can be argued that no fundamental reason for a devaluation existed.

This brings us back to our original list of economic problems besetting the ERM and an assessment of the extent to which they have been corrected.

German reunification: aftershocks still felt until the mid-1990s

To what extent have the problems of German reunification been overcome? The large German budget deficit is set to remain a feature of the European economy for some years and, in this sense, the effects of German reunification have not yet passed through the system. In Figure 1.21 we show the surge in the German government's budget deficit in 1990 and 1991, due to the costs of reunification, and projections for the deficit up to 1994. The overall budget deficit will remain at 4 per cent of GDP, even with a tighten-

---

[1] See Dini 1993 paras 9-10.

[2] See Chapter 16, in which the Banco de Portugal argues that the ineffective operation to restrain the fall of the dollar on 21 August 1992 was important in conditioning market attitudes about the efficacy of intervention shortly before the September ERM crisis broke.

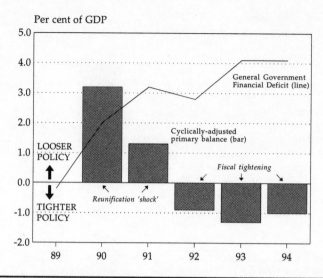

Figure 1.21   German fiscal tightening
Source: OECD Economic Outlook, June 1993

ing of fiscal policy of around 1 per cent of GDP in each year[1]. This fiscal position raises (at least) three important issues. First, the structural tightening will hamper Germany's recovery from its current recession and will perpetuate weak growth in other European countries. Second, the budget deficit will remain above the 3 per cent threshold which has been set as a condition for a country entering into Emu — and which Germany probably takes more seriously than most countries. Third, a deficit on this scale will continue to put upward pressure on German interest rates both directly as a result of demand in the capital market and, indirectly, via the Bundesbank reaction to it. In this latter respect, it is noteworthy that some of the fiscal measures designed to help with reunification make the Bundesbank's task more difficult: in particular, the widespread interest subsidies for investing in the east render the demand for credit much less interest sensitive[2].

[1] *This tightening is shown in the chart by the change in the cyclically-adjusted (i.e. after taking into account the effects of the economic cycle on government borrowing) primary (i.e. excluding interest payments) budget deficit, the best guide to the structural element of government fiscal policy.*

[2] *This point is developed in Chapter 4 by Congdon.*

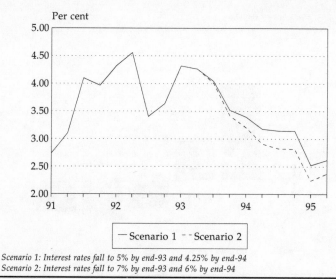

Per cent

Scenario 1: Interest rates fall to 5% by end-93 and 4.25% by end-94
Scenario 2: Interest rates fall to 7% by end-93 and 6% by end-94

Figure 1.22   German inflation projections

The appreciation of the Deutschemark against European currencies since the ERM crisis erupted, which amounts to around 5 per cent on average, will, according to most econometric estimates, reduce German inflation by around 1/2 to 1 per cent over the next two years. Coupled with the sharpness of the current German recession, this will help to produce a fall in the German inflation rate. Even so, it seems likely that it will remain above the Bundesbank's 2 per cent target in the next few years.

This raises the important issue of the Bundesbank's reaction to these developments. There is a risk that the rapid easing of German interest rates, which is generally expected, will not materialize and that the Bundesbank will take a tougher line on interest rates. In Figure 1.22 we show projections for German inflation on the basis of the fiscal tightening which is planned, and assuming a relatively swift reduction in German interest rates to just over 4 per cent by end-1994. Inflation falls to around 2.5 to 3 per cent in 1994, still above the Bundesbank's 2 per cent target, and then rises again as economic activity recovers. If the Bundesbank were to cut rates more slowly — to only 6 per cent by end-1994 — the inflation rate would come down further, but would still not hit 2 per cent. An even tougher stance on interest rates would be needed if the Bundesbank was serious about hitting its 2 per cent inflation target. Such a policy would probably ensure that there was no German economic growth in 1994 (after a drop in output of 2 per cent in 1993). Even in the first case (of a relatively speedy reduction in in-

	Central rate vs. Ecu until 11 September 1992	Rate vs. Ecu on 3 August 1993	Actual revaluation (+) or devaluation (-) vs. Ecu	Implied revaluation (+) or devaluation (-) vs. Ecu
Deutschemark	2.05	1.93	5.9	1.7
Dutch guilder	2.30	2.17	5.9	5.7
Belgian franc	42.17	41.18	2.3	5.9
French franc	6.86	6.74	1.7	1.2
Italian lira	1528.7	1808.4	-18.3	-17.4
Danish krone	7.80	7.67	1.6	-6.6
Irish punt	0.76	0.80	-4.9	-4.9
Spanish peseta	132.9	158.1	-18.9	-0.9
British pound	0.73	0.75	-3.0	-0.8

Figure 1.23   Exchange rate changes since the crisis began

terest rates), German growth is expected to be weak in 1994 (0.5 per cent), and below 2 per cent in 1995.

It is fair to conclude that the aftershocks of German reunification will still be felt for some years to come: the German budget deficit will remain high, frustrating attempts to reduce interest rates; and German growth will remain slow, limiting the scope for other EC countries' exports.

Exchange rate changes have corrected for cumulated inflation differentials

After the exchange rate movements which have taken place as a result of the protracted ERM crisis, it is noteworthy that, for many countries, the exchange rate changes that have taken place are very close to those suggested in Figure 1.8, based on the analysis of accumulated inflation differentials. The Dutch guilder, the Italian lira and the Irish punt have all changed by almost precisely the amount justified by inflation differentials. As far as sterling is concerned, its exchange rate against the Deutschemark in early August 1993 of Dm 2.55/£ is consistent with estimates of its fundamental equilibrium exchange rate presented above. Denmark appears the only odd man out: the Danish krone has appreciated against the Ecu whereas a depreciation seems warranted.

The Walters critique — alive and well and living on the Iberian peninsula

With confidence in the higher-yielding currencies having been shaken by the ERM crisis, the forces of interest rate convergence — the root of the Walters critique of the ERM — are now less strong, but it has been a remarkable feature of the ERM since the September 1992 crisis that, as soon as an element of calm has returned to the system, the high-yielding currencies (particularly the Spanish peseta and the Portuguese escudo) have displayed a tendency once again to be the strongest currencies in the system. For example, on 19 July 1993, a period of calm before the latest crisis, the escudo and the peseta were, respectively, the two strongest ERM currencies with exchange rates which were 3.7 per cent and 2.3 per cent stronger than the Danish krone, the weakest currency in the ERM.

The threat of competitive devaluation

A new post-crisis threat has raised its head: competitive devaluation. During the prolonged period of exchange rate adjustments from September 1992, it was clear at times that the constellation of exchange rates conveyed significant competitive advantages to some countries: when sterling fell to its low-point of Dm 2.35/£, it was quite understandable that there were complaints from French companies who thought that it would be impossible for them to compete with UK producers. Erik Hoffmeyer highlighted the problem when he said in May 1993 that "we have seen a series of major devaluations which were completely out of line with the reasonable pattern in a fixed-exchange rate co-operation". He emphasized that the point of the EMS was to avoid competitive devaluations but that "this has not been the case. What we have seen have been irresponsible exchange rate changes"[1].

This observation raises a long-standing issue in international economics: whether there is indeed a competitive advantage to be gained by devaluation. The pre-crisis accepted view in ERM member countries was that devaluation does not improve trade performance. Devaluation, through one of a number of channels, raises inflation which eventually means that the initial gain in competitiveness is eroded: for example, higher import prices are passed on to consumers and this eventually leads to higher wages, or exporters' profit margins are improved and this wears down their resistance to excessive wage claims. From the monetary policy angle, devaluation would raise the risk premium on the devaluing currency, meaning that higher interest rates would be needed.

Has the orthodox view been overturned? Yes, in part. First, the inflationary feed-through from devaluation has been smaller than expected in many countries, not least the UK. A large part of this is undoubtedly due to the weak state of the economies of the devaluing countries and the high level of unemployment. Second, for countries which have floated, any increase in

---

[1] *'Financial Times' 26 May 1993.*

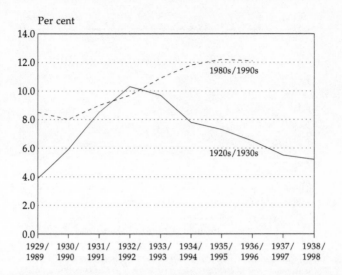

Figure 1.24   European unemployment in the 1930s and 1990s

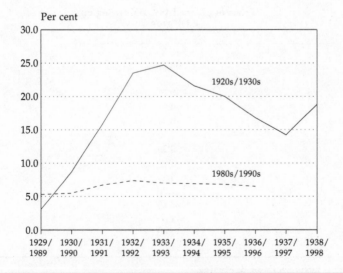

Figure 1.25   US unemployment in the 1930s and 1990s

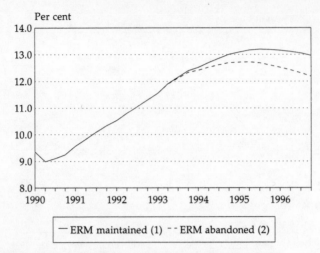

Per cent

(1) ERM remains intact and Germany sets the floor for European interest rates
(2) ERM is abandoned and all countries, apart from Germany, reduce interest rates by 2%

Figure 1.26   European unemployment trends

Country	Effect of planned 1993 tightening on GDP growth
USA	+0.25
Japan	+1.00
Europe	-0.75
France	-0.01
Germany	-0.75
Italy	-2.25
UK	-0.25
Belgium	-1.00
Finland	-2.50
Portugal	-1.00
Netherlands	-0.25
Spain	-1.00
Sweden	-2.00

Figure 1.27   Europe's fiscal tightening...
Source: Oxford Economic Forecasting 1993A

the risk premium on their interest rates has been more than offset by the ability to set interest rates in relation to domestic needs once the ERM constraint has been removed.

If the pre-crisis view on the efficacy of devaluation has, to some extent, been overturned, what of the more important question of whether the ERM is itself perpetuating the slow growth and high unemployment of EC countries?

Would abandoning the ERM help reduce European unemployment?

European unemployment is certainly a problem: as big a problem as it was in the 1930s (see Figure 1.24). The western European unemployment rate in 1993 (10.9 per cent) exceeds the 1930s peak (10.3 per cent in 1932). Moreover, the rate is expected to fall much more slowly than in the 1930s[1]. The parallel with the US is also disturbing (see Figure 1.25). In the 1990s, the US unemployment rate has remained low by international standards, and nothing like as high as it was in the 1930s.

To what extent is the ERM behind this problem? Suppose that EC countries were to abandon the ERM entirely, that is, make no attempt even to stay within the new wide bands and to set interest rates entirely on the basis of domestic conditions. A realistic assumption is that all EC countries — apart from Germany — would be able to reduce their short-term interest rates by 2 per cent[2].

This would have some effect on stimulating demand and reducing unemployment. According to econometric model simulations[3], the unemployment rate would rise less quickly and, by 1996, would be 12 per cent rather than 13 per cent (in the case where ERM parities had been maintained)[4].

The effect is quite small but it could be understated. First, business and consumer confidence may recover sharply — as they have done in the UK since leaving the ERM — and this will provide a boost to growth and employment over and above the effect which can be picked up by the economic model simulations presented above.

---

[1] Data constructed by Andrea Boltho of Magdalene College, Oxford. Forecasts from Oxford Economic Forecasting.

[2] Realistic on two considerations: the UK has rates around 2 per cent lower than they would be in the ERM; the average inflation rate in non-German ERM member countries is 2 per cent below Germany's.

[3] Courtesy of Oxford Economic Forecasting.

[4] Data are for EC countries excluding Germany but including Sweden and are therefore not directly comparable to those in Figure 1.26.

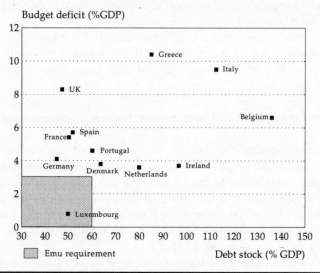

Figure 1.28   ...is still not enough to meet Emu requirements
Source: OECD (1993)

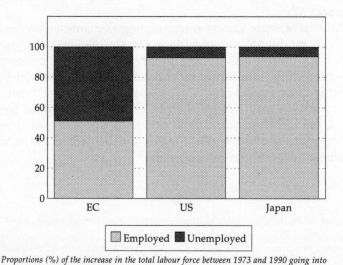

Proportions (%) of the increase in the total labour force between 1973 and 1990 going into employment and unemployment

Figure 1.29   Europe's record at creating jobs is poor
Source: Henderson, 1992

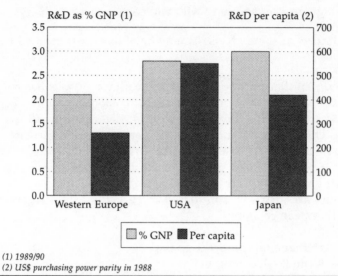

R&D as % GNP (1)   R&D per capita (2)

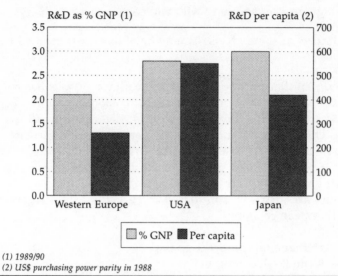

% GNP   Per capita

(1) 1989/90
(2) US$ purchasing power parity in 1988

Figure 1.30   Europe's R&D record is weak
Source: Oxford Economic Forecasting 1993B

Second, if the ERM were abandoned completely then so too might the Maastricht plan for Emu and — with it — its restrictions on government budget deficits. In 1993, all EC countries apart from Luxembourg had government fiscal positions which broke the Maastricht guidelines and the general thrust of European fiscal policy was markedly contractionary (see Figures 1.27 and 1.28). Thus the abandonment of both the ERM and the Maastricht route to Emu *may* lead to some additional easing of (fiscal) policy. With all European governments committed to fiscal restraint — regardless of Maastricht — however, one could not be sure of this effect.

Broadly, therefore, any feasible change in monetary and fiscal policy is unlikely dramatically to change the prospects for European unemployment. Even if it were possible to generate a more stimulative combination of fiscal and monetary policies throughout Europe, its effectiveness would be limited to the extent that unemployment is of a more structural nature.

It was, of course, European structural problems — the *eurosclerosis* of the early-1980s, of which weak employment growth was one symptom — which launched European policy-makers into the single market and the Emu programmes in the first place. So to look at what Europe might gain by breaking free of the ERM and the Maastricht convergence criteria risks missing the main point entirely. Let us therefore turn to the broader structural problems facing Europe and consider: first, the factors that were behind the early-1980s eurosclerosis and the extent to which they might merely have been masked by recent developments; second, the extent to which the single market and Emu will help correct these problems.

The eurosclerosis of the early-1980s may have just been masked by recent developments

There is no doubt that Europe's record at creating new jobs has been poor. Looking at the way in which the increase in the labour force has been used in the period from 1973 to 1990 shows a most disturbing trend (see Figure 1.29). In the US and Japan, more than 90 per cent of the increase was accounted for by an increase in employment. In Europe, the increase was split broadly 50:50 between those going into work and those becoming unemployed: what has been behind that weakness?

Four factors are generally considered to be behind the structural weakness of the European economy[1]:

- low international competitiveness;
- slow technological progress;
- large welfare states; and
- rigid labour markets.

Let us consider each of these in turn.

Low international competitiveness

Labour is expensive in Europe. Estimates for 1993 suggest that it costs up to $20 per hour in western Europe's manufacturing industry, compared with $18 in Japan, $17 in the USA and as little as $1 to $5 in eastern Europe or the newly-industrializing Asian economies. These costs include wages and other costs of employment borne by employers.

Slow technological progress

The explanation for these high labour costs does not reside in the fact that European industry is predominantly highly-productive, making use of the latest high technology and therefore able to afford high wages. European Commission data show Europe moving from a trade surplus in high-tech goods with the rest of the world of one half per cent of GDP in 1978 to a deficit of the same magnitude in 1990. Instrumental in explaining this poor

---

[1] *This section draws heavily on Oxford Economic Forecasting (1993).*

	Europe	USA	Japan
Total public expenditure	48.1	36.5	31.1
of which:			
- welfare state	30.7	17.8	18.1
- education, housing, etc.	12.8	6.1	10.9
- social security	17.9	11.7	7.2
Total public revenue	43.7	31.9	33.1

Figure 1.31   **Public expenditure and its structure (late 1980s, as a percentage of GDP)**
Source: Oxford Economic Forecasting 1993B

| | Regional moves as a percentage of total population | |
	1980	1987
England & Wales	1.1	1.1
France	-	1.3
Germany	1.3	1.1
Italy	0.7	0.5
USA	3.3	2.8
Japan	2.9	2.6

Figure 1.32   **Europe's regional mobility is low**
Source: Oxford Economic Forecasting 1993B

performance is the weak European research and development (R&D) effort. R&D expenditure per capita has been for a long time, and remains, well below that in the US and Japan (see Figure 1.30).

Large welfare states

The welfare state in Europe is much more widespread than in the US or Japan (see Figure 1.31) and its scale is one of the major obstacles to reducing government spending and budget deficits throughout Europe. Even in the UK, where there was an emphasis during the Thatcher years on 'rolling back the frontiers of the state', government spending as a proportion of GDP will be higher in 1993 than it was when Mrs Thatcher took office. In the UK, the philosophy behind the reduction in the state's involvement was that high spending — and the taxes needed to finance it — brought a range of undesirable consequences from the growth of the black economy, to a

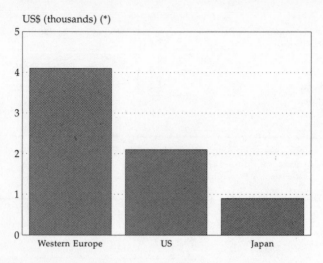

(*) *Purchasing power parity in 1988*

Figure 1.33   Unemployment compensation payments
Source: Oxford Economic Forecasting 1993B

| | Cost as a percentage of total price | |
	Transaction tax	*Total cost*[1]
France	8-10	16
Germany	4	12.5
Italy	10	18
UK	1	5
Spain	6	14
Belgium	17	22
Western Europe	6.5	14
USA	1.5	9
Japan	0.6	5

[1] *including estate agents' and legal fees*

Figure 1.34   The cost of buying or selling a house is high in Europe
Source: Oxford Economic Forecasting 1993B

less entrepreneurial mentality. The same arguments apply, in varying degree, to other western European economies[1].

Rigid labour markets

This generosity of the welfare state goes some way to explain Europe's poor record of creating new jobs. As well as the incentive effects discussed above, a more direct effect stems from the fact that unemployment compensation payments are both higher, and available for longer, than in the US or Japan (see Figure 1.32). Three other aspects of labour market rigidity are cause for concern.

First, state regulations on the ease of redundancies, working hours, the freedom of management to reorganize the workforce, etc. are much stricter in Europe than elsewhere and will become even more strict under the terms of the Social Chapter of the Maastricht Treaty.

Second, trade unions are more important in Europe and, arguably, are organized in a less flexible way. Thus, it has been plausibly argued that the highly-centralized and all-encompassing unions, as those of the Nordic countries or Austria, as well as highly-decentralized enterprise unions, as those of the US and Japan, are much more conducive to real wage moderation and hence to low unemployment levels than are the unions of the major European countries, all of which are organized along traditional industry lines.

Third, Europe's labour mobility is low. Mobility *within* countries is low compared with the US and Japan (see Figure 1.33), and the gap between the highest and lowest unemployment regions is much larger in the countries of Europe. Part of the explanation may lie in the relatively high costs of moving house in Europe (see Figure 1.34), and the more widespread availability of cheap housing provided by local authorities. Adding to the factors leading to low mobility within countries, the linguistic and cultural differences which will be an impediment to movement between countries, it seems doubtful that the degree of labour mobility in Europe will approach that in the US or Japan, even in the medium-term. Two recent studies found that Europe had neither the cross-border mobility of labour, nor sufficient flexibility of wages, to be a good candidate for monetary union[2].

---

[1] *See Robinson (1993) for a discussion of the factors contributing to the difficulties, in the UK, of reducing government expenditure.*
[2] *Connolly and Kröger (1993) and Englander and Egebo (1993).*

Single market		Emu	
Elimination of border controls	0.4	Absence of conversion costs between currencies	0.5
Open public procurements	0.5	Decline in risk and uncertainty	5.0
Free financial markets	1.5		
Greater economies of scale	2.1		
Total:	4.5	*Total:*	5.5

Figure 1.35   The gains from the single market and Emu (percentage of EC GDP)
Sources: European Commission, 1988 & 1990

The single market benefits can be quantified and may well have been underestimated...

The creation of the single market, the '1992' programme, and the move to Emu, are likely to go only a modest way to alleviating these impediments. The single market will help improve cross-border labour mobility, but the most important obstacles — cultural and linguistic — will remain. The extent of involvement by the state is not addressed directly in the Maastricht convergence criteria for Emu — only the size of government budget deficits and debt stocks. And the Social Chapter of the Maastricht Treaty will make labour markets even less flexible.

But the single market and Emu would bring other benefits which could, arguably, counter the structural impediments to growth listed above. The benefits of the single market were quantified in a detailed manner by the European Commission (1988) in the Cecchini report and are shown in Figure 1.35. These gains stem from gains in economic efficiency — in particular greater economies of scale — and may well have been understated. The boost to European growth in the late-1980s owed much to the surge in investment spending, as companies geared up in anticipation of these gains in efficiency, a boost which was not taken into account by Cecchini; and the report may have neglected other gains in productivity as a result of the completion of the single market[1].

[1] *See Emerson (1990).*

...whereas the benefits of Emu are difficult to quantify and rely on a single currency rather than just locked exchange rates

The benefits of Emu are less easy to quantify, but this does not mean that they are any less real or important. The abolition of transactions costs from changing currencies will lead to a clear benefit, but is expected to amount to no more than 0.5 per cent of GDP, according to European Commission (1990) estimates. The Commission provides a list of other benefits and costs — but no quantification of these, apart from the improvement in economic performance which is expected to come from the reduction in exchange rate risk — tentatively put at 5 per cent of GDP.

It is important to stress that these benefits are a feature of the very final stage of monetary union, when all national currencies are eliminated. As Charles Goodhart (1993) has pointed out, this is best referred to as Stage 3b of Emu — Stage 3a, in which exchange rates are irrevocably locked but national currencies still exist, would not confer all of those benefits: crucially, there would still be currency conversion costs. The ERM crisis has demonstrated all too well how easily a previously well-established and stable currency relationship can be put under pressure and this will remain a risk as long as independent national currencies exist — that is, right through Stage 3a[1].

The difficulties of moving from locked-exchange rates to a single currency have been underestimated

The Delors Report and the Maastricht Treaty pay little regard to the difficulties associated with moving from Stage 3a to Stage 3b. It is intended that the move to irrevocably-locked exchange rates should lead quickly to the use of a single currency, but the mechanics have not been spelled out. This might seem a rather academic point given the continuing European currency crisis, but the issue is vital in assessing whether the gains from Emu are worthwhile[2].

How are national currencies to disappear and be replaced by a new European currency? There are two ways which might be considered. The first, 'cold turkey'[3] approach would entail moving from national currencies

---

[1] *Indeed, the example of the Baltic states, who have all moved to issue their own currencies and cease to use the rouble, shows that there is still a risk even when a monetary union has been completed.*

[2] *See Goodhart (1992).*

[3] *The cold turkey approach to Emu would presumably save it from being a dead duck.*

Currency	Central rate
Belgian franc	40.2123
Danish krone	7.43679
Deutschemark	1.94964
Spanish peseta	154.25
French franc	6.53883
Irish punt	0.808628
Dutch guilder	2.19672
Portuguese escudo	192.854
Greek drachma	264.513
Italian lira	1793.13
British pound	0.786749

Figure 1.36   Central rates of EMS currencies versus the Ecu from 14 May 1993

to the new currency — the Ecu — overnight. So from, say, 1 January 2000, there would be no French francs or Deutschemarks, but just the Ecu. The politics of such a move are daunting: could all the EC governments ever agree to such a move? Changes in ERM arrangements have clearly been the subject of heated, and at times bitter, discussions between governments, indicating that the chances of accepting such an approach are slim. Even if they could, the mechanics are awesome. At the moment, for example, the central rate of the Deutschemark against the Ecu is Dm 1.94964 = Ecu 1 (see Figure 1.36). This is a most inconvenient exchange rate. Imagine the popular concern at having goods which were one day priced at Dm 10, costing the next day Ecu 5.129152. There is no example in monetary history of such a change taking place. Perhaps the closest example is decimalization in the UK when shillings and pence were exchanged for new pence. The change took some five years to plan and involved considerable redesign of school books, vending machines etc. Decimalization involved changing just the pound sterling's subsidiary units. The conversion from national currencies to the Ecu would involve changing both the subsidiary units as well as the currency of denomination. Furthermore, that change would take place in every country which moved to Emu, *at the same time*.

A less drastic alternative would be for a phased introduction of the Ecu with, for example, banknotes designed with the national currency value on one side and the Ecu value on the other. Again, however, there is the problem of inconvenient fractions being involved — would a fifty Danish krone note with Ecu 6.72333 printed on the reverse side ever be taken seriously? I doubt it.

There have been some eminently sensible suggestions that the central rates of currencies against the Ecu should be rounded to make as many as possible convenient numbers. So, for example, we could use a Dm/Ecu rate of 2.00; a peseta/Ecu rate of 150 and so on. This would itself require adjustments of all currencies central rates against the Ecu — i.e. an overall re-alignment of the ERM — but the Maastricht convergence requirements expressly forbid any country entering into Emu if it has devalued within the previous two years. Such an adjustment may be more feasible in the aftermath of the 1 August 1993 changes in the ERM, but with the viability of the system in question, the niceties of rounding exchange rates to levels suitable for Emu is presumably not currently a high political priority.

Maastricht Treaty — still a viable plan after August 1993?

This brings us on to the issue of whether, in the light of the ERM difficulties and especially the move to wider bands on 1 August 1993, the plan for the move to Emu set out in the Maastricht Treaty is still viable. Part III of the book deals with the issue in detail, so comments here will be kept brief. Of course, ratification of the Maastricht Treaty is not certain, with the German constitutional court ruling still outstanding but, assuming that it is ratified, a range of other problems raise their heads. The imperfect and incomplete nature of the treaty has been criticized, not least by the two German contributors to this book[1], one of whom calls for an inter-governmental conference soon after ratification to rectify these problems.

The convergence criteria for Emu may also need to be reassessed. These criteria — set out in Figure 1.37 — are subject to some leeway in their interpretation. It has, for some time, been recognized that the 3 per cent and 60 per cent 'rules' on the budget deficit and the debt stock, respectively, will not be applied literally. Indeed, the fiscal criteria have been widely criticized: the contractionary fiscal policies which are being pursued in many European countries, in order to reach the objectives, seem inappropriate in the current European recession; and the 60 per cent debt stock rule is quite arbitrary, being based on a historic average of EC countries' outstanding debt. Attempts at reaching fiscal convergence criteria may well, in many countries, prove counterproductive to the entire Emu process: by perpetuating slow growth, tight fiscal policy can make a currency a target

---

[1] *Seidel in Chapter 5 and Jochimsen in Chapter 13.*

Inflation	The average consumer price inflation rate over the previous year must not exceed by more than 1.5 percentage points that of the three lowest inflation countries, with the exact weighting of the three yet to be determined.
Government deficit	The planned or actual government deficit must not exceed 3 per cent of GDP, unless the ratio has been on a declining path and is approaching the 3 per cent level, or the excess is small and clearly temporary.
Debt stock	The consolidated gross general government debt must not exceed 60 per cent of GDP, unless the ratio is approaching 60 per cent at a satisfactory pace.
	In assessing the two fiscal criteria, the medium-term economic and budgetary position of the member state and whether its deficit exceeds government investment may also be taken into account.
Exchange rate stability	A currency must have adhered to the normal fluctuation margins of the ERM in the two previous years without severe tensions. A member state may not have initiated a devaluation of its currency's central rate in the previous two years. Before the 1 August 1993 widening of ERM bands, 'normal fluctuation margins' were generally understood to be the 2.25 per cent bands, but wider bands may now be considered 'normal'.
Bond yield	The average yield on long-term government bonds over the previous year must not exceed by more than 2 percentage points that on similar government bonds of the three lowest inflation countries.

Figure 1.37   Convergence criteria for Emu

for speculative attack. This was, arguably, a feature behind the recent attacks on the peseta and the French franc. The fiscal criteria also need to be addressed in the light of the great success which has been achieved on the part of the Netherlands and Belgium in keeping their exchange rates stable, even though, on the Maastricht fiscal criteria, it is doubtful that either country would qualify for Emu.

The requirement on exchange rate stability, which was generally understood to be that a currency should have remained in the 2.25 per cent bands without devaluation for two years before being eligible for Emu, may also be re-interpreted in the light of the 1 August widening of ERM bands. If 'normal fluctuation margins' for a currency are now defined as +/- 15 per cent rather than +/- 2.25 per cent bands, most, if not all EC countries would satisfy the exchange rate criterion.

Even on a reasonably liberal interpretation of the convergence criteria, however, shown in Figure 1.38, only Luxembourg and France would currently qualify for Emu.

Partly for these reasons, plans for an alternative route to Emu — based on a small number of countries — may well have to be considered much more seriously. Graham Bishop sets out such a plan in Chapter 7.

Concluding comments

The European currency crisis, which started in September 1992 and has continued with varying intensity since then, has raised many fundamental questions about the nature of the European economy, the operation of financial markets, the role of central banks and the prospects for European

	Inflation	Govt. deficit	Debt stock	Exchange rate	Bond yield	Ready for Emu?
Germany	no	yes[1]	yes	yes[4]	yes	no
France	yes	yes[2]	yes	yes[4]	yes	yes
UK	yes	no	yes	no	yes	no
Italy	no	no	no	no	no	no
Spain	no	yes[2]	yes	no	no	no
Netherlands	yes	yes[2]	no	yes[4]	yes	no
Belgium	yes	no	no	yes[4]	yes	no
Denmark	yes	yes[2]	no	yes[4]	yes	no
Portugal	no	no	yes	no	no	no
Greece	no	no	no	no	no	no
Ireland	yes	yes[2]	yes[3]	no	yes	no
Luxembourg	yes	yes	yes	yes[4]	yes	yes

[1] Yes, because the deficit exceeds 3%, but this is due primarily to the special effects of reunification

[2] Yes, because the budget deficit is temporarily raised by the cyclical position of the economy

[3] Yes, because the debt/GDP ratio has shown a temporary decline in recent years

[4] Yes, assuming definition of 'normal fluctuation margins' is changed due to 1 August 93 band widening

Figure 1.38   Which countries would satisfy the Emu criteria in 1993?

integration. The assessment of the economic factors which we have presented in this chapter indicates that fundamental problems remain: in particular, the effects of German reunification will continue to be felt in the years ahead; the conflict between the domestic requirements of monetary policy and those dictated by the ERM will remain difficult to resolve; and the forces of interest rate convergence once exchange rate stability returns, indicate that the 'Walters critique' is still valid.

Although the two EC official reports have found no 'fault lines' in the ERM there are two operational issues which remain of concern. First, the scale of global financial flows will increase further, and will render central bank's foreign exchange interventions even less effective. Second, the tendency of markets to switch quickly from excessive confidence to equally excessive pessimism about the prospects for a particular market, raises concerns about whether they are acting in a rational manner.

It is too early to judge the significance of the recent move to wider ERM bands — whether this represents a move to *de facto* floating-exchange rates — or whether the move will be temporary. If a floating-exchange rate system (or something very close to it) results, interest rates across Europe will be free to fall further. On the basis of the analysis presented in this chapter, that would help only marginally in reducing European unemployment as this is, to a greater extent, a reflection of underlying structural problems.

References

- Bank of England (1991), Quarterly Bulletin, *The exchange rate mechanism of the European monetary system: a review of the literature*, February 1991

- Connolly, Bernard and Jürgen Kröger (1993), *Economic convergence in the integrating Community economy*, Recherches Economiques de Louvain, Volume 59 No 1-2

- Dini Report (1993), *International capital movements and foreign exchange markets: a report to the Ministers and governors of the Group of Deputies of the Group of Ten*

- Dornbusch, R. (1990), *Two-Track Emu, Now!* in *Britain and Emu*, Centre for Economic Performance in Association with Financial Markets Group, London School of Economics

- Emerson, Michael (1990), *The Economics of Emu* in *Britain and Emu*, Centre for Economic Performance in Association with Financial Markets Group, London School of Economics

- Englander, Steven and Thomas Egebo (1993), *Adjustment under fixed-exchange rates: application to the European monetary union*, OECD Economic Studies Number 20

- European Commission (1988), *The Economics of 1992*, European Economy, Number 35, March

- European Commission (1990), *One Market, One Money*, European Economy, Number 44, October

- Funabashi, Yoichi (1989), *Managing the dollar: from the Plaza to the Louvre*, Institute for International Economics, Washington D.C.

- Goodhart, C. A. E. (1992), *Emu and ESCB after Maastricht* , London School of Economics Financial Markets Group

- Henderson, David (1992), *Europe in the world economy*, paper presented at Merrill Lynch Europe seminar (June).

- International Monetary Fund (1993), *International Capital Markets. Part I. Exchange Rate Management and International Capital Flows*

- Marsh, David (1992), *The Bundesbank: the bank that rules Europe*, Heinemann, London

- OECD (1993), *Economic Outlook*, (June)

- Oxford Economic Forecasting (1993a), *The return of eurosclerosis*, European Economic Prospects (Spring)

- Oxford Economic Forecasting (1993b), *From Euroboom to Eurogloom*, World Economic Prospects (June)

- Robinson, Bill, *Few corners to cut*, Financial Times, July 20 1993

- Temperton, Paul (1992), *UK Monetary Policy: the challenge for the 1990s*, Macmillan, London

- Williamson, John (1985), *The Exchange Rate System*, Institute for International Economics, Washington D.C.

- Williamson, John (1991), *Fundamental Equilibrium Exchange Rates in National Institute of Economic and Social Research Review, December 1991*

Chapter 2

Why the ERM cannot be reformed

Sir Alan Walters
Vice Chairman & Director, AIG Trading Corporation, Washington DC, USA

Writer's note: The following article was written in May and well before the crisis of 1 August 1993. I have left the text unchanged and have merely added a final comment.

What went wrong with the ERM — the official interpretation

We have been showered with reports on what went wrong with the ERM and what needs to be fixed, with the main views being summarized in the April report of Lamberto Dini to the ministers and governors of the Group of Ten (Dini 1993). This is an account by central bankers and finance ministers who are quite naturally anxious to avoid or scotch accusations of blame for Black Wednesday or for the Euro-slump, or for other manifold errors. So it is neither frank nor unbiased.

European government officials and central bankers, we are told by the *Financial Times* (30 April 1993), have emerged wiser, and above all humbler, from the various investigations into last September's crisis. My judgement is that they are a little better informed but certainly none the wiser. As for humility, I find little sign of that, and as Cees Maas, a former treasurer-general of the Netherlands said, "..the mistakes of the last few years could be repeated".

The dominant view was that there is nothing fundamentally wrong with the ERM. No significant ERM reforms are needed. As Alfons Verplaetse, the governor of the central bank of Belgium said: "we can stick with the existing rules".

The chaotic events of September 1992 were attributable to the shock of German reunification and the reluctance of governments to devalue or re-align. Having not conceded to 1991 German suggestions of an appreciation of the Deutschemark and some realignment of the various member currencies, the ERM was stuck with unsustainable rates — or at least only with interest rates that were ruining their domestic economies. As Wim Duisenberg, president of the central bank of the Netherlands, put it: "we should have had the foresight to encapsulate all the five months of realignment into one weekend...we must never let this happen again".

The shock of German reunification

In attributing the fall of the EMS to the conjunction of high German interest rates, in response to the inflation generated by reunification, and the deflation and recession in the rest of the ERM countries, economists such as Rudiger Dornbusch have agreed that the reunion shock was a great surprise and quite unprecedented. (Incidentally, in December 1989, I wrote a paper on German reunification which I sent to the UK prime minister, Mrs Thatcher, and was published in *The Times* on 20 March 1990, in which I thought that, with an average exchange rate of 1 Deutschemark to 4 Ostmarks, the cost would be "as much as $50 billion a year" for at least five years. Although this figure was thought to be quite ridiculously high at the time, the actual outcome has been nearer to $100 billion, that is twice as much!)

But surely any viable exchange rate system should be able to deal with such shocks? A good system not only should mute the shocks of, but should also create incentives to drive the economies back to, non-inflationary growth. A system that will operate satisfactorily only when things are going swimmingly is not much use. As I have argued so often, the ERM is precisely such a system.

The Walters critique, Type One: A high-inflation country pegs its exchange rate to a low-inflation country

The so-called 'Walters critique' of the ERM arose from the argument that the entry of a country with a high rate of inflation, such as the UK, into a system of pegged-exchange rates where the other countries have predominantly low inflation rates, such as the ERM, would give *both* countries perverse signals for monetary policy, would generate instability and would magnify, rather than dampen, cyclical effects. With pegged exchange regimes, theory tells us that speculative capital movements, responding to expectations of movements of the parity, inflation, and to interest rates, will tend to induce policy measures which are solely determined by the peg rather than responsive to domestic conditions.

Consider the example of the UK and the bloc of ERM member currencies which have maintained their exchange rate parities with the Deutschemark — France, Benelux and Denmark — which we can term the Deutschemark zone (DZ). Assume that, with complete independence of monetary policy, the UK has a high inflation rate (10 per cent) and DZ has zero inflation.

Nominal sterling interest rates of 15 per cent and Deutschemark interest rates of 5 per cent then imply the same real interest rate of 5 per cent for the UK and DZ. In equilibrium, sterling will devalue continuously against the Deutschemark by 10 per cent per annum, thus preserving purchasing power parity. Assuming that there are no barriers to the movement of capital and no exchange controls, the real rate of return on financial capital is equal in the two countries and there is no incentive for capital to cross borders.

Now, let the UK join the DZ by pegging sterling to the Deutschemark at the existing purchasing power parity rate (say Dm 2.50 to one pound) and assume that the margin for tolerated variation about the central parity is negligible and that the parity will be held with absolute certainty for a year. Such an exchange rate guarantee will mean that all asset holders will find it profitable to switch from Deutschemark financial assets to sterling assets with less than one year maturity — they will get 15 per cent in sterling instead of 5 per cent in Deutschemarks and they will be able to convert back into Deutschemarks at the same exchange rate of Dm 2.50. At the beginning of the year this large demand for sterling financial assets, and the equally large supply of Deutschemarks, will drive nominal interest rates down in the UK and up in the DZ until there is no more incentive to move from Deutschemarks to sterling — when the interest rates in the UK and the DZ are equal at, say, 6 per cent. Since monetary authorities control monetary conditions through short-term interest rates, this will mean that monetary policy eases enormously in the inflating UK, and tightens somewhat in the stable-price DZ. Monetary growth will expand in the UK and contract in the DZ.

These monetary policies are precisely the opposite of those required for convergence of inflation rates, the ostensible objective of the ERM, and are clearly inconsistent in the medium- and long-term. As the year of fixity passes, the applicability of the exchange rate guarantee becomes correspondingly shorter. Everyone would anticipate that the UK would have to devalue sterling at the end of the year. Sterling interest rates for periods which straddled the devaluation would rise to compensate for the anticipated exchange rate loss. If the devaluation is known for certain to be 10 per cent, then one month money ending the day after the devaluation will require a *monthly* return of about 10.4 per cent (i.e. the 'normal' monthly interest rate, plus a 10 per cent compensation for the size of the devaluation, which amounts to an annualized rate of 228 per cent). (Such apparently outrageous levels of interest rates have become commonplace during the recent ERM crisis, with overnight interest rates of 500 per cent p.a. in Sweden and many thousands of percentage points in Ireland, at times when speculation against the currency was strongest.) Speculators will want to borrow sterling and buy Deutschemark financial asset, so that interest rates at this stage are high in the inflating UK and low in the stable-price DZ. The Bank of England, through its control of monetary policy via the short-term interest rate will be forced to pursue a monetary squeeze more suitable for a country with incipient hyperinflation. After the devaluation of sterling there is no reason why the process should not begin again — particularly if a new peg is established. The induced oscillations of interest rates and the violent swings in monetary policy are an inherent feature of the system. It is a roller-coaster or stop-go policy, the periodicity of which is determined by the holding period of the central value of the exchange rate. Thus, if the holding period were four to five years (approximately what happened in the UK from 1987 to 1992, with shadow ERM membership followed by actual membership), then the roller-coaster monetary policy would tend to exacerbate the normal trade cycle. It is difficult to see how membership of the ERM would reduce inflation in the medium to long-term. The monetary ease of the early months is balanced but not over-whelmed by the monetary squeeze in the last months. (And to add a political effect, it is more likely that governments will allow the reductions of interest rates than they will the rise in rates.)

This analysis of the ERM ignores many of the detailed features of the actual system. First, exchange rates are allowed to vary about their central value by either 6 per cent (for the UK, Spain and Portugal) or 2.25 per cent (for all the other members). This gives a flexibility and an uncertainty of timing of movements which will modify somewhat the certainties of asset yields which are assumed above. However, during the early stages of the peg, this can result in the weak inflationary currency being at the ceiling of its band while the Deutschemark will be at the bottom of the band — with the absurd implication that the Deutschemark is a candidate for devaluation. This is yet another distortion of the signals. Secondly, the date of devaluation or realignment and the actual extent of the realignment are not known with certainty, so asset holders cannot be sure of their return. This will attenuate the speculative activity, the movement of capital and the oscillation of interest rates.

Both the variation around the central value and the uncertainty of re-alignment, however, compromise one of the main claims for a pegged-exchange rate system — namely the reduction in uncertainty of nominal exchange rate movements. If, for example, the effective bands are very wide (say, +/-10 per cent) and realignments are frequent (say, once every eight months as they were in the first four years of the ERM's operation), then there is likely to be little difference between the pegged system and float-ing-rates. Either the pegged system is effective or it is not. The extent to which it is effective is correlated with the amplitude of oscillation of the monetary policy and interest rate cyclicality.

An altogether different tack is taken by those who argue that an active fiscal policy should be used to offset the oscillatory effects induced by the ERM and to enforce convergence. Apart from the massive swings required in the notoriously inflexible instrument of fiscal policy, it is difficult to see why fiscal and monetary policy should fight against each other (Temperton 1991). There are other more effective ways of countering the oscillations — namely exchange controls and, in particular, capital controls. If the hot money flows can be prevented, then the ERM can be effective in stabilizing exchange rates without the perversity in monetary policy. In the early months interest rate falls can be prevented by regulating the capital inflow or by imposing suitably high (and flexible) taxes on capital imports, while in the pre-devaluation stage, capital would be prevented from fleeing or subsidized to remain in place. Although there are many doubts about the efficacy of exchange controls, particularly if they only apply to capital movements — there is little doubt that if they are stringently implemented, then the oscillatory effects can be much muted. This must be set against the costs of exchange controls which include, *inter alia*, the distortion of capital allocation, the administrative costs, and the inefficiencies in the controls on domestic capital allocation, in the form of credit rationing, which are often required to make exchange controls effective. The ultimate control is to take money and capital out of the market system altogether and set up a socialist system of dirigisme...not a system which most adherents of the ERM had in mind.

The Walters critique, Type Two: The difficulty of coping with shocks once inflation and interest rate convergence has been achieved

The Walters critique outlined above hinges on the existence of differences in the rates of inflation between the UK and DZ. If the two countries always had the same inflation, then it would be irrelevant. But consider the state of ERM bliss where there is already complete convergence. First, let us suppose that all the economies in the ERM have had for some time the same rates of inflation and short and long interest rates, then keeping exchange rates pegged will be no problem provided there are no shocks. But suppose that a particular country suffers an unintended increase in monetary growth and its prices rise more rapidly than those of other members. There is now a problem of adjustment in order to get back to the *status quo ante*. To bring monetary growth back to the norm, interest rates must be raised in this particular country. But, given that there is complete confidence in the exchange rate peg, interest rate increases will attract an avalanche of capital from the other members. These capital flows will tend to increase, not diminish, monetary growth and so will exacerbate, rather than reduce, inflation. The critique then applies again. The ERM equilibrium with identical inflation and interest rates is a knife-edge type: it is inherently unstable.

Pegged vs. fixed rates

The argument applies only to *pegged-exchange rate*s controlled by individual central banks or finance ministries. It is not relevant for *absolutely fixed* exchange rates. In the pegged ERM case, exchange rates move substantially within the band and are periodically realigned. Variations in monetary policy are induced by the changes in the probability of realignment or intra-band movement, and monetary changes themselves generate such expectations. If, on the other hand, the exchange rate were absolutely fixed and were believed certain to remain at that value, then there would be no room for any separate monetary policies. This would require suitable institutions, such as strict currency boards, with a fixed parity with respect to, say, the Deutschemark, in each of the states. Each member's emasculated central bank would have to hold sufficient Deutschemarks to honour its obligation to exchange Deutschemarks for the domestic currency at the fixed-rate. In effect, there would be one currency for the ERM members. Only the Bundesbank would have the power to pursue monetary policy.

The Walters critique in practice: ERM developments in the 1980s

Throughout the 1980s, with the exception of the Netherlands and Germany, all ERM countries operated exchange rate controls with varying degrees of severity (Walters 1986, 1990). Italy and France continued rationing and directing credit until the end of the 1980s, so interest rates did not play the same role there as they did in the free markets in the UK. Nevertheless, manifestations of the critique appeared, for example as free eurofranc interest rates rose dramatically at the prospects of various realignments of the French franc in 1981 and 1982. Similarly, the upward pressure on the Italian lira together with the low interest rates induced by capital movements prevented the Italian authorities from pursuing a tight monetary policy which was clearly required in order to contain the burgeoning inflation of 1989/90. From joining the ERM in July 1989 with interest rates about 15 per cent (compared with German rates of about 7 per cent) the Spanish peseta was under persistent upward pressure until the ERM crisis of September 1992. The ERM periodically forced a reduction of peseta interest rates which, together with massive capital inflows, generated great inflationary pressure.

One would expect that the clearest manifestation of the phenomenon would occur as the open capital markets of the UK were integrated into the ERM. In all but name, Britain joined the ERM in January 1987. The chancellor made it clear that he was pegging sterling to the Deutschemark at around Dm 2.93 to Dm 3.00 with interest rates at 11 per cent (with German rates at 6.5 per cent). The next five years' experience saw the first buoyant stage of the Walters critique enacted in the years 1987 to 1988, followed by the consequential double-digit inflation and recessionary stage of 1989-92.

The Walters critique in the light of the ERM crisis of 1992/93

Denigrators of the critique have pointed to the success of ERM members in bringing down inflation and have argued that, notwithstanding a similar performance by non-members, it is of little or no importance in the real world. On the other hand, the argument has been widely accepted by members of the Delors Committee such as Gross and Thygesen (1990), the former president of the Bundesbank Pöhl (1990), and, in the UK, by the NIESR (Temperton 1991).

Throughout the Dini Report (Dini 1993) on the ERM crisis there were references to elements of the Walters critique, and they came near to the essential process in the following:

"...the emergence of exchange market pressure in an adjustable peg system may pose a difficult choice for the authorities: on the one hand, yielding to market pressure would weaken the disciplinary effect of the peg and the credibility of the authorities, possibly inducing anticipations of further realignments: on the other, attempts to hold the parity might require an excessive tightening of domestic monetary conditions and nevertheless turn out to be unsuccessful, thus resulting in an even greater loss of credibility for the authorities."

But what they do not point out is that the reason for exchange market pressure is that the pegged system itself generates that pressure by promoting perverse monetary policies. That is the fatal flaw in the system. Had the Dini Report recognized that fatal flaw, then it would not have been possible for the authorities to propose returning to the ERM. It appears that they could not conceive of any other way of reaching the ostensible goal of Emu.

Possible fixes

First let us consider those devices that have helped hold the ERM together in the past. Throughout its fourteen years of operation the ERM pegs have been held together by exchange rate controls or restrictions on capital movements. As discussed above, until 1990 there were formal capital controls by France and Italy which played an important role in preventing the capital flows that are so destabilizing to the system. At least the Dini report does not recommend a wholesale return to such controls, although Spain and Ireland used them extensively to defend their parities in the wake of the September 1992 crisis. I would suggest, however, that it is likely that the member countries continue to use, and perhaps even extend, *covert* exchange controls such as restrictions on domestic portfolio compositions (Germany) or two-tier interest rates (France). But I doubt if we shall ever see a return to the exchange control system that existed until 1990. The world markets' reaction against Spain, when she briefly imposed tight credit controls in September and October 1992, was a vivid demonstration of the degeneration into a regulated system. And in any case the whole rationale for Emu is that there be no controls over the Community participants.

Secondly, there are suggestions that countries be required to be much more willing to change the parities. The *cri de cœur* of the Dutch central bank was that they ought to have crammed a set of (surprise?) realignments into one weekend. Then presumably settled down to enjoy another ride on the roller-coaster.

Accentuate the flexible in the fixed-but-flexible system

But country authorities were all unwilling to see their currencies devalued against the almighty Deutschemark. Many an earnest editorial has pointed out that this was not consistent with the views of the founding fathers of the EMS. The system was to be fixed *and flexible*. Periodically, there would need to be a realignment to eliminate structural disequilibria. Then the EMS countries would meet and agree to realignments which would restore the viability of the system.

In its essence, this was like the original version of the Bretton Woods system. There was provision for changing the gold bullion parity when there was a structural disequilibrium in the system. Indeed, Keynes (1923), one of the main architects of Bretton Woods, had written his brilliant tract on the great damage that could be inflicted by a country hanging on to old parities (as Britain did in the restoration of the gold standard in 1925) when the Bretton Woods system was established. Keynes clearly wanted a flexible system that, whilst avoiding unilateral competitive devaluation, would readily allow the exchange rate to adjust to new realities.

But both Bretton Woods and the ERM ended up as ersatz fixed systems. Over time they went through a process of calcification. Governments were unwilling to change the peg, even when there was clear evidence that hanging on would severely depress or unduly inflate their economies.

Restore flexibility, cry the reformers, for at least the non-core members of the ERM, or, in the words of one of its enthusiasts, The Economist, create a "soft ERM" alongside the "hard ERM". Frequent, perhaps automatic, adjustments would be made to the central value, and there would be wide shoulders, perhaps +/-10 per cent with provision for moving outside. Such target zones may or may not be disclosed and there is a variety of actions, from monitoring, intervening, interest rate movements and, ultimately, parity changes which need to be settled.

As always the devil does lie in the details. With shoulders as wide as 10 per cent and considerable latitude to adjust the central value, it is difficult to see how the exchange rate system would be different from a dirty or even a free float. It would really only add the uncertainty of the behaviour of the authorities — not, perhaps, a helpful contribution. But in practice I would conjecture that, like the ERM of the 1980s and the Bretton Woods of the 1960s, there would be the same calcification. There will be demands that the government's policy be specified. Uncertainty will be ruining decisions and increasing the premium on interest rates. The 'target zone' will be narrowed to a point and we shall be back at the old Bretton Woods or the late-1980s ERM.

Macho rates and masterly inactivity

The calcification of exchange rate systems is a political and bureaucratic, rather than an economic, phenomenon — although it has, of course, enormous economic repercussions. Once an exchange rate is identified as the central value (in ERM terminology), that rate is elevated as the one that must be defended against predators. The success of government policies are very largely defined in terms of the success achieved in defending that rate as we have lately seen in the 'successful' defence of the French franc. It does not much matter whether the rate is, or is not, appropriate for domestic prosperity. (In the case of France, it is clearly immiserating.)

The fixity of the rate is rationalized by arguing that, notwithstanding domestic conditions, the fixity of the peg is needed to ensure that the rate of inflation is the same as that of Germany. (Strictly, it guarantees only that the prices of tradeable goods are approximately the same as those of Germany.) But it recalls old standards — when sterling was as good as gold — and old anchors of the monetary system. After so many years of inflation, the yearning for some anchor is understandable, even if the anchor occasionally is too tight and pulls the country under water. The parity becomes a macho-issue, defining those governments that are tough from those that drift with the tide.

But I do not think that this is the main explanation for the ersatz fixity. The main cause is surely to be found in the bureaucratic process. Obviously, a change in the parity is a wither-wringing business. It is a very big policy decision, affecting virtually all prices and activities to one degree or another. It denies past promises of 'no devaluation in our time'. Moving an administered exchange rate, even though that is sanctioned or indeed even encouraged by the agreements of the system, involves much eating of words, retraction of statements and changes in procedures.

Such changes are an anathema to entrenched bureaucrats. As a rule, bureaucracies are best at doing nothing. A Gilbert and Sullivan bureaucrat did nothing in particular and did it very well. A policy of 'masterly inactivity'. It takes a long time to change policy and a long time to implement it. Meanwhile, the private sector, fleet of foot, will make its own judgements on whether the authorities will be able to stand an onslaught on the parity. But, notwithstanding the introduction of management methods into the civil service, nothing will be able to change the lugubrious bureaucratic and political process.

Conclusions

My main conclusion is that the ERM, like Bretton Woods, is unreformable. If, as I think most likely, we do see the wayward countries of Italy and the UK returning to the ERM, then it will be the unreformed version. Thus Britain, for example, will be stuck with whatever rate at which she re-enters the ERM in 1993 or 1994, for the run up to Emu.

My conjecture is that the two rogue countries — and Britain in particular — will re-enter the ERM at high parities. After a period of what the French regard as disgraceful 'competitive devaluation', the most influential members of the ERM will not be allowing any such advantage to accrue to such deviationism. A sterling central value of around 2.60 to 2.70 Deutschemarks will seem appropriate, which is consistent with what it might have been had sterling stayed in the system and realigned in an orderly way. (I am sure that it can also be rationalized in the nebulous calculations of the so-called 'fundamental real equilibrium exchange rate'.)

So it looks like another ride on the roller-coaster at least for Britain, Italy, Spain and Portugal. Happy days for the hedging funds are not yet over.

Addendum (August 1993)

I do not think that the ERM was 'finished' by the events of August 1/2 1993. True, the widening of the bands of the ERM to +/- 15 per cent for all ERM currencies except the Deutschemark and guilder looks like a surrender to floating rates. The proximate cause of the widening was the enormous hedging operations of corporations and funds, particularly against a fall of the franc-mark parity below the lower bound. But why did markets believe that such a fall was possible, let alone imminent? After all, we were assured by pundits galore that French 'fundamentals' were sound. But, alas, the only 'fundamental' that was 'sound' was the inflation rate — and, indeed since, taking account of asset values, it was likely that there was *deflation*, the word 'sound' seems misleading, even in that respect. But, in all other respects, France was in desperate straights: unemployment was rising rapidly above 11.5 per cent, output was falling sharply, corporate balance sheets were increasingly fragile. All largely a product of its ERM peg and the high real interest rates required. The French experimented with reductions of interest rates within the ERM in early-1993, but were soon brought back into line.

The market perceived the enormous costs of the pegged franc and conjectured that no government could stand such a punishing regime, and that France would be forced to switch to a British policy of sharply lower interest rates and floating, albeit temporarily, out of the ERM. So the market shorted the franc against the central banks. Reserves and resolution ran out.

But this does not mean the end of the ERM, or the franc fort, or the French slump. France is unlikely, *yet*, to follow the policy embraced by the UK. It is perfectly possible for the French to continue with the *franc fort* policy — keeping interest rates at whatever level is needed to maintain a parity of around 3.5 to the mark. Then, the 15 per cent limits are a mere formality, just as the 2.5 per cent limits were for most of the time before August. I conjecture that this is most likely to be the policy dear to the establishment, and will be pursued by the Ministry of Finance and the Bank of France. With the exception of M. Seguin, on the nationalist side of the Gaullists, the politicians have all lined up to support the *franc fort*. There is too much face to be lost by any wobbling on this crucial issue.

So, I still believe that yet another ERM will be put together in the hope that it will produce a stable convergence, with no realignments, such as we saw from 1987 to 1992. Another five or six years would carry Europe, it is thought, over the hump to monetary union. Wishful thinking, in my view, but we shall see.

References

- Dini Report (1993), *International capital movements and foreign exchange markets: a report to the Ministers and governors of the Group of Deputies of the Group of Ten*

- Gross, D. and Thygesen, N. (1989), *Concrete Steps Towards Monetary Union*, Brussels: Centre for European Studies

- Keynes, J. M. (1923), *A Tract on Monetary Reform*, Macmillan,London

- Pöhl, K.O. (1990), speech given at Munich to the Mont Pelerin Society, 3 September 1990. Reported in the *Financial Times* on 4 September as *"Pöhl warns of danger in rapid moves to Emu"*

- Temperton, P. (1991), *UK Monetary Policy: The Challenge for the 1990s,* Macmillan (London)

- Walters, A. A. (1986), *Britain's Economic Renaissance: Margaret Thatcher's Reforms, 1979-1984,* American Enterprise Institute for Public Policy Research Series, New York and Oxford, Oxford University Press

- Walters, A. A. (1990), *Sterling in Danger: The Economic Consequences of Pegged Exchange Rates,* London (Fontana/Collins/Institute of Economic Affairs)

Chapter 3

How to reform the ERM

Gerald Holtham
Chief Economist, Lehman Brothers International

In the absence of fully-fledged European monetary union, or in the period leading up to it, it is desirable to maintain a system of pegged-but-adjustable exchange rates. Contrary to much contemporary comment, it is possible to stabilize such an ERM-type system and in this chapter we propose reforms to achieve that. The key reform is to abolish the unconditional commitment of central banks to intervene in the foreign exchange market to support bilateral parity limits and to replace it with a conditional commitment. Central banks would be obliged to intervene without limit in support of a bilateral parity, but only if the weaker currency met publicly agreed and stated conditions. These conditions would cover not only the monetary conditions in the weaker economy, but also cover certain real variables. Where the conditions were not met, a change of policy and/or a realignment would be indicated.

A conditional commitment of this type would be preferable to the current arrangement in which the Bundesbank, which is concerned with the impact of foreign exchange market interventions on its own domestic monetary conditions, essentially determines whether a currency is defended or not. Because the commitment was conditional, and more acceptable, it would be more credible to the foreign exchange markets and would therefore be stabilizing. Currencies meeting the conditions would seldom be attacked. Currencies unable to meet the conditions would realign rather than destabilize the rest of the system.

Why a system of pegged-but-adjustable exchange rates is still desirable

The sooner Emu takes place, the more member states of the EC will be excluded. They will, perforce, have to operate some sort of adjustable-peg system of exchange rates. While a common market does not self-evidently require a common currency, it is clearly compromised by volatile floating-exchange rates.

Now, it is a commonplace in current discussion that the ERM is unstable and an adjustable-peg exchange rate system is unsustainable in a world without capital controls. We are told that the only choice is between floating or a common currency. (Or the pipe-dream of a reimposition of controls). I reject that assertion as contrary to the evidence of the past eight years.

Some commentators argue that fixed-but-adjustable exchange rates are the worst of all worlds in that they do not realize all the transaction economies of a single currency, they necessitate continuation of 'risk premiums' on the interest rates of suspect currencies and, being generally fixed, they do not offer the flexibility of floating rates. These commentators ask: 'Why keep separate exchange rates if you do not mean to change them?' That is like asking why keep a fire insurance policy if you don't mean to burn your house down. An adjustable peg provides insurance against large asymmetric shocks (North Sea oil, German unification etc.). Additional transactions costs, compared with Emu, are very small if exchange rates are indeed generally fixed, and any risk premiums may be viewed as insurance premiums. To the extent that the system gains credibility and the probability distribution of shocks with diverse consequences across countries is itself seen to be symmetrical, there would not be any systematic risk premiums. So long as the fixed-rate system works (and there are issues there) it is just as easy to argue it is the best of all worlds. A reformed ERM therefore provides a good fall-back and, hence a 'threat-point' in negotiations over Emu.

This position will, of course, strike some people as odd in view of the recent difficulties of the ERM, which have dragged a number of European countries into recession behind Germany. It is evident, though, that an Emu might have had a similar effect and would certainly have done so if under the control of a body like the Bundesbank. It is true that currency turmoil would not have existed and so the premiums over German interest rates paid by other countries would have been avoided. But German rates themselves would have been quite enough to induce recession in countries with similar or lower inflation rates, as the example of the Netherlands shows. Its rates are at German levels and it is sharing the general recession. The fate of Belgium is similar. On the other hand, an ERM operated differently could have avoided many of those consequences.

The recent turmoil

The ERM has been subject to instability and crisis over the past year or so. Its origins go back to 1990 and German reunification. Reunification happened, unluckily, when the West German economy was already booming and many companies had completed, or were undertaking, heavy investment. Reunification was also followed by the collapse of the economy of the Soviet Union and the loss to East German industry of much of the business for which it was equipped. These two elements of bad luck were more important than policy mistakes in shaping the disaster that followed.

The collapse of East German industry, and the need to provide income support for the new citizens of the German Federal Republic, necessitated a tremendous increase in public expenditure that was entirely pro-cyclical, coming at a time of boom. This shock to the economy raised West German output, and inflation and the Bundesbank responded with higher interest rates. It was clear at the time that the German economy had undergone a massive shock which raised the equilibrium exchange rate. The exchange rate had to rise to divert German goods from satisfying foreign demand, to satisfying the much-increased home demand. It generated a current account deficit whose counterpart was a capital account surplus as foreign funds flowed into the country in response to higher interest rates.

Other European countries, of course, saw some of the effects on their exports of the German fiscal boost but not to the same extent as in Germany itself. While they got only part of the fiscal boost, however, they got all of the monetary restriction that the Bundesbank applied. Their inflation rates, in many cases, fell below that of Germany itself and they subsequently went into an unnecessary recession.

While economic theory specified the solution to this problem — a large revaluation of the Deutschemark at the time of reunification — unfortunately the central bank and monetary authorities concerned did not see it that way[1]. They still saw the fixed exchange rate system as a way of providing a 'nominal peg' for their economies to prevent monetary policy being too expansionary and leading to inflation. Their thinking was dominated by the perceived need to protect their credibility in resisting inflation. A little later, the idea of Emu also came to dominate the thinking of many and a realignment was seen as reducing the momentum for union. The notion of a change to the real as opposed to the nominal exchange rate was unfashionable. The lesson has now been learned the hard way.

An adjustable peg can be adjusted

One lesson is that when large shocks occur, governments must adjust an adjustable peg when necessary. Of course, it is impossible to provide a rule

---

[1] *The Bundesbank is widely reported to have favoured such a move but it was resisted by other countries, notably France. See Appendix 2 for an IS-LM analysis of these developments.*

for such a procedure. Judgement is necessary and it can always be wrong or be misused. That is unavoidable. The search for rules that provide the private sector with perfect assurance, or that prevent mistakes by the public sector, is a vain one. Sometimes politicians have to take decisions. What, after all, is a government for?

While the subsequent ERM crises were largely avoidable, they have thrown up weaknesses in the operation of an adjustable-peg system that need to be corrected if the system is to withstand speculative attacks based on a misreading of government policy.

Resisting speculation

Nearly all speculative attacks have at least some justification in the circumstances of the case. Speculators are there to make money, not to make a point. No single operator can defeat a determined central bank. He does not even try unless he believes a lot of other operators are going to try the same thing. And why should he believe that? Evidently, only if there are public and objective reasons for believing that a central bank's policy is unsustainable. Often, therefore, if the policies are sustainable, there will be no very determined attack. That does not remove all difficulties, however.

If an adjustable peg is to be maintained, a monetary authority must maintain compatible policies. Suppose it is doing so, but suppose that the financial markets do not believe it will continue to do so, for one reason or another. Speculation against a currency could then force interest rates up to intolerable levels. The recent case of Sweden illustrates the proposition. Call it masochism or fortitude, but the Swedish government was prepared to keep interest rates at 10 or 12 per cent indefinitely to maintain the Ecu peg for its currency, in spite of a savage recession. (That is proved by the fact that the government has kept them high even after floating the currency, in order to limit its depreciation). The market's refusal to believe the government would stick to that policy, however, pushed interest rates to 50 per cent and higher, which was genuinely intolerable, in that it threatened many Swedish institutions with bankruptcy. The krona had to be floated. Once a currency is at the bottom of any band defined by the adjustable peg system, it becomes very difficult for operators in financial markets not to take a position against the currency. The upside is so limited compared with the downside that, in effect, very attractive odds are being given to bet on a devaluation. Interest differentials have to be enormous to counteract that. Otherwise, there is the notorious one-way bet.

The market does not need to be utterly cynical about a government's policies to take positions against a currency, just somewhat worried. The flows which can be mobilized are then so large in relation to the foreign exchange reserves which any country holds, that a devaluation may be forced. The market's concern becomes self-fulfilling. It brings about that which it fears, by trying to insure against it.

Any viable adjustable peg system has to have a means of preventing its own destabilization by speculative flows betting on a change of government policy and thereby forcing a change of policy. This can be seen as the need to re-establish democratic control over monetary policy. Governments should be forced to change sustainable policies by the scepticism of the voters not the foreign exchange markets. Unsustainable policies, of course, are always changed anyway.

The role of the 'reserve bank'

In a situation where a currency is under pressure, speculators are selling it for something else. Some other currency is in demand. In recent ERM crises, that currency has been the Deutschemark. The key to the stability of the system is the behaviour of the monetary authority of the country whose currency is in demand. That currency becomes the key 'reserve asset' of the system. No other government or central bank can hold enough reserves to withstand the market, but the central bank supplying the reserve asset (let us call it the reserve bank) cannot run out of reserves because it can print the money in demand. Only the Bundesbank can meet the speculators' demand for Deutschemarks because it can supply an unlimited amount. The stability of any parity in the system, therefore, depends on the attitude to it of the system's reserve bank. Note that the ERM does not have a formal reserve bank as such, though in practice that role has been played by the Bundesbank. Conceivably, that situation could change and another authority could become the true reserve bank, at least for a time.

In principle, under the rules of the ERM, modified by the Basle-Nyborg agreement, the Bundesbank has an obligation to intervene to support any other currency when it reaches its bilateral limit against the Deutschemark. The Bundesbank does not like that obligation because it correctly recognizes that it is incompatible with its own complete autonomy in setting German monetary policy. If the Bundesbank is obliged to meet foreign demand for Deutschemarks by intervention in the foreign exchange market, it obviously cannot control the money supply which will swell in response to foreign demand. In practice it has tried to avoid this obligation by seeking to persuade other countries to devalue when the pressures became considerable. In the case of sterling, senior Bundesbank officials helped to undermine the parity with press briefings. On the other hand, the Bundesbank has judged it politic to express unreserved support for the French franc and to intervene when requested to do so — at least until August 1993. Up until then, the defence of the franc had been correspondingly successful.

Now the present situation is very unsatisfactory. The markets know the Bundesbank is jealous of its autonomy and given to concern about the money supply. The Bundesbank's commitment to any given ERM parity, therefore, lacks credibility. That is the ultimate source of the system's instability. If one could imagine a situation in which the credibility of the Bundesbank's commitment to a parity was complete, it is evident that there would be no crisis and no instability. The important thing is to secure the credibility of the Bundesbank's (or more generally, any reserve bank's) commitment to a set of parities. The essential step in achieving that, paradoxically, is to relieve the Bundesbank of the unconditional necessity to intervene when a currency is in trouble. It is precisely because the commitment is unconditional that it is incredible. No-one believes that the Bundesbank is going to inflate German M3 on behalf of any ERM currency, irrespective of the circumstances. The commitment needs to be limited by being made strictly conditional. That would make the Bundesbank much more comfortable by reducing, if not resolving, the tension between its domestic inflation-controlling duties and its ERM commitments. The conditional commitment would be more credible.

New rules of the game

The basic requirement for ERM reform, therefore, is devising, negotiating and agreeing a set of conditions which any currency must fulfil in order to qualify for unlimited support from the system's reserve bank. The conditions must be such as to persuade the reserve bank that speculation against the currency is not based on fundamentals and can be resisted. That, in turn, means that any expansion of the money supply caused by intervention will be short-lived, since defeated speculators will eventually have to sell the newly-created reserve asset balances (Deutschemarks, in recent practice) back to the central bank in order to liquidate short positions in the currency against which they are speculating. Even the conditional commitment necessarily entails that the reserve bank cannot control its money supply on a day-to-day or week-to-week basis. The conditions should mean, however, that departure of the money supply from target will be temporary and non-inflationary. Why, it may be asked, would an institution like the Bundesbank wish to accept even this innocuous limitation on its ability to control its money supply? The answer is that its current situation of incompatible commitments modified by an invidious exercise of political favouritism is rather worse.

The rules of the game should also stipulate some restrictions on the extent of sterilization of such obligatory intervention. Sterilization occurs when a central bank seeks to counteract the effect on its money supply of purchases of foreign currency by selling other assets. For example, by selling domestic-currency bonds or bills it can soak up the extra deposits it has created. That can, however, drive up interest rates, encouraging capital inflows and necessitating further rounds of intervention. In principle, the reserve bank of a reformed ERM should accept the (temporary) effect on its money supply of obligatory intervention. Of course, if the extra deposits are then used by its commercial banks to extend more credit, leading to a further secondary expansion of its money supply, some sterilization is in order. In practice, it will be very difficult to codify precisely rules of acceptable sterilization practice and some good faith on the part of the reserve bank must be assumed.

What of currencies that do not meet the conditions? The answer clearly is that, if subjected to speculative attack, they must devalue. The adjustable peg adjusts — along, no doubt, with other policies — until the conditions are met. The whole trick now lies in devising conditions that will satisfy the Bundesbank and the markets.

Before setting out such conditions, let us deal in passing with another possibility, namely the reintroduction of foreign exchange or other controls to prevent speculation. Clearly, if different currencies are to exist within a common market, it is important that exchange between them should be rapid, cheap and trouble-free. If converting from one currency to another really is difficult, that will either condemn companies to hold large balances of different currencies or would otherwise limit the efficiency of the single market. And the existence of controls would make it difficult for everyone because there is no clear distinction between 'speculation' and other legitimate commercial transactions. To limit the former, on any definition, would require scrutinizing the latter. That argues against controls. In any event, the operation of controls in a generally liberalized environment is extremely problematic; to be effective they would have to be heavy and well-policed, which entails costs in itself. Not only is the effort to maintain controls likely to be either futile or expensive, I argue that, in a well-run system, it is unnecessary. As long as parities are defensible and the reserve bank's commitment to defend them is undoubted, the system does not need controls.

Conditions for intervention

When is an exchange rate worth defending? One answer is when it is compatible with balance of payments equilibrium over time. That does not mean that the current account has to balance. It means economic agents have to believe that over long periods of time there will be no tendency for foreign debt (be it private or public sector) to rise without limit. Evidently, acceptable current account deficits can occur, for example when a country is investing heavily and importing capital goods, which will be used to generate output and income sufficient to service the debt. Another example is when a country's cycle is out of phase with partners; a period of high activity can lead to a deficit which will be followed by a balancing surplus when activity is relatively low.

Markets, and central banks, have to look forward, however. The current condition of foreign debt and the balance of payments are not adequate indicators. If a country is running a very high inflation rate it can be anticipated that it will become uncompetitive and begin to run unsustainable deficits at a fixed exchange rate. Unless inflation can be reduced, the currency must depreciate. Take another step down the causal chain; suppose a country is running a very loose monetary policy according to certain indicators. For example, interest rates are low, the yield curve is steeply sloping (i.e. long-dated bonds bear higher yields than short-term debt), the money supply is growing quickly and asset prices are rising. It is predictable that, if this continues, general inflation will ensue and the exchange rate will prove to be unsustainable. It would be reasonable for the reserve bank to decline to support such a currency unless policy changes were made, even if the current account happened to be in balance, or surplus and current goods-price inflation happened to be low.

From there, it is possible to argue that the indicators with which the reserve bank should concern itself are monetary indicators. After all, what does it matter if the current account is in deficit and inflation is high if monetary policy is restrictive? Eventually, that restriction will slow inflation and rectify the current account. That argument should, in principle, be congenial to the Bundesbank. Within Germany, it looks primarily at money supply growth when setting interest rates, although it also takes actual inflation and the exchange rate into account. Why should it be any different when it considers international elements? In a world where prices responded readily to fluctuations in monetary demand, without great fluctuations in the level of output and real activity, the argument would surely be correct.

Yet, evidently, things do not work like that. The UK's monetary policy was as restrictive as anyone could wish in September 1992; interest rates were high, the yield curve was inverse, money growth was slowing rapidly — to the point where the monetarists were shrieking for lower interest rates — and inflation itself was falling. Speculation arose because the markets did not think this policy would lead to a rapid decline in UK prices and a restoration of UK competitiveness and output. They believed it would lead to a prolongation of recession or slump, leading eventually to the policy being abandoned. The market thought real activity variables, not prices, would do much of the adjustment and in a politically intolerable way. Moreover the Bundesbank thought so too. Its president, Dr Schlesinger, in a series of press briefings which could be described as unprofessional or Machiavellian, according to taste, made it clear he thought sterling was over-valued.

His evidence seemed to be the UK's current account deficit persisting at a time of deep relative recession. In logic, that situation could be resolved by tight money forcing much lower prices in the UK, but Dr Schlesinger did not believe in that outcome. It turns out that even the president of the world's most independent central bank does not really believe in the neutrality of money, he knows that real-world economies have Keynesian characteristics.

If he were both consistent — and a democrat — he should, therefore, be arguing that his own institution be subjected to democratic control. However, in practice, that will not happen and we must deal with a reserve bank that pretends to be thoroughly monetarist (justifying its constitutional status) while actually holding Keynesian beliefs (a credit to its powers of common observation). That means that purely monetary conditions will not do for a currency to qualify for reserve bank support. Monetary indicators are necessary, but not sufficient.

Implicitly, what everyone recognizes is that certain imbalances may be so great that their rectification requires larger relative price changes than can easily be achieved without changing the nominal exchange rate. The effort to bring about those changed relative prices at a constant nominal exchange rate will, in reality, entail such severe disruption to economic activity and such consequent hardship to many voters, that it is politically unsustainable as well as being severely sub-optimal. Why economies are like that and why key relative prices are so sticky, is too deep a question to be discussed here. Because it is not readily explicable, formally, in simple economic models, some economists have attempted to deny the phenomenon, generally with disastrous consequences when their policy advice was followed. It is sufficient to note at this point that the 'market clearing' model, which assumes relative prices can be rapidly and readily changed without limit and all unemployment is due to mistakes in people's expectations, has gone out of fashion under the burden of a great weight of contrary evidence. Moreover, and decisively in this context, the Bundesbank does not believe it.

Monetary indicators

Both monetary policy and other indicators will be necessary for the reformed ERM. The monetary indicators are the easy part and may be dealt with first.

The Bundesbank's own preference is for a broad-money indicator, like its own M3. Its approach to Stage II of the Maastricht process is to ask that other countries introduce their own monetary targets. There is no reason to resist this request. There are periods of instability in the relation between money and nominal GDP, however, so it would be as well to supplement the monetary aggregate with other indicators of monetary stance. Real short-term interest rates and the yield curve are two such. Other indicators of incipient inflationary pressure are available, notably certain prices that tend to lead the general price level, such as asset prices — equities and property. One, very reasonable, suggestion is to use standard techniques to construct the best available composite leading indicator of inflation and to use that. It would be less likely to send a false signal than any single indicator[1]. Of course, a government cannot change an inflation indicator quickly but observation of the indicator helps to determine whether the monetary stance is appropriate.

Real indicators

As noted above, none of those indicators would have captured the situation faced by sterling in September 1992. The essence of the problem was the perception of real, not monetary, imbalances in the economy that required a change in the exchange rate. The British price level simply could not be expected to adjust to the extent necessary without an unacceptable slump. Chief among the imbalances was the current account situation. This suggests that a key indicator will be a cyclically-adjusted measure of the current account. As a country's level of activity rises or falls relative to that of trading partners, its current account moves into, or out of, deficit. This purely cyclical movement can be measured approximately and the current account can be corrected for it. The remaining, or 'structural,' current balance then becomes a relevant indicator. There is no need to take it too seriously. Balance of payments statistics are notoriously unreliable; indeed, there is a large deficit in the global sum of national balances of payments, which should be identically zero, indicating an error in the data. A deficit of, say, 3 per cent of GDP, cyclically adjusted, might, however be *prima facie* evidence of a problem. It should be looked at in conjunction with the accumulated level of foreign debt (the sum of past current account deficits).

Since the UK was running actual deficits of more than 3 per cent and a cyclical adjustment would have swollen them further, that might have justified the reserve bank in declining to intervene to support sterling. The UK is a creditor country with a positive net foreign asset balance, which would have argued in favour of supporting sterling, but that balance has been declining very rapidly in recent years.

---

[1] *See Stephen Hall and Anthony Garratt, 'A Proposed Framework for Monetary Policy', Centre for Economic Forecasting, London Business School, Discussion Paper No. 0993, 1993.*

Another, more forward-looking, indicator of external competitiveness is the prices of goods that are traded internationally relative to their prices in other countries. If these prices are out of line, it is likely that trade will deteriorate, even if currently in balance. At best, though, this should merely be a supplementary or tie-break indicator, because measures of relative good prices are extremely treacherous. Who is to say that similar goods are really similar to consumers? Attempts to establish that a law of one price prevails for traded goods have failed. The OECD publishes 'purchasing power parities' (PPPs) or measures of difference in price level among countries. When these are used to calculate 'equilibrium' exchange rates, an exercise followed by a number of commercial companies, they produce implausible results. Even floating-exchange rates show no tendency to revert to the calculated equilibrium. PPPs have a role, but it is limited.

So far, none of the indicators is likely to cause any great problems in principle. All the difficulties would come in deciding on appropriate target levels and on relative weights, should the indicators point in different directions. Yet it would be necessary to be as explicit as possible on all these things for two reasons. First, to limit the scope for invidious exercises of judgment by the reserve bank, although these cannot be entirely eliminated; second, to ensure that the reserve bank's decision will generally be predictable by the market. Only when it is so predictable on the basis of published data can unnecessary speculation be avoided.

One, much more difficult, consideration remains. Take the case of Ireland, which was forced into a devaluation and which was refused convincing Bundesbank support, although it had a current account surplus as well as adequately tight money. It was argued, at the time, that Ireland's balance of payments position had been made untenable by the sterling devaluation, but this justification lacked plausibility. The devaluation of sterling, not to mention the peseta and lira, had undermined the competitiveness of all the ERM currencies. The large devaluations of the Nordic currencies had left Denmark in a particularly uncompetitive position, yet the krone was not devalued. The main difference between Ireland and Denmark was that the Irish system of housing finance relies on floating-rate mortgages on the British pattern, while that of Denmark has fixed-rate mortgages in the continental style. That means high short-term interest rates, necessary to defend the currency, do not have the potentially catastrophic effect on households' finances, the state of the economy, employment and, hence, the government's political survival which they do in Ireland and the UK.

If the Bundesbank was correct to cut Ireland adrift, its action can be justified only on the grounds that the effect on real activity made the Irish exchange rate policy unsustainable. In other words an implicit judgment about the real economy and the limits of political toleration was involved. The market speculated against the French franc for months on precisely the same grounds. There is no inconsistency between French monetary policy or balance of payments and the current exchange rate. The entire question is whether it makes sense to subject the French economy to avoidable deflation and whether the French government continue to do so? It remains to be seen how that question is answered after the 1 August 1993 move to wider ERM bands.

If both the Bundesbank and the markets have acted on such considerations they are undeniably relevant to the rules of the game of an adjustable rate system like ERM. Yet they raise peculiar difficulties. How can a foreign central bank judge the limits of political tolerance and the politically acceptable better than politicians, whose careers depend on that judgement? A government with an 'over-valued' exchange rate can generally prevent the overvaluation showing up in a balance of payments deficit by following a very deflationary fiscal policy. That reduces absorption in the economy, almost certainly at the cost of high unemployment. Unemployment then becomes the only obvious indicator that the exchange rate is overvalued. The markets can look at the unemployment and conclude that a devaluation is in order and they can speculate that the government will eventually have one. That describes the situation of the French franc. Should the ERM's reserve bank therefore take account of unemployment rates in deciding whether a currency should be supported, or not? And if it takes account of unemployment rates, why not political opinion polls, too? The market certainly takes account of both.

In reality, it may well be that no agreement could be secured on an 'activity variable' like unemployment being used as a condition for exchange rate support. That would leave doubts in the mind of the market and result in some avoidable speculation remaining likely. A compromise might be to introduce such an activity variable, but to give it very wide bands. For example, unemployment or bankruptcies would have to have risen, say, three percentage points relative to a trend level within a limited time period, say, eighteen months, before being regarded as relevant.

Ironically, the Bundesbank might well resist being asked to take account of a real activity variable in deciding on intervention. It raises too many questions about its own domestic objectives and constraints. In any case, the reformed ERM could operate without an activity variable among its conditions for reserve bank intervention, though it would operate less well.

Double jeopardy

Finally, consider the situation where a currency is not in accordance with the conditions and devalues. Evidently, the effect of a devaluation and of any accompanying policy changes will take time to have their effect. A current account imbalance, for example, is often worsened for a year or more by devaluation. Generally, markets are aware of these lags and do not drive a currency ever lower while the lags work through. Nonetheless, an ERM currency cannot be left indefinitely without formal underpinning. The conditions must include a 'no double-jeopardy' clause. Once a currency has undergone an agreed realignment, it automatically becomes in good order and is subject to unlimited support for an agreed period — say, six months. Thereafter, if it is still not in accord with conditions, its support may be withdrawn. Such a rule would have the effect of turning the ERM into a crawling-peg arrangement for currencies where a fixed peg is not appropriate or defensible, with adjustment each six months. Forward markets and interest differentials would adapt to that situation.

Institutional change

Some will object that even the best and most tightly-defined set of indicators will leave the reserve bank with a large degree of discretion. That is true, but the current situation leaves the Bundesbank with enormous discretion, which it chose to exercise, up until 1 August 1993, on behalf of the French franc and, to a lesser extent, the Danish krone, and against the lira, sterling and Irish punt. Moreover, the discretion then was exercised on no stated criteria whatever. Any degree of objectivity and predictability must be an improvement.

Others, notably French commentators, would object that the reserve bank of even a reformed ERM would remain one of its constituent central banks, probably the Bundesbank, and therefore true multilateral control of European monetary policy would not be achieved. That is true, though it remains an open question how far the German authorities will really be prepared to go in sharing control of their currency, in any case. Once exchange rates are fixed and intervention depends on criteria relating to the situation in other countries, though, any reserve bank is willy-nilly accepting some internationalization of its policy. It would be quite normal if regular meetings were held among central banks to review the state of the indicators in different countries. If such a committee were to decide and declare, for example, that a country's indicators showed its currency was in good order, it would be politically more difficult for the reserve bank to conclude otherwise. Some element of joint decision-making would creep in. This approach does, therefore, provide an evolutionary route to a more European monetary policy. If a reserve bank is obliged, for example, to expand its own money supply via foreign exchange intervention because another country had a slow-growing money supply, and was consequently in compliance with agreed conditions, the reserve bank is, in effect, targeting an aggregate of the two money supplies together. That is, of course, entirely appropriate in a fixed exchange rate system.

Conclusion

Reform of the ERM has two elements: accept the need for realignments in the face of certain sorts of economic shock; and make foreign exchange market intervention in support of a beleaguered currency strictly conditional. Any currency would need to be in compliance with certain conditions but would then receive unlimited support from the monetary authority with the strongest ERM currency. Those conditions would apply to monetary and 'real' economic variables.

Chapter 4

The ERM: incompatible with domestic policies

Professor Tim Congdon
Lombard Street Research

The European exchange rate mechanism has had a troubled history. It is often described as a stepping-stone to European monetary union and a single European currency, and there is no doubt that this was one motive behind its creation in 1979. But the ERM in practice has been accompanied by so many devaluations, realignments and foreign exchange crises that it may have aggravated, rather than reduced, monetary tensions in Europe. The purpose of this paper is to argue that three conditions have to be met if a fixed-exchange rate zone like the ERM is to work, but that these conditions have proved impossible to reconcile, except intermittently, during the ERM's existence. The difficulties in reconciling the three conditions are so deep-seated that doubts have to be raised about the wisdom of trying to fix exchange rates in the manner prescribed by the ERM. The argument here has some affinities to the so-called 'Walters critique', although it covers aspects of the monetary situation which Sir Alan Walters has not discussed in much detail in Chapter 2.

Three conditions for the success of a fixed-exchange rate zone

The three conditions for the success of a fixed-exchange rate zone are that interest rates have to be roughly the same in all member countries (the interest parity theorem), that the prices, and inflation rates, of traded goods have also to be roughly the same in all member countries (purchasing power parity), and that the growth rates of credit and money have to be consistent with purchasing power parity (the monetary theory of exchanges rates). Although the three conditions have been widely discussed, a few words of explanation may be helpful. As will emerge, the problem of inconsistency between the conditions is most interesting between the interest parity theorem and the monetary theory of exchange rates.

One: interest rate parity

The logic behind the interest parity theorem is straightforward. In the absence of exchange controls and significant transactions costs in the foreign exchange market, a simple relationship has to hold between the interest rates in two countries and the exchange rate between their currencies. This relationship is that the difference between the interest rates (for x months) in the two countries equals the forward discount (or premium) between exchange rate today and in x months' time. The forward discount (or premium) reflects, among other things, the foreign exchange markets' expectations about where the exchange rate ought to be. The thinking is that it should not be possible to make an effortless profit by borrowing in one currency, converting the proceeds into another currency on the spot market, leaving the money on deposit in that currency and simultaneously covering the exchange risk by a forward currency transaction. Any scope for profits from such a sequence of transactions ought to be eliminated by arbitrage activity between banks' foreign exchange departments and operators very close to them.

Two: purchasing power parity (PPP)

The rationale for purchasing power parity is also simple. In a free trade area (such as the European Community) the prices of standardized products have to be the same in all countries, after adjustment for transport costs and taxes. If they were not the same, it would be profitable for middlemen to purchase the products where they were cheap, to sell them where they were dear and to make a large return for little trouble. This is not to deny that inflation rates may differ for a considerable period between countries in a fixed-exchange rate system. Inflation can diverge for products and services which do not enter international trade, while it takes time for middlemen to eliminate price differences, even for highly standardized and internationally-traded products. However, the price differences are eliminated eventually. Over periods of several years, inflation rates in traded goods have to be similar in the member countries of a fixed-exchange rate zone. In practice, it is rare for the price levels of one country's manufactured goods (of the kind included in producer price indices) to be continuously over-valued, or under-valued, for more than three or four years.

Three: monetary growth consistent with PPP

The relevance of purchasing power parity to exchange rate levels is widely recognized. The extension of the idea to the monetary sphere further complicates currency relationships and is perhaps a more controversial topic among economists. Clearly, international competition is a strong influence on prices in all countries, particularly in small countries. But there is another dimension to the determination of the overall price level, the behaviour of monetary variables. A commonly-held view, which has considerable empirical support in the long run, is that inflation rates reflect monetary growth. Inflation differences between countries, and also exchange rate trends, should therefore mirror differences in monetary growth. (This view can be termed the 'monetary theory of exchange rates'. It is closely affiliated to the better-known 'monetary approach to the balance of payments'.)

In more theoretical language, the price level in any individual country has to be consistent, not only with purchasing power parity between it and its trading partners, but also with domestic monetary equilibrium. Domestic monetary equilibrium is to be understood as equivalence between the quantity of local-currency money balances and the demand to hold them. It is not sufficient, for the success of a fixed-exchange rate system, that inflation rates in terms of traded goods are broadly the same in all participant countries. There is a further vital condition, that the growth rates of the different money supplies are compatible with that similarity in inflation performance.

Applying the framework to the ERM shows the areas of tension

The requirement that money supply growth rates be related in this sense can be very demanding. It is here that tension is created between the interest parity theorem on the one hand, and purchasing power parity and the appropriate conduct of domestic monetary policies on the other. Money supply growth is dominated, in most countries, by the increase in banks' credit to domestic agents, particularly credit to the private sector. In any one country, the interest rate dictated externally by the interest parity theorem may not be the same as the interest rate appropriate for purposes of domestic monetary control. More specifically, in the ERM context, the interest rate needed to keep a currency inside the grid may generate rates of private sector credit expansion (and so, of money supply growth) which are highly inflationary or deflationary. They may be so inflationary or deflationary as to be both socially unacceptable and at variance with purchasing power parity in the long run.

This is the kernel of the general problem of managing a fixed-exchange rate system and the source of the ERM's particular difficulties in the 1980s. Governments have been forced to choose between their diplomatic commitments to promote European currency integration and their national obligations to achieve satisfactory performances on inflation and unemployment. On several occasions in the 1980s, governments have given priority to their national constituencies and devalued against the Deutschemark. These devaluations have undermined the long-run credibility of both the exchange rate commitments and the ERM itself.

The argument can be expressed in a slightly different way to connect it more clearly with later themes. The ERM contains a large number of countries each of which has its own currency and its own tax system. The distinct currencies have their own histories (of devaluation, inflation, debt repudiation and so on) which largely define their reputations. Associated with a currency's reputation are certain patterns of expectation about future inflation and interest rates. A decision to join the ERM may alter these expectations, but it does not necessarily mean that the inflation and interest rate expectations for every member currency are identical, or even that they converge. Since expectations about inflation and interest rates are an important determinant of the rate of credit growth, the differences in expectations help to explain why — at the common or similar interest rate determined by the interest parity theorem — there can be large differences in monetary growth among the ERM member countries.

Moreover, every European country's tax system is unique in certain respects. This aggravates the problems of currency management, because the demand for credit can be strongly affected by tax considerations. If a country has high tax rates, and most interest payments are deductible from taxable incomes, its borrowers are more tolerant of high interest rates than if it has low tax rates and limited deductibility. Even if inflation and interest rates expectations converge in the way intended by the architects of the ERM, tax arrangements could still motivate differences in credit demand (and of monetary growth) at a common pan-European interest rate.

Systematic differences in monetary growth between countries are associated with contrasting macroeconomic conditions in the short run and diverging price levels in the long run. The divergence in price levels cannot be reconciled with exchange rate stability over a period of years. More concisely, fixed-exchange rate systems such as the ERM suffer from conflicts between the dictates of the interest rate parity theorem and the requirements of the monetary theory of exchange rates. Indeed, unless a quite implausibly long list of conditions (about similarities in inflation expectations, tax structures and so on) are met, these conflicts are inevitable.

The discussion so far has been loosely theoretical. It has identified differences in the demand for credit between countries as a powerful solvent of fixed-exchange rate systems. Much more needs to be said about the origins and character of these differences in credit demand, and about their interaction with monetary growth, before we can examine the real-world background to specific currency crises. We briefly survey the institutions of credit growth and monetary control in three large European economies, those of Germany, France and the United Kingdom.

An examination of the institutions of credit growth and monetary control in Germany, France and the UK...

In Germany, the first page of text in every issue of the Monthly Report of the Deutsche Bundesbank has a table on 'The money stock and its counterparts'. The measure of money under consideration is a broad aggregate, M3, which includes currency and all bank deposits. The dominant counterpart to it is the 'volume of credit', which is lending by both the Bundesbank and the commercial banks to the private sector and public sector authorities. The German notion of the 'volume of credit' is to be interpreted as the sum of 'bank lending to the private sector' and 'the aggregate deficit of the public sector (i.e., the 'public sector borrowing requirement', in UK terminology) minus sales of public sector debt to non-banks'. A large deduction is made for 'monetary capital formation', which represents the incurrence of non-monetary liabilities (such as medium-term bonds) by the banks. (This deduction is conceptually similar to the 'increase in non-deposit liabilities' which appears in the UK's monetary statistics, but it is many times larger, reflecting the greater preparedness of German banks to take on medium-term liabilities.) Other influences on monetary growth — such as changes in 'net external assets' — can sometimes be significant, particularly during foreign exchange crises.

The format of monetary analysis is similar in France and the UK, although the emphasis on a broad monetary aggregate is less pronounced than in Germany. The Banque de France's *Bulletin Trimestriel* includes a table on *Contreparties de M3*, although its Bulletin Mensuel does not. In the UK, the focus of official policy during the late-1970s and early-1980s was sterling M3, an aggregate which included notes, coin and virtually all sterling deposits held by UK residents. The credit counterparts were bank lending to the public and private sectors, adjusted for a number of external and miscellaneous items. (Setting external factors aside, bank lending to the public sector is equal to total public sector borrowing minus non-bank purchases of government debt.) The Bank of England stopped compiling figures for sterling M3 in 1989, and most official discussion of broad money developments now relates to M4. The only important additional counterpart for M4, which includes building society deposits as well as all the assets in M3, is building society lending to the private sector. It follows that the growth of broad money can be largely attributed — at least in an arithmetical sense — to the level of bank (or bank and building society) lending to the private sector.

Governments in all three countries are averse to substantial monetary financing of budget deficits. Differences in monetary growth between Germany, France and the UK can therefore be interpreted, in terms of numbers, mostly to differences in the growth of lending to the private sector. We need to consider what causes credit demand to be of different intensity in the three countries. Some insight into this issue can be obtained by examining the composition of lending. It turns out that, in all three countries, lending for house purchase is the largest single form of credit to the personal sector and, in Germany and the UK, it is also the largest single form of credit to the economy.

In Germany, official figures split lending into two types of loan — 'housing loans' and other (i.e., non-housing) loans. In recent years housing loans have typically been about half the total, although with some tendency for their share to decline. Fluctuations in bank credit are determined to a considerable extent by the behaviour of housing credit. In France also mortgage loans are important, although lending to 'societies' (i.e., companies) is larger than lending to *ménages* (households). Finally, in the UK, mortgage credit is much the biggest element in bank and building society lending to the private sector (which is relevant for M4). It is not the largest component of bank lending alone (relevant for M3), but there were nevertheless periods in the 1980s when the banks were very heavily involved in housing credit, both as direct lenders to home-buyers and through the finance they provided to building societies.

...highlights the importance of housing finance

In all three countries, therefore, housing finance constitutes between a third and a half of all credit intermediated in the monetary sector. It should be possible to understand, and largely explain, the contrast in credit trends if we can identify the motives behind this one type of borrowing. This emphasis on housing finance and conditions in the housing market may seem exaggerated, since house-building is usually only a low proportion of national output. Two points need to be recognized. First, in many non-housing loans the level and rate of change of house prices are vitally important. In loans to small businesses, particularly to new companies where the self-employed entrepreneur often has no assets other than his house, residential property is the most convenient kind of collateral. Indeed, a reasonable generalization is that lending to small businesses is likely to be higher, the stronger are expectations of rapid house price inflation.

Secondly, the housing stock constitutes roughly half of total personal wealth in all three countries. Thus, in the UK, the Central Statistical Office has calculated that at the end of 1991 personal sector wealth was £2277bn, while the value of residential dwellings was £1130bn. Goldsmith has estimated that, in 1976, residential structures in France were worth almost half of all tangible assets (excluding land). (R. W. Goldsmith, *Comparitive National Balance Sheets*, University of Chicago Press, 1985, pp. 216-7.) It is striking, and surely not entirely coincidental, that the proportion of housing to total wealth is similar to the proportion of housing finance to total credit. The variation in the proportion of owner-occupied houses to the total housing stock is admittedly quite marked, with owner-occupation much more common in the UK than in Germany or France. But this is less significant than might at first appear, because many rented homes are owned by landlords who have taken out mortgages.

The causes of the ERM crises in the UK

The time has come to apply our ideas to the analysis of crises in the ERM during the 1980s. Two episodes will be discussed in some detail. Firstly, the difficulties which confronted the UK's attempt to join the ERM in the late-1980s and, secondly, the tensions within the ERM following German reunification. These tensions, between Germany on the one hand and the UK and France on the other, forced the UK's departure from the ERM on 16 September 1992 and the virtual suspension of the ERM on 1 August 1993.

In late 1985, Nigel Lawson (later, Lord Lawson), the chancellor of the Exchequer, urged Mrs. Thatcher (later, Lady Thatcher) to join the ERM and establish this external constraint as the focus of British monetary policy. Although Thatcher opposed the proposal, Lawson decided in early 1987 to conduct monetary policy as if the UK were already a full participant in the ERM. Between March 1987 and March 1988, the pound's external value varied in a narrow band between Dm 2.95 and Dm 3.05. For most of this time, the pound had a tendency to appreciate against the Deutschemark. Reasons for the pound's strength included international enthusiasm for the UK's economic performance under the Thatcher administration and a reaction to a large, and probably excessive, sterling depreciation in mid-1986. However, also important was the gap between UK and German interest rates. UK interest rates were significantly higher than those in West Germany. Although no formal announcement of the exchange rate link was made, the foreign exchanges noticed the steadiness of the Deutschemark/pound rate and assumed (correctly) that Lawson wanted the rate to be semi-fixed. The combination of a semi-fixed exchange rate and a wide interest rate differential created an opportunity for low-risk arbitrage profits, by buying pounds with Deutschemarks and capturing the higher sterling interest rates.

Lawson tried to resist the upward pressure on the pound by cutting interest rates. The interest rate reductions were much criticized at the time and have been judged in retrospect as seriously misguided. They intensified an already-vigorous boom in private sector credit and stimulated very fast monetary growth, which ultimately proved inflationary. By contrast, German monetary policy in 1986, 1987 and 1988 was stable, and there has been little sustained criticism of Deutschemark interest rates in those years. The question arises, 'why was the level of interest rates appropriate to the West

German economy so unlike that appropriate to the UK economy?'. It could be rephrased, to connect more clearly with the themes of this paper, 'why was the level of sterling interest rates compatible with the interest parity theorem in the Deutschemark-dominated ERM also a level of interest rates incompatible with a non-inflationary rate of domestic credit expansion in the UK?'.

The root of the problem was that, in the late-1980s, credit growth was much slower, at the same interest rate, in Germany than in the UK. This difference in the intensity of credit demand can be attributed to the markedly contrasting historical relationships between interest rates and the rate of house price change in the two countries.

The position in the UK is summarized in Figure 4.1. It shows that over the 20 years to 1987, borrowing to buy a house was financially very rewarding. The increase in house prices, as measured by the Building Societies Association 'all houses' index, exceeded the mortgage rate in 10 out of the 20 years. Moreover, the gains in the 'plus' years (i.e., when house prices went up more than the mortgage rate) exceeded the losses in the 'minus' years. When additional allowance is made for the tax relief available on mortgage interest and the amenity value of living in a house (i.e., the imputed rent in national income statistics) taking out a mortgage was — for almost a generation — one of the wisest financial decisions anyone could make. The role of mortgage interest relief in enhancing the gains needs to be highlighted. Without mortgage interest relief the cumulative capital gain (in excess of borrowing costs) would have been worthwhile, but not spectacular. With mortgage interest relief, the arithmetic was dramatically favourable.

The situation in West Germany was quite different. As shown in Figure 4.2, there were only four years out of the 20 years to 1987, in which the increase in house prices exceeded the pre-tax mortgage rate. Although the calculation in the table does not make allowance for tax relief, it is evident that there was nothing comparable with the UK's history of massive and persistent gains. The cumulative 'loss' (i.e., the shortfall of capital gains behind interest costs) for someone who borrowed to buy a house in 1980 had totalled 30 per cent by the end of 1987.

Of course, there are many details which need to be filled in. But we have a plausible general explanation for the difference in the intensity of credit demand between the UK and West Germany in 1987 and 1988. Over the previous 20 years, borrowing to buy houses in the UK had given an excellent financial return. But borrowing to buy houses in West Germany had been costly for the great majority of home-owners. (The activities of investors/speculators who had bought houses on borrowed money, with the intention of renting them out, had sometimes been disastrous.) Memories, particularly when they are memories based on a whole generation of expe-

%	(1) Mortgage rate pre-tax	(2) Mortgage rate post-tax	(3) Increase in house prices	(4) Capital gain above interest costs	(5) Cumulative capital gain
1968	7.46	4.38	8.9	4.3	4.3
1969	8.06	4.74	4.3	-0.4	3.9
1970	8.58	5.05	7.0	1.9	5.9
1971	8.59	6.01	18.1	11.4	17.9
1972	8.26	5.78	37.4	29.9	53.2
1973	9.59	6.71	32.1	23.8	89.6
1974	11.05	7.40	1.6	-5.4	79.4
1975	11.08	7.20	7.2	0.0	79.4
1976	11.06	7.19	7.3	0.1	79.6
1977	11.05	7.29	7.1	-0.2	79.2
1978	9.55	6.40	17.1	10.1	97.3
1979	11.94	8.36	29.1	19.1	135.0
1980	14.92	10.44	15.5	4.6	145.8
1981	14.01	9.81	0.8	-8.2	125.7
1982	13.30	9.31	3.0	-5.8	112.6
1983	11.03	7.72	11.9	3.9	120.9
1984	11.84	8.29	7.8	-0.5	119.8
1985	13.47	9.43	7.7	-1.6	116.3
1986	11.92	8.46	14.9	5.9	129.0
1987	11.56	8.44	16.0	7.0	145.0

Notes:

1. *The house price series used is the BSA's for all houses*

2. *The post-tax mortgage rate is obtained by multiplying the pre-tax mortgage rate by $(1-t)$ where t is the standard rate of income tax. The standard rate in calendar years (e.g. 1957) has been taken as the same as in the dominant nearby fiscal year (1957/58) for ease of calculation*

3. *The 'capital gain above interest costs' in any one year is calculated using the formula:*

$$gain\,\% + \left\{ \frac{100 + \%\ increase\ in\ house\ prices}{100 + \%\ post{-}tax\ mortgage\ rate} - 1 \right\} \times 100$$

Figure 4.1   Capital gains from borrowing to buy a house in the UK over the last 20 years
Source: Building Societies Association 'A Compendium of Building Society Statistics', BSA press releases and 'Annual Abstract of Statistics'

%	(1) Mortgage rate pre-tax	(2) Change in price of residential buildings	(3) Cumulative shortfall
1968	7.05	2.9	7.1
1969	7.20	1.9	8.9
1970	8.56	3.4	2.8
1971	8.50	5.3	1.4
1972	8.29	5.5	3.0
1973	9.89	6.9	5.6
1974	10.47	7.0	8.5
1975	8.69	6.0	13.8
1976	7.84	4.5	17.4
1977	7.01	3.7	19.1
1978	6.42	2.7	19.4
1979	7.66	4.1	18.6
1980	9.55	5.5	17.8
1981	11.06	6.3	21.7
1982	10.35	5.3	25.9
1983	8.45	3.3	30.3
1984	8.31	2.4	34.0
1985	7.79	2.2	37.1
1986	6.87	-0.2	40.8
1987	6.39	0.2	43.2

Notes:

1. *Figures are available for several mortgage rates. The mortgage rate used here is a variable rate and applicable to mortgage loans secured by residential real estate*

2. *The change in the price of residential buildings is calculated from an 'overall price index for residential buildings', including value added tax, published in the section on 'General economic conditions' in the 'Monthly Report of the Deutsche Bundesbank'*

3. *The 'shortfall' in any one year is the excess of interest costs over the increase in the value of houses. It is calculated using the formula:*

$$shortfalls \% + \left\{ \frac{100 + \% \text{ increase in house prices}}{100 + \% \text{ mortgage rate}} - 1 \right\} \times 100$$

Figure 4.2   Capital losses from borrowing to buy a house in West Germany over the last 20 years
Source: 'Monthly Report of the Deutsche Bundesbank' and data supplied by the Bundesbank

rience, influence attitudes. Attitudes then influence behaviour. There should have been no surprise that, at the same interest rate, the pace of credit and money growth in the UK was far higher than in West Germany during the Lawson boom.

In early 1988, a fierce debate about monetary policy developed in the UK. One school of thought urged that interest rates be raised sharply to curb excessive growth of credit and money, and regardless of the likely ensuing appreciation of the exchange rate. Another viewpoint was that the rapid monetary growth would prove harmless, and that priority should instead be given to keeping interest rates and the exchange rate down in order to maintain export competitiveness. Lawson, who favoured low interest rates and the stable Deutschemark/pound exchange rate, was largely responsible for the drop in clearing bank base rates to 7 per cent in May 1988. The result was a catastrophe for the Thatcher government, which lost its reputation for competence in running the economy. With interest rates far too low for monetary control purposes, the increase in domestic demand soared to 8 per cent (in real terms) in 1988, the balance of payments lurched into heavy deficit and inflationary pressures increased. Eventually, inflation went above 10 per cent in the middle of 1990.

Indeed, in 1989 and 1990, the respective monetary circumstances of Germany and the UK changed totally. In the UK many government ministers, including John Major, who succeeded Lawson as chancellor, were inclined to blame overheating in the housing market — rather than the excessive growth of credit and money — for the return of high inflation. The government therefore considered a variety of measures to limit the tax advantages of mortgage borrowing. In addition to this structural change to the housing market, it had to deal with the cyclical problem of rising inflation. It hoisted interest rates to 15 per cent and enforced an extremely restrictive monetary policy, one result of which was a fall in nominal house prices for the first time since the early-1950s. The fall in house prices drastically reduced the value of housing equity, and weakened both the appetite and the capacity to incur mortgage debt in future. At any given interest rate, the demand for mortgage credit was lower than in 1991 and 1992 than it had been in 1987 and 1988. (The phrase 'the demand for credit' may be defined, more precisely, as the rate of credit growth deemed satisfactory by both borrowers and lenders.)

Major also agreed with Lawson that the UK ought to join the ERM. After entry in October 1990, sterling interest rates once again had to take note of those in the rest of Europe, particularly Germany. But Germany in late 1990 was, literally, a different country from the West Germany of 1987 and 1988. After the removal of the Berlin Wall in late 1989 and free elections in East Germany in March 1990, the Federal Republic of Germany and the German Democratic Republic achieved monetary union on 1 July 1990, and full legal and political union on 3 October 1990. German reunification had powerful effects on the macroeconomic situation, increasing tolerance of high interest rates in at least three ways. First, the demand for housing increased in the old 'West Germany' for simple demographic reasons. In 1989, almost 200,000 people moved from East Germany from West Germany, while 360,000 ethnic Germans entered the country from the rest of Eastern Europe. Immigration ran at similar levels in 1990 and 1991, putting further strain on the availability of accommodation. Rents rose sharply. Once again it became worthwhile for landlords to finance the purchase and construction of buildings on borrowed money.

Secondly, the federal government gave fiscal subsidies on loans intended to purchase (i.e., to privatize) and to refurbish the stock of buildings in the new East German länder. The interest rate on such loans was therefore well beneath the commercial rate on equivalent loans in West Germany. In an interesting speech on 2 June 1993 Dr. Helmut Schlesinger, president of the Bundesbank, noted that after monetary union, "our ability to slow down credit and with that money supply expansion by changes in interest rates was made more difficult...[The] demand for credit was, and is, ever more strongly concentrated in those areas which are not particularly influenced by the interest rate level...[The] extensive interest rate subsidies for communal and private investment in East Germany work in this way...About 75 per cent of all investment subsidies for the East German economy today consist of cheap interest loans."[1] It is not fanciful to see parallels between these tax subsidies on mortgage loans in Germany and the system of mortgage interest relief in the UK. Just as the memory of the tax benefits of mortgage borrowing stimulated the demand for mortgage credit during the UK's Lawson boom in 1987 and 1988, so the introduction of tax-subsidized credits for the new länder boosted the demand for credit during Germany's reunification boom in 1990 and 1991.

Finally, monetary union led to a large once-for-all increase (of about 12 per cent) in the economically-meaningful stock of Deutschemark money balances, because the conversion of Ostmark deposits into Deutschemark deposits occurred at an exchange rate which grossly overvalued the Ostmark. Large subsequent increases in social and infrastructure expenditure also enlarged the German budget deficit. Both the once-for-all administered increase in money balances, and the higher budget deficit, exerted upward pressure on real interest rates.

---

[1] *Speech and translation supplied to author by British Management Data Foundation, 19 July 1993.*

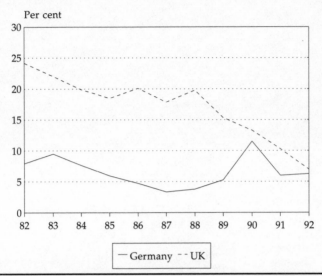

Figure 4.3   Growth rates of mortgage credit, Germany and the UK 1982-92

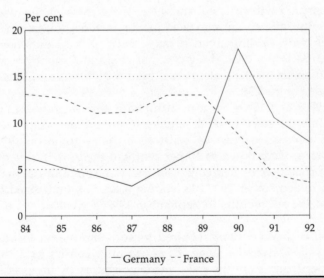

Figure 4.4   Growth rates of bank credit to the private sector, Germany and France 1984-92

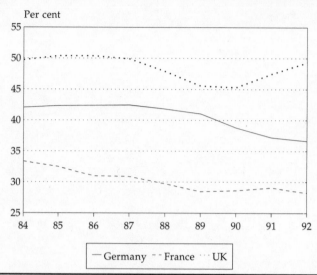

Figure 4.5   **Share of mortgage credit to total credit, Germany, France and the UK 1984-92**

These developments left a clear imprint on interest rates, credit demand and monetary growth. In 1987 and 1988, the growth of the stock of bank credit (and the money supply) was higher in the UK than in West Germany, even with sterling interest rates much above Deutschemark rates. But, in late 1991 and 1992, the growth of credit and money was higher in Germany than in the UK, at interest rates which were increasingly close together (see Figure 4.3).

In the 1970s and 1980s, clearing bank base rates averaged 12 per cent in the UK, while the stock of bank lending to the private sector usually grew by over 15 per cent a year. By contrast, in the autumn on 1992, clearing bank base rates were down to 10 per cent, but the growth rate of M4 lending to the private sector had collapsed and was still falling. Whereas in the six months to September 1988 M4 lending soared at annualized rate of 27.2 per cent, in the six months to September 1992 it went up by only 4.8 per cent.

The level of interest rates required to keep the pound inside the ERM plainly diverged from the level of interest rates consistent with economic recovery. Departure from the ERM, made obligatory by the massive foreign exchange speculation against sterling on 15 and 16 September, permitted a large decline in clearing bank base rate to 6 per cent on 26 January 1993. Signs of recovery became incontrovertible a few months later. The pound's problems — and the eventual need to leave the ERM — would clearly have been less compelling had German interest rates been, say, 2 or 3 per cent per cent (i.e., 200 or 300 basis points) lower. The loftiness of Deutschemark interest rates is largely to be explained by the macroeconomic sequelae of reunification.

The causes of the French franc crisis in July 1993

A similar story can be told about the pressures on the French franc in July and August 1993. As Figure 4.4 demonstrates, the rate of growth of private sector credit — which had typically been higher in France than in Germany during the 1980s — decelerated markedly in 1991, 1992, and early 1993. By early 1993, France suffered from declines in house prices and commercial property values very similar in character to those which had afflicted the UK a year earlier. The state of its domestic economy therefore made it essential for France to lower interest rates, but this could not be reconciled with the franc fort policy in the ERM. The 2 1/4 per cent maximum band of currency variation allowed by the ERM had to be suspended on 1 July.

The purpose of this paper has been to analyse some less well-known aspects of the conflict between external and domestic priorities in monetary policy. In particular, it has shown that the intensity of credit demand (and so the rate of monetary growth) is much influenced by conditions in the housing market. The housing market is in turn affected by a host of variables — including demography, the tax system and other institutional factors — which have no direct connection with the traded sector of the economy. A number of potential inconsistencies have been identified between the domestic and external objectives of monetary policy. Most obviously, at an interest rate which satisfies the interest parity theorem, the rate of credit and money growth in one member of the ERM may be much higher or lower than in others. Either the domestic objectives of policy have to be compromised, or the country concerned has to break ranks from its ERM partners. This breaking of ranks may involve devaluation, revaluation or, in the extreme, departure from the system.

Capital controls may be the only way to overcome ERM tensions

Is there any simple means of overcoming the tensions between the three conditions (interest rate parity, purchasing power parity, the monetary theory of exchange rates) for the success of a semi-fixed-exchange rate system like the ERM? One answer would be restrict currency convertibility on capital account. Indeed, the widespread presence of such restrictions may have helped the Bretton Woods system endure longer than would otherwise have been possible. The ERM may also have been easier to defend before the dismantling of exchange controls in Italy, France and Spain in 1990 and

1991. However, it would be an ironic and deeply unsatisfactory outcome if the ERM, intended to promote European monetary union, were able to survive only on condition that the member countries separated their capital markets and banking systems.

PART II

*The Maastricht Treaty
— still a viable plan for a single currency?*

Chapter 5

The European Community after Maastricht

Professor Dr. Martin Seidel
Legal Advisor to the German Federal Ministry of Economics[1]

The Treaty of Maastricht ('the treaty') signed by the twelve member states of the European Economic Community and the two other Communities, that is those on Coal & Steel and Atomic Energy, consists of about three hundred typewritten pages; in terms of volume, it is thus by far the most comprehensive treaty the member states of the European Communities have ever concluded to strengthen European integration. But it is up to the future to assess and to judge whether this highly controversial treaty, if it comes into force at all, will be, from a political point of view, the most important step towards European unification, as it is widely acclaimed by its supporters.

To enter into force, the treaty has to be ratified by all the twelve member states according to their national constitutional provisions. Although the European Parliament has not yet consented or ratified the treaty, it approved of it politically in 1992. Much to the surprise of political insiders, the European Parliament did so, though with certain reservations, despite the fact that many of its wishes and proposals were not accepted by the Maastricht conference.

The twelve member states agreed that the process of ratification was to be completed in 1992 and that the treaty was to become Community Law from the beginning of 1993. The ratification process, however, has not progressed according to that plan.

---

[1] *This contribution is based on a presentation at a seminar for institutional investors organized by the Westdeutsche Landesbank Girozentrale on 6 May 1993. The views expressed are personal and not necessarily identical with those of the federal German government. The analysis is a legal, rather than political, one.*

The treaty does not meet with broad public acceptance in many countries...

Although the treaty has now been ratified in the United Kingdom, there — and in many other member states — it does not meet with broad acceptance. In France, only a small majority of the people approved the treaty when they were asked to do so on the basis of a referendum. Members of the new governing political parties in France seem to be doubtful as to whether the road to political union, and economic and monetary union, is appropriate for their country. So, Jacques Chirac, whose party has the greatest weight in the French National Assembly, showed himself to be highly sceptical about the proposals and the future of the treaty. He is said to have declared that the prospects of the treaty remain uncertain, the solidarity of the member states in the field of monetary policy is breaking up, the conflicts of interest among members states are becoming more acute and that the current economic depression favours and justifies the emergence of national interest[1]. Instead of the simply-assumed march of triumph, member states are now confronted with the danger that their achievements of the last forty years will fall into pieces.

In the United Kingdom, the treaty seems to be very unpopular, despite the special status granted to the UK with respect to economic and monetary union, as well as the Social Chapter of the treaty. The irreversible mechanism for entering into the third stage of monetary union, as agreed upon in Maastricht, does not commit the UK and Denmark. Even when assuming that the UK fulfils the criteria for entering into the third stage of monetary union in 1996 or 1998, it will be free to stay aloof from the monetary union.

Despite the fact that the two chambers of the German Parliament approved the treaty with a broad majority, the treaty is highly unpopular among the population. The German government and political parties will probably not be able to deny the German population the right to be asked for approval on the basis of a referendum. The German population may not accept that the citizens of nearly all the other member states are deemed fit to approve or disapprove the treaty, whilst it does not have the right to give its opinion.

In Germany, a number of private individuals have recently challenged the treaty in the Federal Constitutional Court in Karlsruhe with the aim of obtaining a ruling that it is not reconcilable with the Basic Law. The Federal Constitutional Court has not yet decided on the matter — the outcome is uncertain and a matter for speculation.

---

[1] *According to the 'Frankfurter Allgemeine Zeitung' of 23 March 1993.*

state in which the powers are divided between the central state and the
member states. The European Communities, i.e. the first mainstay of the
union, do not form a federation, but a confederation. Later, we will be able
to see whether monetary union has changed the structure of the European
Community into one of a supranational entity. The two other mainstays of
the European union do not necessitate the creation of a confederation.
European union, which could just as well be described as 'European political co-operation', is no more than a procedure for co-operation among the
member states, and for co-operation between the member states on the one
hand and the European Communities on the other. Legally, the member
states have not transferred their foreign and security policy to the union,
they have only agreed to co-operate in this field within the framework of
European union. Any real transfer of competences to the union in the field
of foreign and security policy, or in the field of justice and home policy,
would require a new agreement to be adopted by the member states and its
ratification according to national law.

...does not create a European superstate...

Those who contest this analysis of the legal structure of the European union
should be aware that the treaty very clearly states that the 'organs' of the
union as mentioned in Article E, namely the European Parliament, the
Council, the Commission and the Court of Justice, only exercise their functions according to the provisions in the treaties of the Communities. The
Treaty of European union does not assign to the four organs any additional
competences, the treaty transfers new competences only to the European
Council. Even this competence is restricted to giving new impulses to integration without any legally binding effect. Maastricht has by no means created a superstate as many people feared. Prime Minister John Major has
been criticized that, in Maastricht, he had helped to degrade the UK to a
simple member state within a new supranational federal state. He — quite
rightly and convincingly — replied to the Commons and to the British public that he had kept out the Commission, the Parliament, the Council of
Ministers and the Court of Justice. Not even the structure of the European
Community had been built into European union.

...or, at least not yet

But, of course, European union is a programme and a political pledge to a
further step towards a more integrated confederation, or even federation, of
European states. And this is the basic message to the people of Europe.

The December 1991 conference on political union which led to the treaty
did not restrict itself to the creation of European union and to entrusting

the union with the two fields of co-operation. It has introduced a lot of new provisions into the Treaty of Rome, among which, the transfer of new competences in special fields are of some interest. These fields are education policy, vocational educational policy, cultural policy, social policy, youth policy, health policy, consumer-protection policy, industrial policy, policy of economic and social cohesion, research and technology policy, environmental policy and development policy. All these transfers of competences seem to be very comprehensive, but are, if one analyses them very carefully, not comprehensive at all. In terms of the Community's constitutional development, these transfers either complete or enhance already existing competences of the Community. These transfers are based on the existing structure of the Community, a structure which says that, basically, the members states have the competence and responsibility for the policies concerned; policy-making by the Community has to restrict itself to co-ordinating member states' policies, perhaps to adopting additional measures of the Community and to financing national programmes by the Community. These transfers of competences do not precondition that the structure of the Community has to be changed into a real federation or a federal state.

Therefore, conversion of the European Community into a federal state was not a general aim of the conference on political union, nor was such a conversion a subject during the negotiations. On the contrary, there was a tacit agreement among the participants to the conference that the basic structure of the Community should not be touched. In accordance with this, the strengthening of the competences and powers of the European Parliament was a minor subject of subordinate importance of the conference. The ideas of the participating member states were restricted to the concept that the European Parliament should have certain scope for wider participation in the legalistic process of the Community. The conference introduced the so-called procedure of 'co-decision' which replaces the procedure of co-operation as introduced by the Single European Act, in some fields. But, this new procedure does not basically touch upon the position of the Council as the general bearer of legislative responsibility of the Community. Even after Maastricht, the Community will be governed by the heads of state and government as the supreme policy-making institution of the Community.

One of the most important demands of the European Parliament to the conference was that the procedure to alter the treaty as laid down in Article 236 should be changed to the effect that any change of the treaty shall need the consent of the European Parliament in the future. The member states did not fulfil this basic demand — the conference deliberately reserved the power to deny any further amendment of the Treaty and the power to correct Court of Justice rulings to the member states. The member states are the masters of the Community and the masters of the union. There is no place — and no need — to include the European

Parliament since, at least in the near future, the Community and the union should not give up its structure and its nature as a community of independent and sovereign states.

The move to economic and monetary union...

The second Maastricht conference of December 1991 was assigned the task of transforming the European Economic Community into economic and monetary union. The documents to prepare this conference were the Delors Report, written by a group of monetary experts under President Delors, and the draft statute of the European System of Central Banks (ESCB) drawn up by a study group composed of the governors of the central banks.

The conversion of the Community into economic and monetary union (Emu) is based on the precondition that the single market is fully established. Completion of the single market means not only that all the measures enlisted in the 1985 programme for the completion of the internal market have actually been implemented, but also that all the other necessary measures (which were not listed in the programme) are implemented as well.

...is not made conditional on the completion of the single market

The conference did not expressly lay down that the member states join economic and monetary union, especially its third stage, only under the condition that the single market is completed. This is a shortcoming — it would have been wise if the conference had expressly laid down that the single market must have been completed. Such a provision in the treaty would have legally forced the member states to complete the internal market. They would have been forced to abolish, in particular, the remaining controls on capital movement, and they would have to create an integrated competition-based market in the fields of transportation and energy.

Member states may still impose import restrictions between each other...

Unfortunately, the treaty does not abolish Article 115 of the Treaty of Rome, which enables member states to introduce import restrictions against other member states. This safeguard clause is not at all compatible with the fact that the European Community has exclusive competence in external trade. If Article 115 of the Treaty of Rome had been abolished, the member states would have had difficulties in continuing to pursue national trade policies *vis-à-vis* third countries (for example, self-restraint agreements in textiles, cars and electronics).

...and there are other obstacles to the completion of a real single market

The treaty stipulates freedom of capital movement within the Community and in relation to third countries, but it introduces new safeguard clauses for capital movements.

The envisaged European currency would only become a generally trusted hard currency, appropriate for commercial and investment purposes alike, if monetary union is based on a genuine single market that is absolutely open, both internally and *vis-à-vis* third countries. The Deutsche-mark owes its strength to the fact that a common legal framework has been in place for any kind of economic activity in the Federal Republic and that all its borders to third countries are open.

Economic union, if it is to function well, requires that the principles of the market economy and competition are legally guaranteed within the Community as well as in its member states. The treaty obligates member states to ensure that their economies are organized and run in accordance with the principles of market economy and competition. If member states do not respect this obligation, they may be sued by the Commission or by any of the member states before the Court of Justice. Other provisions would have been necessary as well, directly applicable within the member states, granting rights to individuals and enterprises. The Maastricht conference did not adopt such provisions which would be the only ones capable of guaranteeing that the single market is respected as an economic system. But such clauses would — and should — be adopted by the next conference, scheduled to take place in 1996.

The elements forming a liberal economic system are the freedom of ownership, the freedom of occupation including choice of working place, the freedom to act, equality of status in competition and, above all, the freedom of assembly and of collective bargaining. These fundamental rights guaranteed by the Court of Justice are, however, not sufficient as instruments ensuring market economy. According to the still-prevailing doctrine, the fundamental rights and freedoms can only be enforced against the Community itself — they do not have restraining effects on the member states if the member states do not act within the scope of Community Law, but within their own competences. Individuals and enterprises cannot call for the protection of property as guaranteed by the Court of Justice if they are expropriated by a member state on the basis of a national measure. Appeal to the instances of the Community, especially to the Court of Justice, is not possible if fundamental rights and freedoms do not bind the member states too. Of course, there is national jurisdiction and there are national courts but, for a variety of reasons, national jurisdiction in favour of foreign nationals does not suffice to make up for litigation in the Court of Justice.

A single market and European economic and monetary union require that any national indexation of prices and wages be under the control of the Community. Completion of economic and monetary union, as envisaged by the EC member states, would make it necessary to forbid indexation of wages and prices — such a measure is tolerable only under the condition that it has been approved by the European System of Central banks.

Economic and monetary union also requires some Community control of national price fixing. Here, too, the treaty does not contain provisions to that effect, so that the next conference in 1996 will have to fill the gap in this context, too.

European economic and monetary union presupposes convergence of the member states' economic development, which is a responsibility of the member states themselves. Without it, a stable common currency would not be attainable and participation in European monetary union unthinkable. The only way towards convergence for those member states whose economic development cannot compete, is to orientate their wage and income policy to the domestic level of productivity. The treaty does not explicitly require those member states to do so.

Last but not least, an effective competition policy of the European Community must be free of political influences. Therefore, an anti-trust and cartel office of the European Community has to be installed if the economic community and the single market are to function well.

Considerable power over monetary policy has been transferred to the European Community...

The second conference has transferred competences to the European Community on a considerable scale. This transfer was made on the basis of the existing structure of the Community, not counting that by transferring monetary sovereignty to the European System of Central Banks an embryo of a federal state was established. But, in the long run, the Community will only be able to function as an economic and monetary union if it changes its structure and becomes a real federation, in the sense that it has been granted centralized-state authority to a limited extent.

...although all other aspects of economic policy remain at the member state level

Indeed, even after Maastricht, economic policy remains, contrary to monetary policy, a competence and responsibility of the member states. Whereas monetary union is characterized by a central and exclusive competence in the field of monetary, credit and interest policy, economic union restricts its activities to co-ordinating the economic policies of the member states whose competences in this field remain basically untouched. The basic reason is that, if the Community were to have central-state authority in economics, it would also have to have independent budget authority. This would imply, for the member states, that they surrender to the Community their defence policy, their social policy, their educational policy and, above all, their infrastructure policy. Without such transfer of authority from the member states to the Community, it would not be conceivable for the Community to have budget authority. Transferring all these policies would imply legislative powers of the Community in nearly all fields of economic and social policy relevance. In order to finance its expenditures, the European Community would need wide-ranging taxation authority. Transferring national economic policy to the European Community, which may be referred to as creating a 'real' economic union, would necessarily imply a substantial transfer of national sovereignty to the Community. Such a transfer of sovereignty would presuppose conversion of the Community from a union of states, that is to say from a confederation having the member states as its masters, into a real federation — that is to say, into a federal state.

For the time being, member states are not willing to change the structure of the European Community and to create such a federal state. The German federal government has quite rightly argued before the Constitutional Court in Karlsruhe that there is no consensus among member states to such an integrational step within the near future. Against this political background, economic union is reduced to decentralized responsibility in the field of economic policy and to co-ordination of national economic policies by the Community.

Co-ordination of national economic policies has already been provided for in the Treaty of Rome. The Maastricht Treaty contains additional provisions for co-ordinating national economic policies; these new provisions are much more stringent than the provisions of the Treaty of Rome and are, to some extent, legally binding. The economic policy of the member states will be governed by so-called 'general and special guidelines' of the Community. The most important guideline obligates the member states to pursue an economic policy that leads to economic convergence. Notwithstanding the financial assistance which can be granted by the Community (in special cases and to a limited extent), member states are responsible themselves for attaining 'convergence'. Neither the Community, nor any of the member states, is liable for failure and collapse of the economic policy performance of any of the other member states. At present, the way such liability has been structured in the field of economic policy is totally different from the one normally found in the case of a federation; the liability structure of a federation is based on solidarity, so that the central state and its members are liable for the failure of economic policy performance of any of the members.

Furthermore, the treaty strictly prohibits funding public budgets by central bank loans or capital market loans in excess of three per cent of the gross domestic product. Compliance with this three per cent limit is subject to strict monitoring under a surveillance procedure which enables the Community to take sanctions against member states.

Overall, the new provisions governing economic union considerably restrict the sovereignty of the member states but these provisions and rules, contrary to the provisions governing monetary union, do not create real sovereign power at the Community level.

Monetary policy powers...

Concerning monetary union, the treaty transfers the respective competences to the European Community in a different way. In future, currency policy, including credit policy and interest policy, will be an exclusive competence of the European Community. This exclusive competence of the European Community will manifest itself without any mediation on behalf of the member states. Transfer of monetary sovereignty will not take place by one step, but on the basis of a three-stage procedure, although this three-stage procedure presents a mechanism which makes the process more or less irreversible. The final stage will begin either in the year 1996/1997 (provided that at least seven of the twelve member states fulfil the so-called 'convergence criteria') or, in any event, in the year 1998/1999, notwithstanding how many member states then fulfil the relatively strict criteria governing entry into monetary union.

The criteria are well known. They require a low inflation rate, no excessive credit-financed public budgets, no excessive public debts, a relatively low long-term bond yield and participation in the European exchange-rate system for two years without devaluation. These strict criteria are preconditions not only for entry into the final stage of the monetary union, but also for remaining a member of the monetary union. These criteria shall guarantee that member states who participate in the monetary union are able to secure economic convergence without changing their exchange rates and without devaluing their currencies. The members of the monetary union are not permitted to vary their exchange rates as a means of economic adaptation.

...will be transferred to the European System of Central Banks

The monetary competences at the level of the Community will rest with a European System of Central Banks (ESCB) to be established for this purpose. The ESCB will exercise its political and regulatory powers and competences without any mediation on behalf of the member states; it will exercise the competences directly *vis-à-vis* private banks and enterprises. Contrary to nearly all the other policies of the Community, the member states will not have any chance of taking part in the shaping of monetary policy by the Community by way of additional national currency policy and currency measures. The monetary policy, which includes credit and interest policy, will be exercised on behalf of the European Community by the ESCB in the same way as member states exercise their monetary policy functions. The way the European Community and the ESCB will operate means, for individuals, enterprises and private banks, that their relationships with the European Community will acquire a new dimension. This new relationship will, in the long run, probably substitute their traditional relationships with national authorities. The ESCB will be independent: the members of the governing board of the System, i.e. the Council, will not be subject to instructions from national governments or Community organs, not even from the European Council. The ESCB consists of the European Central Bank (yet to be established) and the national central banks. In order to ensure independence of the ESCB and a common monetary policy, the national central banks will be taken out from the national administrations insofar as their functions of national central banks are concerned. Insofar as they exercise the policy and implement decisions of the ESCB, the national central banks will function like Community organs. They will exercise Community power, for example, when implementing minimum reserve provisions.

While responsibility for guaranteeing monetary stability will primarily rest with the ESCB, the European Council will have responsibility for exchange-rate policy towards third countries.

Central bank independence is only one element of German monetary stability...

Responsibility for monetary stability, however, rests also with government, trade unions and employers' associations. A central bank cannot guarantee, even when it is completely independent, the stability of currency and prices, if its policy is not backed and actively supported by the government, which is responsible for budget policy, and by the two sides of industry, who are responsible for wage policy. All three bear responsibility for monetary stability collectively.

When one looks at Germany's Constitution, one will not find any provision to the effect that the Deutsche Bundesbank, the federal and the state governments and the two sides of industry are collectively responsible for the stability of prices and that they have to act by consensus. Constitutionally, the three mainstays of stability are only united in the view that price and monetary stability is of a high political value. This basic political consensus originates in a centrally organized opinion-formation process. Without a basic political consensus, which has a special tradition in Germany, monetary stability can probably not be guaranteed. The general consensus on monetary stability comprises and legitimizes independence of the central bank.

...and, in itself, is not enough to ensure monetary stability at Community level

At the Community level, the structure of responsibility for monetary stability is very different. Besides the ESCB, responsibility for economic and monetary stability rests with the twelve member states. Responsibility for wage policy has not been transferred from the member states to the Community by the treaty. Wage and income policy remains a national responsibility. The question is whether the ESCB will be strong and powerful enough to come to terms with the twelve national governments as partners in responsibility for monetary stability and wage policy. There are justified doubts as to whether the ESCB will be able to stave off the pressure of public opinion in the member states, and as to whether national governments would not feel tempted to use their influence for getting a hold on the ESCB. Therefore, if the ESCB is to function in a way enabling it to attain the basic aims of its policy, it must be free from possibly opposing national influences. The question is whether the ESCB can attract a Community-wide political consensus on price and monetary stability, as a high common value.

Such a consensus does not exist for the time being, and cannot come into existence on the basis of the existing decentralized national communication systems. The national communication systems are entrusted and restricted to more or less national functions — they are shaping national interests and are fighting for national interests within the Community. Because of the divergent influences, the decentralized structure hardly supports a common monetary policy with the exclusive aim of price stability. The existing opinion-formation structure is to be regarded as a danger to the well-functioning of the ESCB, rather than a supporter. Above all, the existing structure of opinion-formation can never function as a real legitimating factor for the ESCB and its monetary policy. It will probably work the opposite way and get into conflict with the ESCB. In this case, member states would not support the ESCB so that it would have national governments and trade unions, not as its supporters, but as its opponents.

The danger of a conflict between the ESCB and national governments

Some argue that the European Community, in its capacity of economic union, has the task of co-ordinating economic policies of the member states and that the member states, under the treaty, have undergone several obligations aimed at supporting a stability-orientated common monetary policy. Co-ordination of national policies by the Community takes place within the institutional framework of the European Community. Within this framework, the member states are only subordinated to the Community to a very small degree. As mentioned above, the Conference of Maastricht did not restructure the European Community in a way that it can be regarded as a federation and can exercise its competences in the same way as a federal state.

The history of the European Community shows that its co-ordination function is not very effective — co-ordination of national policies has rather continued to be dependent on the good will of the member states. Therefore, the competences of the European Community in the field of co-ordinating national policies cannot be regarded as an absolute guarantee against any undermining of a stability-orientated common monetary policy. The danger of an undisciplined and uncontrolled national economic budgetary and wage policy continues. A Community-wide political consensus on price stability can only originate from an integrated Community-orientated framework for communication and for political discussion. Such a framework can only be built up, and can only be established, on a very long-term basis. Its building-up presupposes restructuring of the European Parliament into a representation of citizens, as distinct from the peoples of the member states. Therefore, the principle of equal voting rights has to be introduced. Furthermore, building up such a framework for Europe-wide opinion-formation on the value of price stability presupposes the appearance of integrated political parties, of new Community-wide mass media coverage and all the other institutions which normally form a part of this process of shaping public opinion. A necessary precondition would be that, first of all, the European Community itself be transformed from a Community which is dominated by its member states, into a state which is dominating the member states.

But the appearance of such a structure necessary for public opinion-formation is not, in itself, a guarantee that the Community-wide consensus on monetary policy matters would give absolute priority to monetary stability. There might be a consensus on the value of political aims other than monetary stability. Nobody can foresee how great the risk is that the new political consensus has other priorities and might not work as legitimating factor for the ESCB when it pursues a policy basically and primarily aiming for price stability. This is the risk involved in the creation of a monetary union which replaces national monetary policies with a common monetary policy. This risk is part of the general risks which are inherent in the process of integration as reflected by the Treaty of Rome and, more recently, the treaty.

Subsidiarity

Finally, a few observations on the principle of subsidiarity which dominates public debate within the Community. The principle of subsidiarity is enshrined in Article 3b of the treaty, and it is to ensure that the European Community exercises its competences, unless exclusive competences, only if national authority does not produce the same desired effect and if these effects can better be attained at the Community level.

Basically, the principle of subsidiarity is not so much meant to block the exercise of a competence, but it is a determinant which governs the creation of a federal constitution. By this principle, the founding states are to transfer to the central level only such competences and decision-making powers as they cannot exercise themselves. When they transfer powers and competences to the central state, they must describe these competences and decision-making powers in a precise and clear way. They have to do this because the process of transferring competences is irreversible, and because they need to have a guarantee to the effect that the central level can only exercise the competences transferred and, above all, no judgement can be passed against them by the Court of Justice in the case of conflicting interests. Furthermore, the exercise of competence requires two legislative chambers to be involved to this end, that is to say the Parliament, and a second chamber, composed of representatives of the founder states.

If one looks at the Community constitutional system, one notes that it corresponds to the second device. All legislative and political competences which have been transferred to the European Community rest with the Council which is composed of members of the national governments. But one also notes that nearly all the competences of the European Community have been described in a very loose way, so that, in a case of a conflict between a Community organ and a member state, the latter cannot be sure that the Court of Justice in Luxembourg will go along with its reasoning. For example, the necessary regulatory powers for creating and ensuring the well-functioning of the single market are just broadly defined. The extent and the structure of the competences, which are necessary for the creation and the functioning of the single market, are permanently discussed between the organs of the European Community and the member states. Neither the national constitutions, nor the literature, can give exact answers on the extent and scope of the single market. It is the unclear and imprecise description of the competences of the Community which has given rise to an understanding of the principle of subsidiarity to be a means of blocking any excessive exercise of the existing competences. Within the Community, the principle of subsidiarity is only discussed as a means of blocking excessive exercise of competences. For the member states, it is a dilemma that, when transferring competences to the Community level, they also transfer the power to interpret the extent of the competences to the Community level. Lastly, the European Court of Justice has to decide to what extent the Community has legitimacy for exercising special competences. Even the decision on whether or not the legislator has respected the principle of subsidiarity as laid down in the treaty, will lastly be taken by the European Court of Luxembourg, not by any national court. Those who know the mentality of the Court of Justice, and the basic lines of its jurisdiction, are doubtful whether the Court of Justice will ever declare null and void a legislative Act of the Council for disregarding the principle of subsidiarity. Such a legislative measure will always imply that, according to the opinion of at least a qualified majority of the member states, the political aim of this act cannot be attained at the national level. The European Court will very rarely disagree with the opinion of the majority of member states.

The demand for subsidiarity can also be understood to mean that decisions of the Community have to be sufficiently transparent before they are taken. Subsidiarity in this sense means policy-making by the organs of the Community must be understandable for everybody, and must be deemed necessary by the majority of people. In exercising its competences the European Community presents a political process for creating a new social and legal order within the member states. This new legal and social order must be embedded in a programme which must be presented to the people and must be publicly discussed. Not only the programme, but also the single measures, must be profoundly discussed within the framework of a democratic process since they must be accepted by the people if they are adopted and implemented. It is this aspect of the principle of subsidiarity which lies as a burden to the process of integration. If this aspect is not solved, the process of integration would probably not continue. The Community after Maastricht will only survive if its Constitution changes in response to the need for greater transparency. The treaty may be difficult to understand, but the Conference of Maastricht ought to be referred to as a milestone towards more enlightenment within Europe.

Chapter 6

The future of Maastricht

Dick Taverne
PRIMA europe Ltd.

The longer-term impact on the future of the European Community of the collapse of the old ERM can best be judged by looking at the attitudes of the pro- and anti-ERM camps before the traumatic events of July and early-August 1993.

Long before the collapse, the prevalent view in Britain — which had a growing number of adherents abroad — held that the treaty would prove to be dead as soon as the ink had dried on the signatures of ratification. The other view, which prevailed in the European Commission and was reflected in the official attitudes of most EC governments, held that the treaty was alive and well and that, in due course, no doubt after the occasional hiccough, the EC — or at any rate the majority of EC member states — would progress inexorably towards economic and monetary union.

The weight of evidence and argument behind the critics of Maastricht was impressive.

It is now widely recognized that, in their desire to move as quickly as possible to monetary union, the politicians ran ahead of public opinion in a substantial number of EC member states. Not only did the Danes first vote against the treaty; they were only persuaded to accept it the second time round after Denmark had been allowed to opt out of Maastricht's central feature, the commitment to a monetary union. The French referendum may well have been an inaccurate reflection of the real level of support for Maastricht — it is often said that in every French referendum the French vote on a different issue from the actual question asked. But no one can argue that the French vote demonstrated popular enthusiasm for monetary union in France.

The Germans have not held a referendum. However, every test of popular opinion suggests that the German public dislike the idea of losing their Deutschemark and handing over the control of inflation from their much-respected Bundesbank to a European Central Bank. British public opinion, likewise, has not been officially consulted. But the attitudes of the government, of an apparent majority of Conservative MPs and the results of occasional opinion polls, all suggest that there is little support in Britain for joining a monetary union.

Recent events can only have weakened public support for the Maastricht programme.

Intellectual, as well as popular, opinion seemed to grow increasingly critical. There were, from the start, widespread doubts among economists about whether the convergence criteria made sense at a time of recession. It was argued that, devised as they were in happier, pre-recession days, the criteria require deflationary policies that will make recession deeper and unemployment worse. It was also strongly argued, before the old ERM collapsed, that the mechanism could not survive in principle or practice. In principle, it was said that exchange rates which are not permanently fixed are incompatible with the abolition of exchange controls, at least while the economic performance of member states remains diversified. In practice, it was argued that the weight of speculative money would inexorably overwhelm weaker currencies and force a succession of devaluations, which were incompatible with the effective working of the ERM. Further, in a monetary union — the critics argue — the weaker countries will be worse off, because an effective monetary union requires a large central fiscal budget to offset local weaknesses; but the EC member states are unwilling to grant the Brussels' authorities the necessary fiscal powers.

Lastly, as proof that monetary union was nothing but a distant hope, the Maastricht critics pointed out that, far from converging, EC economies diverge by the day. Compliance with the Maastricht criteria recedes far into the distance, as even countries like Germany, which are essential to Emu, head for budget deficits more than double the Maastricht maximum, with little hope of an early return to the fiscal rectitude prescribed by the treaty.

This catalogue of criticisms contrasts sharply with the view from Brussels.

In the Commission, in the meetings of Ecofin and in the detailed preparatory work being done by the Committee of Central Bank Governors in Basle, steady progress to implement Maastricht was taken for granted.

"We have looked at the system [the ERM] with a magnifying glass", said Wim Duisenberg, chairman of the Committee of Central Bank Governors, "but we have not found any fault lines". There could be improvements in the way the system was applied, according to the official findings of a central banks' study group, with better co-ordination and, perhaps, a greater readiness to realign currencies when basic circumstances require adjustment. But the system itself was sound.

A very similar conclusion was reached by eleven out of the twelve finance ministers (Britain dissenting), who rejected the British claim that the
ERM needed drastic revision to amend its fault lines.

When charged with the earlier upheavals of the last year, the departure
of the pound and the lira, the devaluations of the peseta and escudo, and
the attacks on the French franc, the defenders of the ERM pointed out the
reasons why the ERM was likely to survive:

- (i) The crisis of September 1992 had, as its root cause, the consequences of German reunification, which was a unique event. Nothing so traumatic is likely to shake the stability of the ERM in the
  future.
- (ii.) The realignments of 1992 and the departure from the system of
  the lira and the pound were disorderly. Governments were not in
  control. By contrast, the more recent devaluations of the peseta and
  escudo had been orderly, showing that the ERM could cope with
  realignments.
- (iii.) Realignments were previously thought to be dangerous to the
  credibility of the system even if they were economically desirable
  and overdue. Since the goal of Emu had been firmly accepted by all
  EC members except Britain and Denmark (and was likely to be accepted by the new EC applicants from Efta), there was less need to
  establish the credibility of the system by hard parities. A more relaxed attitude could be taken to realignments as they became necessary.
- (iv.) The most important relationships within the ERM were those
  between the core currencies which would form the first group of
  Emu members. These relationships had remained stable, despite a
  temporary but vigorous onslaught on the French franc.

These arguments have now been disproved by events. Most important of
all, the core link between the Deutschemark and the French franc has effectively been broken. At all points, the anti-ERM and anti-Emu brigade has
apparently emerged victorious. Were the ERM defenders then wholly mis-
taken in their arguments, and is Maastricht, the ERM, and the whole programme for monetary union, now dead? If Emu is now nothing but a
dream, the Community will be the loser. Indeed, if in the foreseeable
future, there are in effect no fixed-exchange rates (except, perhaps, between Germany and the Netherlands) within the EC, the whole single market may prove to be in jeopardy.

First, the merits of the *aim* of monetary union itself have not been affected by recent events. The arguments in favour of the goal are still the
same, as powerfully set out by the Commission in *One Market, One Money*.

A single currency will not only save substantial cost, it is the coping stone on the single market; it provides stability, enhances confidence and increases the Community's influence in dealing with the dollar and the yen. Ironically Britain, which has been most reluctant to commit itself to the goal, would seem to have most to gain from Emu. Britain has suffered more than any other country from the instability of its currency. Britain has also suffered from the existence of a separate national balance of payments. The abolition of national balance of payments would not exonerate British industry from the need to compete. It would, however, remove the need for special measures, such as high interest rates, which have had to be taken to protect the pound at times of large external deficits. These protective measures have had the perverse effect of making industry less, rather than more, competitive and making future balance of payments crises more likely.

Next, the intermediate steps required by the Maastricht programme, the need to make central banks independent, and the convergence criteria, mostly made sense, even when judged on their own merits.

The need for central bank independence, for example, has not yet been accepted in Britain (although it has been accepted by recent chancellors of the Exchequer); but independence is being actively promoted in France, Belgium and Spain and has been, to a substantial extent, achieved in Denmark, Ireland and Portugal. The case for independence, while not theoretically incontestable, is a powerful one. It is supported by clear evidence of the coincidence between central bank independence and successful anti-inflationary policies. Over the last 20 years, the record in terms of inflation rates — and unemployment rates as well — has been substantially better in Germany, Switzerland and the USA, the countries with the most independent central banks, than in Italy, Britain and France, where central banks were least independent.

Of the Maastricht convergence criteria, the most important are probably the limits on public sector deficits and public debt. Obviously, there are times when larger and smaller deficits are appropriate and there is an element of arbitrariness in fixing figures of 3 per cent for the deficit and 60 per cent for the debt. (This arbitrariness is, however, modified by an element of flexibility allowed for by the treaty which critics argue make the limits meaningless!).

Again, however, even if the treaty had not imposed these limits, it is doubtful if similar disciplines would not have had to be observed in any event. A monetary union cannot be formed between states with substantially different underlying rates of inflation. But even those who may not want to join a monetary union will still need to control inflation. Few economists now argue that there is any trade-off between growth and inflation (except over a very short time-scale). All governments in advanced industrial countries now seek to control their public sector borrowing, although some control it more successfully than others. All are concerned about the level of their public debt.

It was perhaps significant that, when the French prime minister, Edouard Balladur, recently announced his economic programme to reduce the budget deficit to 2.5 per cent by 1997 and to make the Banque de France independent, he said the aim was not just to conform to the Maastricht Treaty, but to do what was in any event in the interests of France.

The gaping hole that has been blown in the Maastricht Treaty is, however, in the programme for ever-closer links between the exchange rates of would-be Emu members, ending with two years of relaxed existence within very narrow bands before exchange rates were irrevocably fixed. For the ERM, it will never be 'glad, confident morning' again. If monetary union is still a desired objective, a different route will have to be devised.

No doubt the conventional wisdom will now proclaim that even the aim should be abandoned as unreal or, in many people's eyes, undesirable. To begin with, public opinion — it is said — will be less enthusiastic than ever.

However, one should remember that, to date, the EC has never been a truly popular creation. While most people support the Community in principle, according to periodic polls conducted by Eurobarometer, major new steps on the road to closer union have been government-led, not the result of pressure from the people. This was almost inevitable given the nature of the steps: abolishing tariffs and removing non-tariff barriers to trade, promoting competition, or creating the European monetary system, were hardly the subject matter of regular debate in pubs.

It is true that popular support becomes more important as the EC's impact on people's lives becomes more pervasive. Nevertheless, it will be popular acceptance, rather than positive enthusiasm, which will be needed. This, it seems reasonable to predict, will depend on the economic environment. At times of economic hardship, public support for the Community slumps; at times of prosperity, it revives or flourishes. At a time when all governments are unpopular (when some, it has been observed, would lose a referendum if they asked voters to vote in favour of motherhood), it would be surprising if Brussels were held in high regard. Lack of popular enthusiasm for Maastricht at a time of growing unemployment was almost inevitable. In more prosperous times, it is unlikely to be a lasting obstacle to any progress towards a monetary union.

Next, there are good reasons why one should no expect the effective floating of EC currencies to continue forever. Not all EC governments may have been committed to the aim of monetary union, but *all* governments are determined to see the single market succeed. The success of the single market will be greatly hampered by the instability of exchange rates. During the lifetime of the old ERM, the single market made progress, but its progress was bound to be limited by the continued possibility of currency realignments. The possibility of hedging qualified, but did not remove, the difficulties of fixing long-term contracts in currencies whose values might change. Floating currencies, however, will not only cause havoc to the Common Agricultural Policy and the EC budget, but could have major disruptive effects on intra-Community trade. This danger provides a powerful incentive to put what were previously the hard core currencies — those of Benelux, France and Germany — together again, when interest rates are lower and fundamentals are more in line.

Most EC governments still favour a monetary union. If the determination of most EC countries to maintain the goal of monetary union survives, but if the route via the old ERM is now blocked, what alternative route can be devised?

What must seem an attractive possibility to several of the core states must be a Schengen-type Emu. It could, theoretically, be achieved quickly and avoid the problems associated with an ERM-type half-way house.

There is, however, no evidence that the necessary parties to such a dash for Emu have so far seriously considered it or, if they have, regarded it a feasible option. The Bundesbank would be prevented from co-operating in such a venture by its statute, which would need reform. No formal or institutional relationship could exist between a 'Schengen' Emu and the European Parliament, or the Commission, or the EMI. It would be incompatible with the Maastricht Treaty as it stands. It would be strongly opposed by Spain, Portugal and Italy. Germany has so far shown deep reservations.

The difficulties have not disappeared with the ending of the old ERM, but since there will now have to be a major restructuring of the European Community, a Schengen-type Emu must be considered one of the options. The inter-governmental conference in 1996 has suddenly become a crucial date on the political calendar.

The immediate aftermath of a traumatic crisis is not the best time to foreshadow future developments. But the political determination of the main governments involved cannot be disregarded. Not all the Maastricht programme is ready for burial. The old ERM route through Stage Two may have become impassable, and the timetable may have become irrelevant. But several features may survive or be at least partially restored. The aim of monetary union is unlikely to be abandoned. The convergence criteria will continue to be pursued. And the EMI may well develop as a key institution, when the time comes to lead the way back from floating currencies to the currency stability which Europe badly needs.

Chapter 7

Is there a rapid route to an Emu of the Few?

Graham Bishop
Salomon Brothers, London

Summary

The Treaty of Maastricht is on the verge of ratification. If it is not ratified, many of the signatories will look for an alternative route to reach their goal of European monetary union (Emu). Even if ratified, the treaty's long drawn-out timetable risks a loss of momentum that could still lead financial investors to doubt whether Emu will ever be achieved. Recognition of this risk has already triggered discussion about creating a fast track to some form of monetary union by the core countries, because fiscal problems suggest that the explicit convergence criteria of the Maastricht Treaty will not be met for some years, thus delaying the formal implementation of Emu until around 1999.

In this report, we look at the environment that would exist for a fast track if the treaty is ratified and examine the concepts underlying a practical route to achieve it within the letter and spirit of the treaty. After the turbulence in the exchange rate mechanism (ERM) — culminating in the widening of the bands to 15 per cent — a transparent, credible and robust structure is required if policy-makers wish to rebuild the confidence of market participants in the Emu process. This confidence-building exercise would not represent a substitute for the eventual single currency but rather a temporary step, which may even encourage progress towards Emu by demonstrating the ability and willingness of a few states to move towards this goal.

The economics of this route are straightforward; the necessary legal changes should be simple for all European Community (EC) member states with the political will to proceed, because the changes would only anticipate the steps ultimately required for treaty compliance. Nonetheless, the political implications are profound for participants and the impact on financial markets will be dramatic, given the probable narrowing of yield spreads that would occur.

Constraints on the fast track to Emu

Any plan for a rapid move to monetary union by the core countries must satisfy many constraints simultaneously. Therefore, the plan must include the following basics:

- Comply with the letter of the Treaty of Maastricht.
- Match the spirit of the treaty. The process must be open to any EC member willing and able to sustain price stability, and whenever they reach that goal. This should make it acceptable throughout the Community — a prerequisite for implementation.
- Happen naturally, because it is accepted in the financial markets, rather than be imposed by law. The magnitude of Europe's recession means that the required quorum of states satisfying the treaty criteria will not be achieved for some time so the formal route to Maastricht's *de jure* Emu is blocked.
- It must be sufficiently robust to withstand the inevitable storms — there must be minimal risk of a repeat of the currency crisis of September 1992 and July 1993. Yet failure must not prejudice those who have succeeded in their policies. Instead, the penalty of failure must be paid only by those whose policies fail.

These constraints point to a pragmatic and evolutionary system that harnesses market forces rather than creating a new institution. Therefore, it must require few changes in law, other than those needed to comply with the treaty anyway. Instead, existing practices in the financial system should adapt and extend to the changed circumstances so that the eventual result amounts to an effective locking of exchange rates. The question of implementing one currency for the whole community, by changing national notes and coins, would not arise until Stage Three occurs.

The most fruitful approach may be to build on the successful parts of the existing ERM by adding a range of measures to build up mutual trust among countries that want to maintain an ERM peg for their respective currencies. This may be facilitated by the only institutional change set by the treaty for Stage Two: the creation of the European Monetary Institute.

The environment for the EMI

On 1 January 1994, a new EC institution, the European Monetary Institute (EMI), is scheduled to come into existence, as stated in the Maastricht Treaty. However, the opening could be postponed by the delay in treaty ratification. The treaty-makers originally envisaged that the institution would have only a brief existence, serving to prepare the way for the European Central Bank (ECB) to commence operations. However, the role of the EMI during a lengthy transition to full monetary union may turn out to be somewhat different from the original concept.

Developing the influence of this institutional forum could open a way to coordinate the policies of the independent members so closely that they will achieve an effective monetary union to bridge the Stage Two gap until the conditions of the treaty are formally fulfilled.

The EMI is the creature of the treaty, whose guiding economic principles are clear:

- price stability and sound public finance,
- an open market economy with free competition and
- subsidiarity.

There are numerous references to these principles throughout the treaty as well as in the EMI statutes.

The EMI's tasks

The EMI is set up by Article 109f of the Maastricht Treaty. In paragraph two, this states that "The EMI shall:

- strengthen co-operation between the national central banks,
- strengthen the coordination of the monetary policies of the member states, with the aim of ensuring price stability, and
- monitor the functioning of the European monetary system."

These general tasks are fleshed out in paragraph four: "The EMI, acting by a majority of two thirds of the members of its Council, may:

- formulate opinions or recommendations on the overall orientation of monetary policy and exchange rate policy,
- submit opinions or recommendations to governments . . . on policies which might affect the internal . . . monetary situation in the Community and, in particular, the functioning of the European monetary system, and
- make recommendations to the monetary authorities . . . concerning the conduct of their monetary policy."

The EMI has an additional 'primary task': according to its statutes it shall also "normally be consulted by the national monetary authorities before they make decisions on the course of monetary policy in the context of the common framework for *ex-ante* co-ordination".

The treaty makes provision for the EMI to be given additional tasks "for the preparation of the third stage" but this requires unanimity among EC members. Therefore, the EMI could be given new tasks temporarily as a result of current economic realities. However, we believe that members would block any plans that might exclude their participation in an early Emu.

The EMI Council will be independent

The EMI will be run by a council consisting of a president and the 12 governors of the member states' central banks. The statutes specify that the governors shall "act according to their own responsibilities" even though they are representative of their institution. As a group, the EMI is required not to take instructions, nor may the governments "seek to influence the council".

Inevitably, there will be questions about the ability of the governor of a dependent central bank to be independent in the EMI forum. Fortunately, there are successful precedents from earlier periods in EC history, and this issue is likely to diminish over time as more central banks are granted independence. This process is happening more rapidly than the treaty timetable requires: Legislation is completed in Belgium and underway in Spain; the new French government is committed to giving the Bank of France independence before year-end; and the Danish, Irish, Italian, and Portuguese central banks now have a substantial measure of independence. Interestingly, with the semi-independent banks, the required two-thirds majority of the EMI Council would exist to "formulate . . . submit . . . and make recommendations" to the monetary authorities on monetary and exchange rate policies.

The result: a substantial influence on policy

The EMI statutes explicitly state (Article 3.3) that the institution's activities will be conducted "without prejudice to the responsibility of the competent authorities for the conduct of the monetary policy within the respective member states". However, the EMI's tasks of ex-ante coordination suggests that its council's discussions will be influential.

If the EMI makes an explicit recommendation, it would be curious if the Governors who supported the recommendation were unable, or unwilling, to persuade their respective central banks, especially if these are independent, to accept it. The response of the dependent central banks may be uncertain. However, a formal recommendation from the EMI will have a substantial impact upon EC member state policies if it is backed by *all* of the independent central banks. In practice, that would be close to effective power. If any central bank exercised its inherent right to ignore such a recommendation, the financial markets would serve as the judge in the competition of credibility.

However, the treaty does not resolve the logical conundrum: If 'independent' central banks co-operate too closely with each other, they will no longer be independent. In any event, this issue will have to be clarified soon. Inevitably, that will raise the question of whether or not to use the EMI to encourage a form of *de facto* monetary union among the states that desire it and can sustain it.

The plan for fast track Emu of the core countries

The plan set out below is not a detailed blueprint, but merely suggests the concept of a package of practical steps that attempts to balance the risks and rewards to each party involved.

Principles

The principles of this plan are straightforward, and simply extend existing arrangements. They start with the existing ERM rules, which require unlimited intervention by the pair of central banks whose currencies are at opposing ends of the maximum fluctuation margin.

Problems

The weakness of the existing ERM system is that the central bank of a country receiving a currency inflow has no certainty that the central bank of the country whose currency's value is the lowest of the ERM group will tighten monetary conditions enough to stop its capital outflow. There is no guarantee that the combined money supply of the two countries will not rise and eventually threaten price stability in the 'inflow' country.

Solution

This risk could be eliminated by an 'Agreement' between participating central banks to coordinate monetary policy much more closely than what is stipulated in the general framework set for the EMI. As stated in the treaty of Maastricht (Article 3a), this agreement would be made "in accordance with the principle of an open market economy with free competition" and would maximize the role of the national central banks. However, it would be to monetary union what the Schengen Agreement is to the free movement of people — a temporary solution.

Specifically, the participating central banks would:

- treat the changes in their aggregate balance sheet as a matter for common agreement, and respond to the opinion, and perhaps recommendation, of the EMI;
- focus on the money-creating components of their balance sheet (for example, banks' deposits and repurchase agreements, or repos) and the availability of foreign exchange reserves; and
- offer repos in other members' currencies to any EC credit institutions (see below).

Safeguards

These agreements may only be concluded between qualifying central banks that have:

(1) a legal obligation to achieve price stability, and
(2) the independence and powers to achieve this goal.

The powers should include the right for each bank to influence its domestic currency's central parity in the ERM and to cut off the intervention obligation in case of abuse threatening the primary duty of achieving price stability. Independence would not exempt the central banks from proper democratic accountability.

- The ERM intervention obligation would be suspended automatically if the central banks acted in concert to purchase more than about 15 per cent of the 'outflow' country's broad money supply. Such a level of intervention would imply that there had been a serious loss of confidence in the sustainability of policy, rather than reflect a temporary speculative surge. That outflow cap would range from Ecu 30bn for the Netherlands to Ecu 120bn for France.

  The need for any type of limit on outflow, let alone the size, is debatable. However, the existence of a cap is the key to enhancing participants' confidence that they could not be trapped in some way. The size would need to be large enough to assure the markets that only a major crisis would force a breach in the limit. Market participants' confidence would be reinforced if some potential flows were eliminated by exchange risk guarantees.
- Participation must be fully supported by the domestic government, which would only agree once the inflation rate had met the Maastricht

treaty's criterion: not more than 1.5 percentage points above the 'three best-performing member states' over a one-year period.

- The domestic government should demonstrate its own commitment to price stability by offering purchasers of new government debt the right to have redemption proceeds adjusted for any difference in the exchange rate of the government's domestic currency between (1) maturity and (2) the lower ERM limit at issue. This guarantee would apply against the currency of any country participating in the Agreement, and would be a powerful signal of a government's confidence in its policies.

   This protection for savers would cost nothing to a government committed to achieving ultimate monetary union with other countries that have stable prices. Moreover, this mimics the situation that will exist in Stage Three of Emu, when member governments begin to issue debt in a currency that is entirely under the control of an independent central bank. If the national central bank failed in its duty to maintain the value of the currency, then the government would have to retain the right to sanction the central bank before its error caused taxpayers unnecessary losses. If the government failed to act, it could hardly complain about any negative consequences.

- The hard-currency link is not absolutely essential but it has multiple, and powerful, purposes: enhancing credibility between participating central banks, assuring credibility of the central banks in the eyes of the financial markets, as well as reducing potential outflows.

- The existing ERM band widths (2 1/4 per cent above or below the central parity) should be retained as a shock absorber. As the currency of the 'outflow' country fell towards its floor in the ERM, most investors in the government's bonds who wanted to divest their holdings would lose the incentive to sell, because their hard-currency link would afford adequate protection. Other speculative sellers would be aware of their risk of serious loss, given the authorities' incentive to return the currency to the central rate. Narrowing the band widths would remove this potential penalty.

How the 'Agreement' would work in practice

Two member states, which we refer to here as countries A and B, decide to give their respective central banks the legal power to conclude this type of agreement and offer a hard-currency link on all new public debt issues. In line with the Maastricht Treaty, the two central banks would participate in the EMI's tasks of strengthening co-operation and co-ordination.

It is crucial the two central banks agree that any central bank which no longer has access to foreign exchange for intervention will immediately freeze the money-creating components of its balance sheet. However, this is more of a convenient psychological break-point than a real economic problem. There are several ways of obtaining extra foreign exchange reserves, including foreign borrowing by the government, ensuring a trade surplus by squeezing the domestic economy or even loans from the other central bank. In practice, any currency crisis would have three phases.

Phase I: The crisis starts

- Holders of country A's money become fearful of a currency devaluation. They start selling their holdings back to central bank A, thus causing a sharp contraction in A's money supply.
- Despite the efforts of A's central bank, and presumably supporting steps by the government, the currency continues to depreciate and the capital outflows deplete all of the central bank's foreign reserve assets.
- If no further resources become available, the currency will fall to its ERM floor and the agreement with B's central bank will be set in motion.

Phase II: The crisis becomes acute

A's central bank freezes the aggregate of the money-creating items on its balance sheet (The definition of these items would be agreed in advance, based on the characteristics of the national financial system). In practice, the central bank has now lost the competition in credibility despite its independence.

- At the intervention point, country B's central bank purchases A's money — in exchange for issuing more of its own money. However, this action does not remove the sudden shortage of country A's money within its own borders, unless its citizens are prepared to use country B's money for day-to-day activities.
- The simple solution is for B's central bank to recycle the A money it has just purchased. Since the financial markets would obviously attach greater credibility to B's central bank, it should live up to its responsibility through a more cautious monetary policy; in other words, B would set A's interest rates, but at a higher level.

- B's central bank is now the marginal supplier of the A money drained from A's commercial banking system by the currency outflows. This places it in a powerful position to set A's domestic short-term interest rates because central bank A's ability to act is frozen.
- B's central bank uses the A currency it has purchased to buy A government bonds via repos. However, B is protected against loss by the hard-currency link, because the repo pact would leave any windfall gain on a devaluation with B's central bank (see Appendix for a detailed technical description). B would sell enough repo pacts to allow interest rates to settle at a level that cuts off further outflows from A.
- Simultaneously, B's central bank takes steps to offset the increase in its own money supply that results from the intervention. This would be achieved through its existing mechanisms, ensuring that monetary conditions within the combined geographical area remain consistent with price stability.

Phase III: The crisis abates

Once the crisis begins to abate because of the credibility of central bank B's policy, premium interest rates cause money to flow back to A's central bank. As its foreign reserves start to rise again, it automatically regains control, because central bank B's monetary instrument — repos — would expire within a few weeks.

Comments

- At first sight, the concept of a foreign central bank formally setting domestic interest rates seems radical. Yet most parliaments have now ratified the Treaty of Maastricht and accepted that an independent central bank shall set monetary policy so as to achieve price stability. Thus, each member state will see its monetary policy set by an institution controlled by non residents. In practice, all the other central banks participating in this Agreement are likely to receive currency inflows and therefore participate in the repo auctions which will determine interest rates in country A. Therefore, the process will be analogous to the deliberations which the European Central Bank will eventually undertake.
- There are built-in safeguards against abuse. For example, if country A voted in a new government that did not intend to follow policies consistent with sustained price stability, B's central bank would push strongly for an early currency realignment. In this case, the

intervention obligation, although unlimited in terms of everyday market fluctuations, would be capped at the point where it was obvious that a serious loss of confidence was imminent, although the sizeable repo portfolio would be protected against devaluation. There would be a credit risk, but a formal default in these circumstances would be much more than a minor economic event.

- Another potential for abuse of the system would occur even without this plan: An independent central bank may have the incentive to engineer currency appreciation to fulfil its duty to maintain domestic price stability. Ceding influence on the central ERM rate to the central bank would enhance this risk, which may have to be subject to constraining rules.

Which countries could participate in the 'agreement'?

The hurdles to participation should reflect the rigor of the treaty convergence criteria as closely as possible while recognizing the temporary nature of this proposed solution. Therefore, in this instance, long-term problems, such as the scale of each country's public debt, have less significance.

- The first hurdle is inflation. The treaty is ambiguous on the exact measure: Is it the average or the highest rate of the 'three best-performing member states'? Moreover, it specifies that the CPI used is "on a comparable basis, taking into account differences in national definition". Based on our current forecasts for the published national indexes, the hurdle rate would be 3.3 per cent or 3.6 per cent in 1993 and 3.0 per cent or 3.2 per cent in 1994. The tougher examination this year would include France, Belgium, Netherlands, Luxembourg, Denmark, and Ireland, but not Germany, which should be included in either definition next year.

    This plan makes sustained convergence of inflation a precondition of entry, thereby avoiding the particular risk of lost competitiveness from relatively high inflation, which has just caused so much anguish in the EC.

- The independence and objectives of each country's central bank are the next criteria. Naturally, the Bundesbank already satisfies the Maastricht criteria, as does the Netherlands Bank. The statutes of the National Bank of Belgium were recently modified to gain formal independence, but the bank continues to perform functions rather than have tasks, such as achieving price stability. The changes to the statutes of the Bank of France will be key given

France's crucial role in the EC. Current proposals suggest that both its independence and tasks will fully satisfy this criterion.

* Control of the ERM central rate is currently outside the power of any central bank, and exchange rate policy has been carefully left as a grey area in the Maastricht Treaty. Even the Bundesbank's hands are tied — although the exact extent was never made clear when the ERM was established in 1979.

This control function is crucial, because it is a vital part of the system of checks and balances. Since the reward for successful participation is clear, there must also be a corresponding penalty for failure. It is the hard-currency link of public debt that provides this penalty, and the system would be seriously weakened if it could be avoided simply by political pressure rather than a proper economic policy response. All potential participants would have to provide an adequate check-and-balance mechanism such as that defined in Article 109 of the treaty. This provides for the European Central Bank to "recommend" change in central rates.

Linking public debt to the hardest participating currency is the final hurdle. In reality, this will only be a question of degree for many members. France has already undertaken to issue 15 per cent of its debt in Ecu, while Belgium, Denmark and Ireland have substantial foreign currency-denominated borrowings. In Germany and the Netherlands, the principle might pose a theoretical problem, but neither would be borrowing in foreign currency and the risk would only crystallize if they abandoned their price stability objective. This activity would still be a step short of the commitments implicit in the treaty.

There would be a bonus with this form of borrowing: The saving on interest costs would be substantial if the goal of fast-track Emu were achieved and the credibility of policy enabled interest rate spreads to narrow sharply. If a country failed to sustain policy, then, in effect, the interest saved would have to be paid as a lump sum at maturity. This payment would be substantial and represent a highly visible penalty for failure.

The currency protection afforded to government bondholders could be designed to enhance this incentive. It might start at say 1/2 per cent below the central ERM rate, and be scaled up to give full protection at the lower ERM limit. Each government would then have a strong incentive to support its central bank's policy of targeting minor fluctuations about the central parity for its currency. This would encourage market participants to view the currencies as virtual substitutes for one another under normal conditions — with correspondingly narrow yield spreads.

The German stance

Germany's viewpoint will be crucial to the success of such an agreement, because current capital flow patterns suggest that the Bundesbank is likely to be the recipient of most flows. Long-term, Germany may have strong interest in participating in a zone of exchange rate stability as the shock of unification wears off and the need arises for a gradual reduction in the real value of the Deutschemark, with the resultant risk of it losing its hold as the anchor of Europe's monetary order. In effect, this plan would broaden the number of currencies constituting the anchor.

The practical steps needed to implement this approach are few:

(1) Control of the central ERM parity. When the ERM was founded in 1979, the Bundesbank strongly resisted the fettering of its power to set the Deutschemark's exchange rate. Legislation may not even be required for the Finance Ministry to cede more of this power to the Bundesbank.

(2) Linking the value of public debt to the hardest currency will inevitably strike a raw nerve in Germany, in light of its experience of hyperinflation. However, this proposal does not require debt issuance in foreign currencies, and can be viewed as little more than a first step towards the Emu goal of a single currency. This goal has been sanctioned by the Maastricht Treaty's ratification, so larger steps are already mandated. Moreover, it offers German savers additional protection against the risk that unification may still spark a sharp rise in inflation, because their savings will be linked to the hardest currency, whichever that may turn out to be.

(3) Bundesbank repo operations in a foreign currency. Formal amendments to the Bundesbank Law in connection with repo operations would take time and would raise suspicions that more substantial changes are being slipped through. To the layman reading the Bundesbank Law, the Bundesbank already has great flexibility.

- Article 15 of the Bundesbank Law allows the bank to establish the principles governing its credit and the open market policies to regulate the amount of money in circulation.
- Article 19 appears to limit the Bundesbank's transactions with banks to "banks in the area of validity of this Act". Although this may conflict with the principles of the single market, which calls for freedom of services, it is not a practical problem, given the large number of foreign banks operating in Germany. Moreover, the

Bundesbank can make loans to other central banks that could act as its agent in other countries.

- Article 19(1) 8 gives the Bundesbank the power to "buy and sell payment media denominated in foreign currencies, including . . . claims and securities".
- Article 21 regulates the Bundesbank's dealings on the open market, permitting it to buy and sell "other bonds determined by the bank".

In recent months, as in past years, the Bundesbank has made substantial changes to its procedures and instruments, including the build-up of securities repos and the introduction of *Bulis*, a type of short-term liquidity paper. In September and October 1992, the speed of capital inflows to Germany was more rapid than the expiration of the Bundesbank's securities repos, so it undertook foreign exchange repos. Having demonstrated this flexible response to changing market conditions, the Bundesbank appears to have the necessary legal powers to participate in such operations if it so wishes.

(4) The economic capacity of the Bundesbank already seems adequate for the task. Repos have accumulated in the last few years, reaching Dm 150bn in mid-1992, while lending via bills to domestic credit institutions amounted to nearly Dm 60bn. The value of Bulis in issuance could grow to Dm 50bn. By allowing these short-term assets to expire and by fully utilizing the opportunity to sell short-term paper, the Bundesbank could sterilize more than Dm 250bn of inflows without exceptional difficulty. If the intervention obligation were capped at 15 per cent of other participants' M3, the maximum exposure to France, for example, would be about Dm 235bn.

The message to financial markets

This package of concepts would permit several EC members to start a rapid move towards an effective monetary union in the reasonably near future, rather than beyond the market's time horizon when a quorum of the Maastricht Treaty might be reached. The move would start with members that:

- have already achieved adequate price stability,
- are determined to sustain it,
- are prepared to take bold steps to achieve the benefits of an effective monetary union, and
- are prepared to pay a significant penalty if they fail to stay the course.

Credibility must be built up with several policy blocks. The foundation stone would be to give the members' central banks the goal of achieving the monetary conditions necessary for price stability and the necessary means: independence of action. Credibility would be raised another notch by giving up the benefit of inflation — erosion of the real value of public debt — through linking it to the currencies of other stable-price countries.

A major building block of credibility would be the willingness to cede control of domestic monetary policy in the event of a significant crisis of confidence — from the independent domestic central bank to the central bank judged most credible by the market at the time. This would occur when the domestic central bank's foreign assets were exhausted and its balance sheet constrained at the moment sellers of its currency forced intervention to begin at the lower limit of the currency's ERM band. This transfer of control is the crucial difference from the existing ERM policy.

The potential scale of intervention would be two or three times greater than that undertaken during the sterling crisis of September 1992. Moreover, the hard-currency link would remove a major source of sellers — holders of government bonds. In effect, this intervention would be unlimited, unless dramatic events caused a major crisis of confidence among a broad segment of society.

The hard-currency link has the dual purpose of reducing potential outflows and enhancing a government's credibility by applying a heavy, visible penalty for failure. This currency linkage represents a possible mechanism to achieve these two goals.

These arrangements could be implemented relatively easily through Agreements among the independent central banks. Once the EMI begins operation in 1994, it will provide an appropriate forum to discuss monetary policy and a lead on the specific requirements needed to achieve the goals enshrined in the Maastricht Treaty. The creation of such a plan, and steps towards its implementation, would send a powerful message to the financial markets that an effective monetary union is likely among some EC members.

Appendix: The repo system in practice — technical description

The following example illustrates how the repo system would work and shows that the intervening central bank would be fully protected against loss unless the devaluing government defaulted on its debt obligations. The default would have to be general rather than targeted, because the government would be unable to identify readily the bonds temporarily held by the intervening central bank.

The calculation below approximates the Bundesbank's setup for its existing repo system but with an additional condition: if an ERM devaluation occurs during the life of the repo pact, the repurchase price increases by an amount commensurate with the change in the exchange rate when the repurchase obligation falls due.

For devaluations of less than 4 1/2 per cent in the central rate — the current Community intention — the currency's new upper band will be above the old lower band. Intervention will only occur at that lower band. History suggests that the improved credibility of policy (and short covering) will leave the currency, initially, in the upper part of the band. Thus, there is a good chance that the exchange rate will be only slightly below, and could even be above, the old intervention point.

Our assumptions, based on current typical values for the government bond markets of the 'narrow' ERM band currencies, are as follows: the average maturity of the bond market is six years, the average yield is 7 per cent and the short-term interest rate is 9 per cent.

In terms of mechanisms, the intervening central bank takes a portfolio of bonds from a commercial bank at the underlying price, thus excluding accrued interest. For bonds which pay annual interest, this represents a significant discount to the market price and is effectively a credit enhancement for the central bank. A simple illustration of this follows:

Underlying bond price: 100.00 (the level at which the central bank makes the purchase)

Commercial bank repurchase price in 30 days: 100.75 (the implicit short-term interest rate is 9 per cent)

Memorandum
Market price at start: 103.5 (reflects average accrued interest)

Market price in 30 days: 104.1 (includes addi-
                                                   tional accrued inter-
                                                   est)

A currency devaluation of 2 1/4 per cent occurs before the repo has
matured during this pact. This means that the old floor of the currency's
ERM band becomes the new central rate.

Scenario I

The currency moves in the upper half of its ERM band. When the repo
matures, the market exchange rate will be above the level recorded at the
beginning of the pact. Therefore, no adjustment in the repurchase price is
made.

■ *Results*
- The intervening central bank makes a profit on its foreign exchange
  holdings.
- The commercial bank gets its bonds back at the original price and
  may even make a minor gain on the transaction, because the redemption value may be uprated somewhat, depending on the exchange rate at maturity.

Scenario II

The currency moves in the lower half of its ERM band. Assuming the worst
case — a fall to the new floor — the repo agreement will require that the
repurchase price rises by $2^1/4$ per cent (the difference between the intervention point — the old floor — and the new market rate). The new repo
arithmetic is:

Adjusted repurchase price in 30 days: 103.0 (operation of
                                                   devaluation clause)

Memorandum
Underlying price in 30 days: 101.5 (adjustment of
                                                   principal to 102.25; re-
                                                   flects the devaluation)

Market price in 30 days: 105.6 (includes ac-
                                                   crued interest)

The bond's underlying price would not rise to reflect fully the 2.25 per cent increase in the maturity proceeds, because that date is still six years away, and will be appropriately discounted.

■ *Results*
- The intervening central bank will still expect the commercial banks to repurchase their bonds at a discount of 2.6 points to the new market price. Therefore, the major banks have no incentive to default on the more costly repurchase obligation, leaving aside any question of damage to their reputation.
- The commercial banks would rather obtain funding by reducing debt elsewhere in the domestic economy. That contraction would only shrink domestic credit by less than 0.5 per cent, a significant but bearable amount. The banks also miss the opportunity to profit as the bonds rise in price, since this profit reverts to the intervening central bank. If the banks did not wish to risk surrendering this profit, they could bid up domestic short-term interest rates until they compensated for the devaluation risk. This process would be halted by the competing attractions of funding via the repo agreements.

PART III

Central bank independence and a single currency — necessity, hindrance, or alternative?

In Denmark, the second referendum overturned the original 'No' vote, with a vote in favour of the treaty. This followed the European Council meeting at Edinburgh in December 1992, at which three special arrangements for Denmark were agreed. Firstly, Denmark need not introduce the single European currency and will retain its monetary policy autonomy (indeed this was merely a reaffirmation — such an opt-out is stipulated in the treaty). Secondly, Danish nationality will not be replaced or affected by the union. Thirdly, Denmark will not participate in the elaboration (and implementation) of decisions with defence implications. The Edinburgh decisions, insofar as they relate to Denmark, are notes of interpretation, as distinct from formal proposals for a modification of the treaty. Therefore, the Edinburgh decisions, which the Council regards as compatible with the treaty, will not be ratified in the other member states, although they will be part of the ratification procedure in Denmark and the UK.

...possibly because it is difficult to read and understand

Many problems and difficulties which arise from the treaty are due to the fact that it is difficult to read and understand. Many interpreters argue that there is no system which underlies the multiplicity of new provisions and stipulations. My reply would be that there is certainly a system underlying the treaty, but we have not been able to identify it until now.

The system underlying the treaty, which creates European union...

On the basis of the treaty, a variety and multiplicity of competences and regulatory powers are to be transferred to the European Community. But the competences to be transferred are different in dimension and quality: there are the tasks and functions to be transferred within the framework of European union on the one hand and competences to be transferred to the European Community on the other.

The nature and structure of European union cannot be described by a single sentence. The treaty defines European union as a 'single institutional framework' and says that the bases of the union are:

- the three European Communities — i.e. the European Economic Community, as well as those on Coal & Steel and Atomic Energy;
- co-operation among the member states in foreign and security policy;
- co-operation among the member states in domestic and justice affairs.

When one looks at the structure of European union, especially these three mainstays, it is evident that, at the Maastricht conference, the member states did not create a state — not even a federal one — that is to say, a

Chapter 8

An introduction to the debate

Paul Temperton, Editor
The Independent Economic Research Company (TIER)

Central bank independence, viewed in the context of the move to Emu, can be seen as a necessity, a hindrance, or an alternative.

Central bank independence is a necessity if a country wishes to take part in Stage Three of the Maastricht plan for Emu. This will enable the country to let its central bank governor take his seat on the European Central bank council. The requirement for each national central bank to be independent is written in to the Maastricht Treaty. European central banks which have not been independent in the past will have to pass legislation to grant independence to their central bank a move which has been taken by both Belgium and France in 1993.

Central bank independence can be seen as a hindrance to plans for Emu, however, before Stage Three is completed. The Bundesbank, for long the world's pre-eminent independent central bank, is blamed by many as the cause of the ERM crisis, doggedly pursuing counter-inflationary policies which have made it ever more difficult for other countries to retain their ERM parities. Bundesbank independence might actually reduce the chances of an eventual Emu being formed. More generally, central bank independence might compromise a balanced approach to economic management. For example, if an expansionary fiscal policy is aggressively offset by an independent central bank (the US experience of the early-1980s or the Bundesbank experience more recently) the policy mix might not be the most appropriate one. As Gerald Holtham points out in Chapter 10, Australia has not wanted an independent central bank precisely for this reason.

Central bank independence can be seen as an alternative to membership of the ERM and the Emu convergence criteria. If a country is seeking a way of keeping inflation under control then giving the central bank an unequivocal counter-inflationary mandate is an obvious method which has a proven track record. Apart from the Bundesbank, the US Fed and, more recently, the Reserve Bank of New Zealand provide excellent examples. In this sense, central bank independence is an alternative to ERM membership, which can be characterized as piggy-backing off the credibility of another central bank. The point was not lost on Nigel Lawson who, once he had tried to convince Margaret Thatcher of the case for UK ERM membership, tried to convince her of the need for central bank independence as an alternative[1].

The economic literature on the success of independent central banks has produced relatively mixed results, partly because the notion of independence is itself rather nebulous and rests on a variety of considerations such as legal status, the way in which the governor is appointed, his term of office etc. Nevertheless, a quick look at Figure 8.1 bears out many people's prejudices: the country with the lowest inflation rates in the post-war period (Germany) has the most independent central bank; the one with the worst record has the least independent central bank.

In the UK the debate on central bank independence is particularly intense at the moment. Two of the last three chancellors (Nigel Lawson and

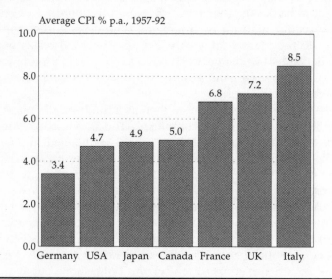

Figure 8.1   Inflation in the G7 countries

[1] *See Lawson, Nigel 'The View from Number 11', especially Chapter 69 and Annexe 2.*

Norman Lamont) have said, in their resignation speeches, that they had tried to convince the prime minister of the case for central bank independence. Robin Leigh-Pemberton, on retiring as Bank of England governor in June 1993 set the challenge of devising a scheme for bank of England independence which would guarantee enough accountability to government. A House of Commons Select Committee and a Centre for Economic Policy Research study group are both studying the issue at the moment.

In the next two chapters, Erik Hoffmeyer, governor of the Danish central bank, sets out the case for central bank independence; Gerald Holtham explains why the case is overstated.

Chapter 9

The case for central bank independence

Erik Hoffmeyer[1]
Governor, Danmarks Nationalbank

I have been involved in work on the ideas leading to the proposal and in drafting the Statute of the European System of Central Banks, ESCB, and of the European Central Bank, ECB, embodied in the Treaty of Maastricht. So I am a partisan in the debate on central bank independence and its role in the blueprint for an economic and monetary union, but I shall nonetheless try to make my case soberly, and in such a way that flaws in the reasoning can be easily detected.

During the post-war period, now almost 50 years, there have been wide changes in the conventional wisdom regarding determinants of macroeconomic magnitudes and in the scope for economic policy activity. This is not least true of the causes of inflation and the assignment of monetary policy. The period has seen a pendulum swing in policy prescriptions from simplistic Keynes epigones to monocausal Friedmanites. Politicians have gladly adopted both.

The debate on the role of monetary policy and on central bank independence has been coloured by these changes in prevailing attitudes. Evidence on both issues has been provided by empirical research although, until now, the findings have been quite ambiguous. During the last couple of years, Emu has been drafted on the basis of present thinking, part of it, however, in a way that to me is not entirely satisfactory.

In the following three sections, I discuss:

- inflation and the role of monetary policy
- the question of the 'advantages' of independent central banks
- the stability of the proposed monetary union

[1] *This chapter is based on the 1992 Mais Lecture, delivered at the City University Business School on 6 May 1992.*

The issues raise a wide range of problems, but I shall try to concentrate on essentials.

Inflation and the role of monetary policy

It was remarkable how quickly the doctrines of Keynesian thinking permeated the political system after the Second World War. It appeared that these doctrines were exactly what was wanted.

The epigones of Keynes managed to simplify economic problems and prescribe a recipe for managing the economy. It is true that Keynes did not present an overly-simplified model, and that you can find almost anything in the writings of such a prolific mind, but it is also true that he was fascinated by the role of a stable consumption function versus volatile investment behaviour and an interest rate level that seemed possible for the authorities to manage. It is also true that the background of the depression of the 1930s gave little basis for concern about demand pressure and inflation. Much of this thinking was, however, blurred by his last article from 1946 in The Economic Journal, which was far more market-orientated and less inclined towards intervention and regulation. Keynes' followers took his basic concepts and simplified the model to the point of destruction, but simplicity gave it a market value to the political system that was quite outstanding.

The doctrines can be summarized in the following brief sentences.

- Economic policy instruments were free goods. They could be applied without cost.

- Total demand could be determined by fiscal and monetary policy.

- Inflation was dependent on trade union discipline, as maintained in the Beveridge Report. I have a favourite quotation from the report which casts a sharp light on attitudes and the way of thinking when plans were drafted for the post-war economic system: "If trade unions under full employment press wage claims unreasonably, maintenance of a stable price level will become impossible; wage determination will perforce become a function of the state. If the private owners of business undertakings under full employment set out to exploit consumers by organizing monopolies ... the private owners cannot for long be left in their ownership". Such a presentation almost amounts to a threat of introducing a Soviet system if people do not behave properly — centralized wage determination and abolition of private ownership of capital.

- Monetary policy had only one purpose — to determine the interest rate level and thereby influence investment and total demand. The Radcliffe Report (1959), contained that message in the extreme. Monetary measures were not considered to have a strong impact. They "can help, but that is all" was the famous statement. Or, "monetary measures are aimed at the level of demand, but by their nature they are incapable by themselves of having an effect sufficiently prompt and far-reaching for their purpose, unless applied with a vigour that itself creates a major emergency". This emergency scenario is not described in detail.

In short, monetary policy had no perceptible impact on inflation and interest rate levels could be fixed autonomously. Even though it would probably be difficult to find such extreme simplicity in professional presentations it did represent a dominating line of thinking. It had the effect of pushing the role of central banking into the background. The so-called Keynesian consensus broke down during the 1970s. In the UK it was marked by the 1976 IMF crisis which has been described in such a colourful way in the recent publication by Burk and Cairncross with the dramatic title *Goodbye, Great Britain*.

It is difficult to say why the consensus disappeared. There was the first oil price explosion, which is often erroneously used as a major cause. There was the end of the post-war boom and the widespread hostility against the growing public sector and the disappointment with expansionary policies that led to stagflation. To this must be added that experts became increasingly disillusioned by the inappropriateness of relying mainly on demand management and the inefficiency of a policy of fine tuning based on often unreliable short-term forecasts.

Time was ripe for a change of opinion and in such cases the pendulum often swings to the opposite extreme. The quantity theory of money which was resented by Keynesians reappeared and conquered the scene in the Friedman formulation according to which employment and growth — at any rate in the long run — were seen to be independent of monetary policy, which in turn would determine inflation. In other words, there was supposed to be a monocausal relation between monetary policy and inflation.

This way of thinking was just as willingly bought by authorities and quickly gained widespread support. It has been instrumental in the endeavours to use money supply targets as a simple means to achieve an acceptable level of inflation. Central banking was all of a sudden seen as being highly important. Such simplicity does not work either.

Reality is cumbersome and unclear in the sense that economic relations are uncertain and policy instruments unreliable. It has not been possible to estimate a clear and reliable connection between one or two economic variables and inflation, and it has proved impossible to apply economic policy measures without repercussions from the market. In other words, economic policy proved not to be a free good. The latter aspect is, to a large extent, due to the role of expectations and the interaction between expectations and policy measures.

Given the fact that expectations play an important role, a heavy burden is put on authorities to create credibility regarding a certain course of policy. Otherwise, policy measures are likely to create instability. It is a truism that price increases stem from excess demand in individual or all markets. In our system there are strong forces that tend to create excess demand.

Thus, the trend of growing demand for public services and for private consumption, puts a sustained pressure on public budgets and on income creation, with the consequence that requests for wage and salary increases contribute to create excess demand.

The final outcome, with respect to price performance, is a result of expansionary and restrictive forces. Monetary policy is almost everywhere assigned the task of working for stability of the currency, aiming at a low rate of inflation. This means that the cost and availability of money are elements that have an influence on inflationary performance.

The next step in this line of thinking is consequently what kind of institutional set-up is best suited to providing monetary policy efficiency. Should monetary policy be conducted by independent central banks or be integrated as a part of the political decision making system?

The 'advantages' of independent central banks

During the period of the Keynesian consensus until about the middle of the 1970s the predominant view was that for efficiency reasons central banks should be tightly incorporated in the policy-making system. The main target for economic policy was full employment, aiming at around 3 per cent unemployment, with a reasonable trade-off regarding price increases on the basis of the Phillips curve philosophy. The policy-mix between fiscal and monetary policy was not at all a burning issue, but rather one of expediency.

It might be said that independence of central banks was a disadvantage to the formation of a coherent and consistent economic policy. At that time advocates of independence were considered to represent an archaic attitude. The swing towards monetarism — based on the old quantity theory — led in some cases to a similarly extreme attitude. It was argued that discretion regarding money supply would inevitably result in a too permissive policy and a too rapid increase in inflation. Therefore, central bank activity should be substituted by an inflexible rule. It meant that monetary policy should be outside the reach of both politicians and central bankers. Money supply should be increased by, for example, 3 per cent per year.

Such rules were proposed in spite of the fact that the transmission mechanism is far from fully understood — except that it is recognized that time lags are variable.

Instead of the two extreme models of inflation, the more down-to-earth view of the inflation mechanism has changed attitudes gradually, but decisively. Inflation is created by forces in all the markets in the economy, which are not at all easy to analyze. As mentioned, the outcome is determined by the balance between expansionary forces and barriers to cost and price increases. One can enumerate a long list of expansionary forces, from political promises and considerations to institutional ambitions among income groups as well as to individual behaviour. But where are the constraints?

The list is pretty short but, as one major item, it includes monetary policy. In this setting the question of strengthening the scope for monetary policy becomes evident, and a way of tying one's hands is to make central banks more independent. Then the question of policy-mix becomes essential.

A sequel to this change of attitude is that it becomes highly relevant to collect evidence about the consequences of central bank independence in order to assess the importance of this aspect. Is it possible to measure the degree of independence and relate it to inflation performance? If so, researchers could present politicians with a rational choice. Politicians would so to speak be able to choose their preferred combination of the degree of independence and inflation. In a sense this exercise becomes a substitute to the previously mentioned trade-off between employment and inflation. This sounds rather naive, and unfortunately it is. There have been a lot of investigations in this field during recent years.

I have no intention of reviewing the literature but wish to acknowledge the seriousness of the work done by Bade and Parkin (1987), Alesina (1989), Grilli, Masciandaro and Tabellini (1991), Capie and Wood (1991) and Swinburne and Castello-Branco (1991).

Investigations have not been rewarded with any clear theorem regarding a relation between inflation and central bank independence. A strong barrier is the question of measurement. Some analysts believe that formal criteria are a sufficient indicator when measuring the degree of independence — who takes decisions, can instructions be given, what is the length of tenure, etc. Others are sceptical of whether such criteria give a reasonably reliable picture. Even within the formal criteria there is disagreement about classification, and results are significantly sensitive to, for example, the classification of Japan which formally is highly dependent on the political system.

It is also necessary to point to the fact that formal independence cannot always prevail over strong political priorities, as was seen in connection with the German unification that has led to a substantial increase in German prices.

Altogether, attempts to measure central bank independence by formal criteria seem to be unrealistic. If subjective criteria are used, one runs into a jungle of identification problems. The statistical approach also faces the problem of changing priorities.

When, during the immediate post-war years, the overriding objective was to create and maintain full employment, price stability was considered much less important and intended to be handled by incomes policy. But this turned out to be an uncertain, or unreliable, policy instrument.

Mainstream attitudes gradually changed, however, during the 1970s. As mentioned, it is difficult to explain or analyze exactly when and why it happened, but it is indisputable that priorities have shifted in favour of stability at the expense of employment.

In the early-1970s, most industrial countries embarked on an expansionary economic policy in order to maintain growth and employment. In broad terms the outcome was higher inflation, slow growth and rising unemployment. This experience had a profound impact on attitudes and was instrumental in the change of priorities in favour of stability. It was increasingly pointed out that, by delegating monetary policy to an institution with inflation averse obligations, a device could be created that permitted a lower rate of inflation to be sustained than would otherwise be possible. In other words, an independent central bank was expected to behave more predictably and this could in itself create greater stability.

The mere fact that stability achieves a higher priority means that the position of the central bank — whatever its formal degree of independence — is strengthened. It becomes more risky to go against the opinion of the central bank. Measurement and identification problems in relation to central bank independence thus tend to obscure the path to clear objective conclusions. Statistical evidence does not provide unambiguous answers.

So we are left with personal judgements. On that score I have no doubt about my own experience. Over the many years I have been in the business there have been so many instances in my own work in Denmark, and likewise regarding colleagues in other countries, that I do not hesitate to state that formal independence strengthens the hand of a stability orientated monetary policy.

In other words, if governments are free to choose their favourite policy at any given time in order to accommodate the aspirations of the electorate, then policies will inevitably have an inflationary bias. Thus, as argued previously, in the search for more stability it is rational to strengthen monetary policy as a counterpart to the underlying expansionary forces of the economy, but this does not mean that an independent central bank is a guarantee for stability. It is one player in the game — but not the only one, and not even the dominant one.

It is an unbalanced and unfortunate view that stability can be achieved and maintained largely by monetary policy measures. This is, to a certain degree, the philosophy in the treaty version of the economic and monetary union, which is the final part of my presentation.

Stability of the proposed monetary union

Pierre Werner and Jacques Delors were given the same task by politicians: Give us a blueprint for an economic and monetary union to be implemented by stages. The answers were not exactly identical.

The Werner Report of 1970 prescribed a gradual convergence of economic policy and economic performance, ending up in a system where national decision making regarding both monetary policy and fiscal policy was transferred to common institutions. This meant that, in the end, national parliaments would have to abide by instructions regarding fiscal policy. It is well known that the Werner plan had some impact on the formation of the EC exchange rate system from 1972, but on the whole the plan was immersed in the tensions of the mid-1970s. When politicians asked again almost 20 years later the answer was less ambitious.

The Delors Committee had a heavy monetary lopsidedness with 12 central bankers and 3 monetary experts, plus 2 members from the Commission. The majority was willing to concentrate on the monetary aspect of an Emu, assuming that this would be the driving force towards broader economic policy integration, but a strong minority could not accept such simplicity. To them a common central bank would be necessary but the co-ordination of fiscal and other economic policies was of equal importance. The compromise was to sever the two. The cutting instrument was the principle of subsidiarity. In operational terms, it is certainly not a crystal-clear concept, but one that has to be developed in a pragmatic way. It means that for instance in the fiscal field as much as possible shall be determined at the national level, provided there are no adverse repercussions on the cohesion and functioning of the Emu. So we are left with a concept that has the obvious purpose of protecting the independence of national parliaments. It is not surprising that the report — completed in 1989 — was welcomed by politicians and its main ideas were eventually incorporated in the Maastricht Treaty.

The philosophy of central bank independence was adopted along the German model that over the years had proved its effectiveness. Independence based on that prescription had of course not been the subject of disagreement within the Delors Committee with all its central bank members, or — it would appear — at the inter-governmental conference leading to the treaty proposal. The principle of subsidiarity was, not surprisingly, canonized in the treaty.

This means that, in two respects, the common system will differ from the national systems. The two are the accountability aspect and the counterpart aspect. The first — the accountability problem — relates to the question of ultimate political control.

In the national systems, the central banks have at least two formal strings to the political system. First, the rules have been stipulated by parliaments and can be revoked by parliaments. Second, central bank leadership is nominated politically and in almost all cases for a limited period. In addition monetary policy decisions are subject to public opinion in the sense that they have to be understood and, in the long run, accepted by the public. That is the reason why it is so important to explain monetary policy to the public at large. The central bank statutes of monetary union can of course be changed by the politicians, but it would require a change of the treaty, which, by implying ratification by all member countries, could be expected to be far more complicated than a change of national law. Furthermore, the nomination of the leadership will probably be much more inclined to compromise candidates than the present selection at the national level. The accountability problem is important but, to my mind, much less so than the counterpart problem.

At the national level, monetary policy decisions have at least to be understood —- if not applauded. The most important feature concerning monetary policy is that in the broad field of policy decisions, monetary policy is almost always the residual. When all other decisions have been taken monetary policy consequences follow almost by necessity. It can also be said to have its justification in its inevitability. But it is not a one-way relationship. There is fortunately a feedback, in the sense that policy decision-makers in other fields of economic policy have to consider the possible monetary policy answers to their own decisions. Such a close relation would seem to be difficult to establish in Emu, comprising up to 12 national decision making units in fields other than monetary policy. This feature raises the same problem that was considered by the Werner group and was left unsolved by the Delors group and in the treaty. Even though the Maastricht provisions regarding fiscal policy put strong demand on member countries' economic performance the counterpart or feed-back relation will be much weaker than at the present national level. But this does not imply that the system will be unable to function.

It will be possible to create lines of liaison to important policy-making units but such lines will be weaker than they currently are at national level and this implies that the system will be more vulnerable. There will be a higher risk that tensions will create dissatisfaction at the national level. Therefore, one of the most important tasks will be to ascertain that treaty conditions on budgetary policy, etc. be strictly observed, and that the economic surveillance exercise be effectively geared to that end.

In other words, although I find the system to be weaker than appropriate, it is definitely a workable proposition. At present, we in the Committee of Governors are involved in work to establish the institutional infrastructure for the European Monetary Institute, EMI, that is planned to start functioning at the beginning of 1994. I am convinced that it will be possible to finish this work properly — it is largely of a technical nature, which I shall refrain from bothering you with on this occasion. There are, however, two important policy aspects that deserve to be included in my presentation.

The first is our continuing obligation to improve the co-ordination of monetary policy among member countries. Our first annual report contains a presentation of the methods we are ;reports of Governors Committee using[1]. In essence, we are comparing and discussing forecasts, but have to observe the constraint that decisions must be taken at the national level and, for that reason, genuine negotiations are impossible.

In Stage Two, when the EMI starts functioning, there is an obligation to further improve co-ordination of monetary policy, but it seems to me that we have come rather close to the limit already now. Given the fact that there will be no transfer of decision-making power from the national level to the EMI, the only way to improve co-ordination is even more open and frank discussions leading to, at any rate, a better mutual understanding. This is, however, complicated by the second policy aspect I wish to mention — the varying degree of independence of member central banks.

If there is a very limited degree of independence, the central bank representative has a similarly limited possibility of participating in a debate leading to concrete steps to enhance economic convergence. My conclusion is, therefore, that in order to improve convergence, it should be recognized that formal independence of national central banks should be accomplished early in Stage Two instead of postponing it until the end, just before entering Emu, by when it must be adopted. Let me summarize my arguments in the following way.

A realistic view of the process of inflation makes it appropriate to strengthen the hand of monetary policy, which is an important instrument in containing inflation. It has not yet been possible to provide statistical evidence of the advantages of formally independent central banks. When seeking to contain the inflationary bias in our economic systems there is,

---

[1] *'First Annual Report' of the Committee of Governors of the Member States of the European Economic Community.*

however, to my mind little doubt that there are clear advantages connected with central bank independence.

Stability cannot be achieved solely by monetary policy. There seems to be a skewness in the Maastricht Treaty in that monetary policy will be highly centralized but other policies decentralized, thereby disclosing a lack of counterpart relations. This drawback will have to be overcome by developing relations with national policy decision-makers in a pragmatic but efficient way.

Finally, for the purpose of increasing monetary policy co-operation in Stage Two it is advisable to make national central banks independent at an early point in time and not to postpone this until just before transition to the final stage.

References

- Alesina, A. (1989), *Politics and business cycles in industrial democracies*, Economic Policy, April

- Bade, R. and Parkin, M. (1987), *Central bank laws and monetary policy*, University of Western Ontario Department of Economics Discussion Paper

- Burk and Cairncross (1992), *Goodbye, Great Britain*, Yale

- Capie, F. and Wood, G. (1991), *Central bank dependence and performance: an historical perspective*, City University Business School Discussion Paper, July

- Grilli, V., Masciandaro, D. and Tabellini, G. (1991), *Political and monetary institutions and public financial policies in the industrial countries*, Economic Policy, 13

- Beveridge, W.H. (1945), *Full Employment in a Free Society*

- Radcliffe (1959), *Report of the Committee on the working of the monetary system*, Command 827

- Swinburne and Castello-Branco (1991), *Central bank independence*, IMF Working Paper Number 91/58

Chapter 10

Central bank independence: an overstated case

Gerald Holtham
Chief Economist, Lehman Brothers International

The idea of an independent central bank has become exceedingly fashionable. At present, it is a *sine qua non* for taking part in any European monetary union. In their simplest form, the arguments for it are wrong; a more subtle argument has some justification, but its practical empirical importance is open to doubt.

The simple argument is just that politicians manipulate monetary policy to win elections, or are at least prone to taking the soft option. As all loose money does is cause inflation, it is better to take monetary policy out of party politics. An independent central bank will then yield lower inflation on average. The problem with this reasoning is that, while loose money generally just causes inflation, too-tight money does more than cause price deflation; it causes recession that often has permanent real effects on the economy. If Mr Volcker had let US banks and the government of Mexico go bust in 1982, by maintaining tight money, are we really to believe the world would have been the same a few years later except for a lower price level? The belief that monetary policy is 'neutral' in the long run, and affects only the price level, is an economist's superstition.

If, in spite of that, monetary policy can be taken out of politics, why not take fiscal policy out, too? As a matter of fact, there is much more international evidence of fiscal policy being manipulated for electoral ends than there is of monetary policy[1]. Before the last British general election, for example, the government greatly increased its expenditure, leading to a large budget deficit, while keeping interest rates high despite their unpopularity.

---

[1] *Alberto Alesina, 'Politics and Business Cycles in Industrial Democracies', Economic Policy, No.8, 1989.*

That is a common pattern. Yet no-one proposes that fiscal policy should be put in the hands of independent functionaries; it is too obviously anti-democratic. Once the neutrality of money is recognized as a fiction, the argument for democratic control of monetary policy becomes equally compelling.

Moreover, the evidence that independent central banks lead inevitably to lower inflation is unimpressive. It consists of a sample of one: Germany has lower inflation than other countries (the US with an independent central bank, by the way, does not). Some academics have imputed 'degrees of independence' to central banks and found these to be correlated with low inflation[1]. That is unimpressive both because the proxies for independence are generally imperfect, and sometimes subjective, and the variation of inflation rates across countries is also due to many other factors not specified in the correlation exercise. Moreover, in a small sample of countries, there is no reason to think these omitted factors somehow average out. The results are only persuasive to people whose prejudices they support.

So much for the simple arguments. The more subtle one depends on the idea of credibility. Politicians may mean to keep inflation down but other economic agents, especially in financial markets, know they have an incentive to inflate before elections. Accordingly, inflation expectations, and therefore the costs of controlling inflation, will be higher than in the case where the monetary authority is not thought to have any such incentive. An independent central bank will have different incentives from politicians, so its anti-inflationary policy will be more credible and so less expensive in terms of lost output than that of the toughest politician.

As an argument that is perfectly plausible — but how important is it? The Bundesbank, for all its credibility, has had to induce a substantial recession in Germany this year in order to reduce inflation. Wage bargainers were not frightened, or impressed, into moderation by the mere threat of tight money, even in nation-wide negotiations. The more decentralized the wage bargaining system, the less likely are deals to be influenced by the expected stance of the monetary authority, anyway.

We are left with the argument that, given an independent central bank, the financial markets would expect lower inflation — so nominal and real interest rates would be lower. What is that worth? There is a test case.

In New Zealand, the Reserve Bank was made statutorily independent in 1989. Since then, New Zealand's inflation has fallen below 1 per cent and this is, naturally, widely regarded as a great vindication of the independent

---

[1] *Vittorio Grilli, Donato Masciandoro and Guido Tabellini, 'Political and monetary institutions and public financial policies in the industrial countries', Economic Policy No.13, 1991.*

central bank. In fact, the true picture is more complicated, as a comparison of New Zealand and Australian experience makes clear.

The Reserve Bank's independence is actually a less controversial model than that of the Bundesbank, or the proposed European Central Bank of Europe under the Maastricht Treaty. The government still sets the target for inflation, normally for a five-year period, but with the right to step in and change it. This must be done publicly, however, and otherwise the Bank has complete independence to pursue the current target as it sees fit. The Bundesbank, of course, sets its own targets.

New Zealand's central bank is independent...

Since 1990, the New Zealand economy has begun to recover and, in 1992, grew at 2.3 per cent. As Figure 10.1 shows, this comes after a long period in which real growth averaged zero. Indeed real GDP in 1991 was about 1 per cent below its level of 1986. Growth of 2.3 per cent in 1992 has restored

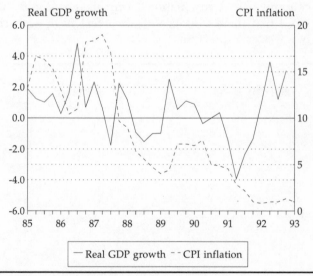

Figure 10.1   Inflation and GDP growth in New Zealand

GDP to the level of 1989. Forecast growth of 3 per cent this year would not, in the circumstances, look like a miracle. The disinflation resulting from this long period of stagnation began in 1987 and has continued since 1990. Meanwhile, unemployment has risen from 4 per cent in 1987, to 7.9 per cent in 1990, and to 10.7 per cent currently.

Obviously, proponents of the Reserve Bank Act hope that the arrangement will contribute to inflation staying low, while growth continues and unemployment ultimately falls. We shall have to wait and see. Many other structural reforms in New Zealand have been held up as an example to the rest of the world since 1984 but the results of that whole reform programme, at the macro-economic level so far, have been poor. The effects on income distribution and, perhaps, the level of crime have been worse.

...Australia's is not

The New Zealand unemployment rate would have been still higher were it not for heavy net emigration in these years to Australia. In Australia, there have been some structural reforms, but on nothing like the New Zealand scale, and the Reserve Bank is not independent. Indeed, a number of its senior officials have said they do not want independence, which might make the co-ordination of fiscal and monetary policy more difficult. Australia's reluctance to jump out of the frying pan of corporatism into the fire of reform (recently endorsed by the electorate) has brought criticism from newspaper columnists and international organizations, who have apparently not noticed that those voting with their feet have been crossing the Tasman sea in a westerly direction.

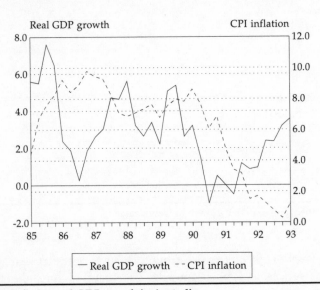

Figure 10.2   Inflation and GDP growth in Australia

Figure 10.2 shows growth and inflation in Australia since 1985. Inflation there is also around 1 per cent. Last year, it was the lowest in the OECD. Disinflation started later than in New Zealand — in 1990, when inflation was at 8 per cent. There has been an output cost, but it has been relatively mild and apparently short-lived. GDP declined in 1991, but grew by 2 per cent last year and is currently growing at about the same rate as in New Zealand. Australia also has an unemployment problem (though with net immigration); the rate is currently around 11 per cent, up from 6.9 per cent in 1990. The level of GDP last year was just over 1 per cent above its 1990 level and nearly 17 per cent above its 1986 level, in real terms.

Evidently, it is too soon to judge the relative advantages of the New Zealand and Australian arrangements for their respective Reserve Banks, although other New Zealand reforms are not showing up well on the face of it. Nonetheless, if Reserve Bank independence is to yield any of the advantages claimed for it, it must have a substantial effect on people's expectations, particularly their expectations of future inflation. The natural place to look for such an effect is the financial markets.

Spot the difference

Figure 10.3 shows 5-year bond yields in Australia and New Zealand, with the current year-on-year inflation rate subtracted. It is therefore a conven-

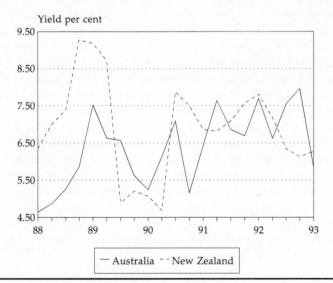

Figure 10.3   A comparison of real yields

tional measure of real yield. One of the most important influences on this variable will be expectations of future inflation. Reserve bank independence, if it affected inflation expectations, might have resulted in a drop in real yields. As the chart shows, that has not happened. Real yields are higher today than they were in 1990 and substantially higher than in 1986. Moreover, real yields have moved closely together in the two countries. Looking charitably at the graph, one can perhaps detect a small relative decline in New Zealand yields compared to Australian but it is well within the range of past variation, and most recently Australian yields have been falling faster. Even if the difference does reflect a lower inflation risk premium, due to the different institutional arrangements, it is exceptionally hard to believe that such a small difference could have any substantial effect on the behaviour of operators in the real economy, wage bargainers, for example.

What can we conclude? The truth is that history has yet to speak on the merits of the New Zealand Reserve Bank reform. So far there is no evidence that it has had any significant benefits at all.

Nonetheless, it must also be accepted that some degree of central bank independence is a *sine qua non* for German participation in Emu. A New Zealand style monetary constitution, which gives the central bank independence in general, but has a provision for an explicit political override, is a minimum requirement. Some supporters of central bank independence have suggested that the bank's overall priorities should be set by a qualified majority of the European Parliament — not by the executives of member States[1]. The Parliament could then change the priorities if it achieved the requisite majority, say, two-thirds. Politicians from a number of different countries would obviously find it much harder to agree to follow procedures leading to an override of the central bank than would politicians in a unitary state. Any central bank in a federal Europe would inevitably, therefore, have considerable independence in practice. Such an arrangement would also give the European Parliament a clear *raison d'être*. Yet, currently, prospects for asserting even a minimal degree of democratic control do not look promising. However, the future holds two elements of hope. First there is an ambiguity in the Maastricht constitution hinging on the role of the Council of Finance Ministers, Ecofin, in determining policy towards the exchange rate. In principle, this compromises the central bank's independent control of monetary policy, and much will depend on how this ambiguity is worked out. Second, the Bundesbank will be placed in an im-

---

[1] *Alesina op.cit.*

possible position in years to come by events in Germany, where sharper conflicts with the political authority are highly likely. This may result in a loss of its prestige and a more flexible German attitude to the monetary constitution.

The possibility should be faced, nonetheless, that German attitudes may remain irreconcilable and a hard choice will be necessary. In my judgement, it would then be better to avoid Emu. An exchange rate peg to the Ecu could be maintained and a system negotiated for the countries in that position. My proposals for reform of the ERM in order to make such a system more satisfactory are discussed in Chapter 3.

PART IV

*Perspectives on the crisis
— ERM member countries*

Chapter 11

A Belgian perspective

Alfons Verplaetse
Governor, Belgian National Bank

Before the foreign exchange crisis

Traditionally, Belgium has always assigned very high priority to the maintenance of stable exchange rate relationships. For a small, open economy in
which around 40 per cent of total expenditure is covered directly or indirectly by imports, the exchange rate is in fact one of the most important
factors determining the movement of domestic prices and costs. Furthermore, owing to the generally applicable automatic price indexation of
wages, salaries and other incomes, including social benefits, the effect of
any external price shock is propagated rapidly throughout the economy. It
is therefore clear that, in Belgium, the internal and external value of the
national currency are closely interlinked.

During the 1980s, Belgian exchange rate policy gradually became more
ambitious, this having been made possible by the favourable development
of the fundamentals of the Belgian economy and by a number of structural
improvements in the operation of the financial markets.

With economic growth keeping somewhat above the European average,
it was possible, from the second half of the 1980s onwards, to maintain
inflation rates which were among the lowest in the European Community.
At the same time, the current account of the balance of payments of the
Belgo-Luxembourg Economic Union (BLEU) was showing a strikingly stable surplus of around 2 per cent of GDP, so that the BLEU was able, year
after year, to accumulate net claims on the rest of the world.

At the same time the Belgian authorities took a wide range of initiatives
designed to modernize the Belgian financial markets and make them more
competitive and also more accessible to the widest and most varied possible
investing public. Without any attempt to give a complete account, mention
may be made here of the abolition of the two-tier exchange market in
March 1990, the introduction in 1989 of so-called 'linear bonds', referred to
here as OLOs, which are easily-negotiable dematerialized government

bonds designed to meet the specific requirements of institutional investors, and also of the reorganization, at the beginning of 1991, of the primary market for short-term Treasury bills and the creation of a liquid secondary market, stimulated by a body of primary dealers. In addition, the organization and operation, as well as the supervision, of the stock exchange were reformed and the Belgian Futures and Options Exchange (BELFOX) was created. Furthermore, the government had decided, in 1990, to lower the withholding tax on interest income from 25 to 10 per cent, a measure which appreciably increased the attraction of assets expressed in Belgian francs, particularly for resident investors.

It was against this favourable background that the Belgian authorities gradually shifted their exchange rate objective from keeping the exchange rate for the franc stable in relation to the average rate of the EMS partners to the maintenance of a stable exchange rate relationship against the anchor currencies of the exchange rate mechanism (ERM). Lastly, in the spring of 1990, the government decided officially to ratify that 'hard-currency policy' by formally and publicly entering into the undertaking to peg the franc to the anchor currency of the ERM, namely the German mark.

This undertaking contains two commitments:

- Firstly, that the central rate for the franc against the mark will not be changed in the event of a general realignment of the ERM.
- Secondly, that the National Bank will ensure that the fluctuations of the franc around its central rate with the German mark will be consistent with this new orientation, which means, concretely, that the Bank will henceforth observe, in relation to the German mark, much narrower fluctuation margins than the ± 2.25 per cent band applicable within the framework of the ERM.

The elimination of a number of structural handicaps and the gradual growth of confidence in the Belgian franc are clearly reflected in the shifts which have taken place, over recent years, in the structure of the balance of payments of the BLEU. While current transactions had, in fact, resulted in surpluses since 1984, these were exceeded up to 1989 by net outflows of long-term capital. The basic balance which comprises current transactions and long-term private capital transactions was thus still leaving a deficit, financed mainly by a surplus in short-term capital transactions. The latter surplus was made possible by the deliberate maintenance of a positive interest rate differential between short-term investments in francs and in marks. In that period in the financing of the deficit on the basic balance of payments, eating into the official reserves or government foreign exchange loans still played only a subordinate role, while the franc was declining

		1991	1992 Jan-Aug	Sep-Dec	1993 Jan-Apr
1.	Current account	156	210	91	119	116
2.	Long-term capital transactions	48	21	133	-112	182
	of which: securities	(59)	(45)	(113)	(-68)	(104)
3.	Basic balance (1+2)	204	231	224	7	298
4.	Short-term capital transactions	-152	-20	-242	222	-344
5.	Errors & omissions	-23	47	40	7	-19
6.	Balance of official settlements (3+4+5)	29	258	22	236	-65
	- changes (- = increase) in the government's foreign currency debt	(6)	(103)	(19)	(84)	(4)
	- changes (- = decrease) in the net exchange reserves of the NBB	(23)	(155)	(3)	(152)	(-69)

Figure 11.1   Balance of payments of the BLEU on a cash basis (in billions of francs)

only slightly in value against the mark — between the middle of 1985 and the middle of 1990 it fell by only 2.25 per cent

The growing confidence in the franc and the reduction of the rate of the withholding tax on interest income led, in 1990, to a spectacular turnaround in the balance of transactions in securities. From then on, long-term capital transactions resulted in substantial surpluses, which were further contributed to by the expansion of the market for linear bonds issued by the Belgian government. These developments, together with the continuance of a positive current account balance, turned the basic balance into a substantial surplus.

This made it possible to keep the exchange rate for the franc very close to the central rate against the German mark and, at the same time, completely eliminate the remaining positive interest rate differential in relation to short-term investments in marks, which still amounted to around 2 percentage points at the beginning of 1990. Permitting the disappearance of that short-term interest premium set in motion net outflows of short-term capital which thus constituted a spontaneous counterbalancing factor for the substantial surpluses in the basic balance.

This generally comfortable and stable situation continued until the summer of 1992. It also provided a favourable context for the radical changes which were made at the beginning of 1991 in the operational implementation of monetary policy.

As, on the one hand, the credibility of the firm exchange rate policy increased and, on the other hand, the position of the German mark weakened somewhat, owing to domestic economic disequilibria, Belgian short-term interest rates like the corresponding Dutch rates displayed a tendency, as early as 1991, but particularly in 1992, to fall below the German interest rate level. Although this development, partly owing to the lower inflation rate in Belgium, was not in principle unwelcome, the monetary authorities initially curbed, rather than encouraged, it. This was because they were convinced that, despite a temporary upsurge of inflation in Germany, the markets hardly believed that any depreciation of the German mark would be permanent. In the absence of any such expectations and in a context of completely liberalized capital transactions, it was not to be ruled out that a slightly excessive interest rate reduction would set in motion substantial capital outflows and thus compromise the credibility of the hard currency policy. This cautious attitude on the part of the National Bank was seen by the markets as a sign of its determination, thus allowing the Belgian franc to occupy the strongest position within the narrow band of the ERM throughout the greater part of 1992.

During the exchange rate crisis

In September 1992, the credibility of Belgian foreign exchange policy was put to a decisive test upon the outbreak of the most severe foreign exchange crisis experienced by the EMS since its creation. In contrast to the periods of foreign exchange unrest in the 1980s, the Belgian franc was never seriously threatened during the latest crisis, but on the contrary, together with the German mark and the Dutch guilder, served as a refuge currency. This is evidenced by the radical shifts which took place in the balance of payments of the BLEU from September 1992 onwards. A very substantial net demand for francs developed on the foreign exchange markets, chiefly owing to the leads and lags in the settlement of current transactions and to the dramatic reversal in short-term capital flows.

The exceptionally large current account surplus on a cash basis during the period September-December 1992 was partly due to a speculative reduction in net commercial claims on foreign countries. When resident importers expect certain foreign currencies to depreciate it is, of course, in their interest to postpone their payments in those currencies while, conversely, foreign importers may find it advantageous to pay for their imports from the BLEU more quickly, that is, before their own currency depreciates. In this way, the foreign exchange crisis exerted an influence on the payment periods which are customary in international trade.

The repercussions of the foreign exchange crisis on the balance of payments of the BLEU were, however, mainly observable in short-term capital transactions, which gave rise to net capital inflows during the last four months of 1992 of over BFr 220bn, in sharp contrast to the substantial export of short-term capital which had been recorded from 1990 until August 1992. The unprecedented volume of these short-term capital flows was partly attributable to the large positions which investors had built up in currencies offering high interest rates during the preceding period of stability within the ERM. As expectations of depreciation of these currencies developed, these investors preferred to cover their positions, thus setting-off considerable capital flows — mainly in the form of forward transactions — in the direction of currencies considered to be strong, such as the Deutschemark, the Dutch guilder and the Belgian franc. In this way, predominantly defensive strategies in fact had a destabilizing effect on the foreign exchange markets. Of course, deposits in francs were also formed for purely speculative reasons and foreign currencies were sold forward in the hope of being able to repurchase them later at a lower rate.

The previously-observed net inflow of long-term capital continued during September and October 1992, but during the last two months of the year the inward flow of capital was replaced by quite considerable outflows. This was chiefly connected with the fact that the long-term interest rate differential with Germany, which had reached a peak of about 100 basis points in the course of September, subsequently narrowed sharply, partly because an important international rating bureau reported that it had assigned its best rating to loans in Belgian francs issued by the Belgian government. Towards the end of the year the long-term interest rate differential against the mark reached a temporary low of only about 50 basis points and Belgian long-term interest rates had also fallen appreciably below the French rates. These relative interest rates levels and the prospects of larger rises in the prices of bonds of countries which had been obliged to raise their interest rates sharply during the foreign exchange crisis appear to have been the main reasons for this temporary reversal in long-term capital transactions: they induced non-residents to sell Belgian linear bonds in favour of mainly French OATs, while residents, too, were inclined to revert to buying more foreign currency bonds.

From September 1992, short-term capital transactions no longer counterbalanced the surplus shown by the basic balance but, on the contrary, added to it. Consequently, the entire burden of the compensatory financing of the balance of payments fell on the National Bank. The latter was obliged, as were the Deutsche Bundesbank and De Nederlandsche Bank, to intervene on a massive scale on the foreign exchange market in order to support other ERM currencies. The extent of these interventions can be approximately deduced from the surplus on the balance of official settlements, which reached BFr 236bn over the last four months of 1992 and which was also influenced, apart from by the interventions, by the interest received on

the National Bank's official reserves. This accumulation of reserves was unavoidable, since it would have been too risky to attempt to counteract the
massive inflow of short-term capital by a unilateral lowering of interest
rates. In this turbulent period, the primary concern of the Belgian monetary
authorities was to safeguard the credibility of the exchange rate policy for
the medium term. Therefore, the National Bank's interest rate and liquidity
policy had to be very accurately attuned to the changing market conditions.
In the wake of the German mark and the Dutch guilder it proved possible,
from the middle of September 1992, to set in motion a downward movement of money market interest rates, and even to maintain — almost constantly — a slightly negative interest rate differential against the German
mark. Only for a few days in September did the interest rate on Belgian
eurofranc deposits rise above that on euromarks. This was, however, chiefly
attributable to a technical reason: because of the massive formation of euro-
mark deposits, the interest rates for these declined appreciably below German domestic money market rates. This unusual situation was, however,
rectified towards the end of September under the influence of the Bundesbank's neutralization operations.

The unruffled course of interest and exchange rates cannot, however,
conceal the fact that the extensive official interventions on the foreign exchange markets had major repercussions on the National Bank's domestic
money market management. Purchases of foreign currencies by the central
bank are in fact coupled with the creation of additional liquidity in the national currency, which will ultimately be used by domestic credit institutions in order to reduce their liabilities to the central bank or increase their
assets with the central bank. Much the same applies if foreign central banks,
within the framework of the European Monetary Co-operation Fund
(EMCF), resort to their very short-term credit facilities with the National
Bank in order to use the borrowed francs to finance interventions in support of their own currencies. This is because the Belgian francs which are
sold by the foreign central banks are not held by their foreign counterparts,
but will flow into the Belgian money market.

There is thus a danger that, owing to their expansionary effect on the
money market, interventions in support of other ERM currencies will tend
to thwart the central bank's provision of liquidity to the domestic money
market, and it is precisely via that channel that the National Bank puts a
large proportion of its interest rate policy into practice. It was therefore
necessary to neutralize or sterilize the repercussions of these interventions
on the domestic money market to the greatest possible extent in order to
ensure that the credit institutions remained dependent on the central bank
and that the National Bank, for its part, fully retained its grip on interest
rates.

		31 Aug 1992	31 Dec 1992	30 Apr 1993	30 Jun 1993
1.	Initial money market deficit or surplus	-104	44	-21	-42
	origins:				
	a. Banknotes in circulation (-)	-423	-430	-426	-442
	b. Net foreign reserves of the NBB[1]	307	459	390	387
	c. Miscellaneous (net)	12	15	15	13
2.	Sterilizing swap transactions (-)	-5	-140	-78	-71
3.	Adjusted money market deficit (1+2)	-109	-96	-99	-113
4.	Granting (+) or absorption (-) of liquidity by the NBB	99	99	98	107
	a. Mobilization of commercial bills	10	4	4	4
	b. Granting of credits by tender	45	25	20	30
	c. Direct money market interventions	44	70	74	73
5.	Residual money market surplus or deficit (3+4)[2]	-10	3	-1	-6

[1] *Spot and forward, valued at buying exchange rates*

[2] *To be absorbed or covered through different end-of-day facilities with the NBB*

Figure 11.2   Money market management by the National Bank of Belgium (outstanding amounts in billions of francs)

There were various lines of action to choose from for this purpose — skimming off the excess liquidity by the introduction of some kind of compulsory monetary reserve, using the foreign currencies acquired for redeeming part of the government's foreign currency debt and carrying out specific liquidity-tightening operations on the money market.

In Belgium, unlike in most other European countries, the credit institutions are not required to maintain compulsory reserves with the central bank, and the National Bank in fact endeavours to avoid using an instrument which is hardly in conformity with market principles. Actually, advantage was taken — in consultation with the minister of finance — of the possibility of using part of the foreign currencies acquired through interventions for the purpose of repaying foreign currency loans previously contracted by the Treasury. Indeed, it seemed logical that this debt, which had been accumulated at the end of the 1970s and during the 1980s in order to help finance the current account balance of payments deficits and the outflows of private capital with which the country had to contend at that time, should now, in the opposite situation, be repaid and replaced by instruments of indebtedness in the national currency. Over 1992 as a whole, these redemptions of foreign exchange debt amounted to BFr 103bn so that, of the total surplus on the balance of official settlements, amounting to BFr 258bn,

BFr 155bn gave rise to a growth in the National Bank's net foreign exchange reserves. Of this, BFr 135bn was sterilized by means of currency swaps, in other words by selling the accumulated foreign currencies spot on the market and repurchasing them forward against Belgian francs. This enabled the rise in the cash foreign exchange reserves and thus its repercussion on money market liquidity to be ultimately reduced to about BFr 20bn.

That residue was absorbed by curtailing those forms of liquidity provision that are least necessary for the fine-tuning of money market conditions — thus the National Bank reduced its lending via auctions, the frequency of which was reduced from twice to once per week from November 1992 onwards, while the facility for the mobilization of commercial paper was halved from December onwards (from over BFr 10bn to around 5bn).

During the first four months of 1993, the structure of the BLEU's balance of payments became more similar to what it had been before the ERM crisis. On top of the still-considerable current account surplus, a substantial positive balance in respect of long-term capital transactions reappeared, so that the basic balance again turned into a very large surplus. This development was partly attributable to the reappearance, from February to April, of a growing positive interest rate differential in relation to long-term investments in German marks, on the one hand, and the disappearance of the negative long-term interest rate differential in relation to the French franc on the other, causing investment in foreign securities to become less attractive again.

Against the basic balance of payments surplus there were also again, in the first four months of 1993, substantial net outflows of short-term funds. These outflows were due partly to the reversal of short positions taken up during the preceding months of violent foreign exchange upheavals and partly to a temporary weakening of the international markets' faith in the Belgian franc, as a reaction to the uncertain domestic political situation. In fact, provisional data indicate that BLEU residents, who had set in motion a substantial net inflow of short-term funds at the end of 1992 by the liquidation of their foreign currency positions, had stepped up their formation of deposits in foreign currencies again at the beginning of 1993. Non-residents, for their part, appear to have largely covered the substantial positions in Belgian francs which they had built up in the preceding months by forward sales of Belgian francs.

The temporarily reduction of confidence in the Belgian franc was also reflected in the fact that, in the course of February 1993 and again for a short period towards the end of March, the exchange rate for the Belgian franc slipped slightly below its central rate against the German mark. The National Bank did, however, react very promptly and vigorously to these signs of weakness.

The pressure on the franc which started at the beginning of February was due to several factors: the reversal of the previous speculation against the French franc, the Danish crown and the Irish punt, the perhaps somewhat excessively sharp narrowing of the long-term interest rate differential in January 1993 and the uncertainty about the reduction of the Belgian government deficit. Under those circumstances, the National Bank appreciably cut down its provision of liquidity to the credit institutions, making the latter more dependent on the Bank's residual financing facilities. The Bank also made recourse to its overnight facilities more expensive by widening the spread between its upper and lower intervention rates to 2 percentage points, against 1 percentage point previously.

At the end of March, there was a certain resurgence of the pressure on the franc, when the government was unable to reach agreement on a package of measures for consolidating the budget deficit and even tendered its resignation an offer which was, however, kept under consideration by the head of state. The National Bank again reacted by making its liquidity assistance to the credit institutions considerably more expensive: the central intervention rate was raised by half a percentage point, from 8 to 8.5 per cent, and the rate for overnight advances was even increased by a whole percentage point, from 9 to 10 per cent When it became evident, after a short time, that the political crisis could be averted, the position of the franc strengthened again and the Bank was able to discontinue its defensive interest rate measures.

During the first four months of 1993, the evolution of the balance of official settlements was dominated by a decrease of some BFr 69bn in the National Bank's exchange reserves, reflecting repayments in Belgian francs of EMCF loans which other central banks had previously contracted in order to support their own currencies. In accordance with the EMCF rules, however, another part of these loans was repaid, not in francs, but in Ecus and other foreign currencies. Consequently, there is a danger that part of the increase in the amount of foreign currencies in the Bank's balance sheet due to the foreign exchange crisis might become permanent. In that case, as a result of such an increase, there would be no reversal of the associated contraction of the Bank's assets in Belgian francs. Until such time as this expansion of the money market is cancelled out by other factors, the Bank will be obliged to go on carrying out sterilizing currency swaps in order to safeguard the effectiveness of its action on the domestic money market.

After the foreign exchange crisis

In comparison to what other European currencies with sound fundamentals have had to contend with during the last few months, the tensions in connection with the Belgian franc have, on the whole, remained very limited.

That was most probably the reflection of the fact that, since the middle of 1990, the Belgian authorities have not allowed there to be any doubt about their exchange rate objective and have also always acted consistently in accordance with it. Furthermore, the markets knew that the Belgian hard currency policy is based on a broad political and social consensus and is implemented by an autonomously-operating central bank.

The Belgian franc thus seems to have emerged strengthened from the February/March mini-crisis. It very quickly became possible for money market interest rates to be brought down again below German rates without this adversely affecting the exchange rate. On the contrary, when, in the period May-June 1993, the Bundesbank temporarily curbed the downward movement of interest rates because of the continuing monetary and budgetary pressure on the level of domestic inflation, the Belgian franc and the Dutch guilder had in the meantime acquired a strong enough position to allow a course of action somewhat more independent of German interest rate policy. The National Bank and De Nederlandsche Bank, in close consultation with each other, have taken advantage a few times of this admittedly limited scope for manœuvre in order to lower their own interest rates, without this being matched by a corresponding movement in Germany. Moreover, towards the end of June 1993 — for the first time for more than two decades — French short-term interest rates were also reduced to below the German level.

Thus, for the time being, there appears to have come into existence again a hard core within the EMS which is sufficiently broadly-based to be able to serve as a pole of attraction for other Community countries. In fact, despite the retrograde steps which have had to be taken, economic convergence remains the key condition for lasting monetary integration. The EMS can undoubtedly continue to play an essential role in that convergence process as a disciplinary factor, at least provided that the exchange rate mechanism is looked upon primarily as an instrument and not as an aim in itself, since the most serious mistake made during the last few years was to regard the EMS as a monetary union *avant la lettre*, which had the effect, in a number of countries, of thwarting, rather than encouraging, policy adjustments directed towards convergence.

Chapter 12

A Danish perspective

Erik Hoffmeyer
Governor, Danmarks Nationalbank[1]

European monetary integration after the September 1992 crisis

Since its establishment, the European monetary system (EMS) — and in particular its exchange rate mechanism (ERM) — has been through two periods that have been distinctly different. The first was the disorderly, incoherent years from 1979 until March 1983, with uncoordinated national economic policies and frequent and large exchange rate adjustments. It almost ended in collapse. During the second period, from March 1983 until early 1992, the system gradually experienced growing exchange rate stability with improved co-ordination of economic policies in member countries, increases in membership, and — since 1987 — no exchange rate realignments. However, the system exploded in September 1992 after the heaviest exchange market pressure experienced so far. Interventions to defend the system became so huge that Italy and the United Kingdom eventually decided to leave the ERM temporarily while Spain devalued by 5 per cent but remained in the ERM.

It is natural to ask why the successful development of the system came to suffer from a crisis of credibility last September and how serious this setback is for the move towards further European monetary integration. Fundamentally it deals with the interconnection between rules of behaviour, performance and expectations. Particularly regarding analysis of expectations I have to warn you that this issue is highly conjectural — almost subjective, and I have no claim to be closer to the truth than others.

---

[1] *This contribution is based on a speech at the European Finance Convention on 23 November 1992. A short addendum on page 174 comments on the events of August 1993.*

Let me begin with the basic policy rules of the EMS as they were originally formulated with the aim of creating a 'zone of monetary stability in Europe'.

The rules were laid down in the Brussels Council Resolution of 5 December 1978. These rules, *inter alia*, stipulated that, when a currency crosses its threshold of divergence there will be "a presumption that the authorities concerned will correct this situation by adequate measures, namely:

- a) diversified intervention;
- b) measures of domestic monetary policy;
- c) changes in central rates;
- d) other measures of economic policy."

It was, of course, recognized that economic performance had to converge if the system should remain stable, but the focus of attention was initially on the parity grid of exchange rates and the divergence indicator.

If a country, for one reason or another, diverged from the rest it had to adjust. In general terms, divergence was measured by the market exchange rate of a currency in relation to an average of all other EMS currencies. It was a one-dimensional test that was presumed to trigger action. I think it is well-known that this blueprint did not work at all. For various reasons, the divergence indicator never played a significant role as a trigger mechanism. Nor did divergent countries seriously embark on stability-orientated policies. On the other hand, the exchange-rate instrument was used frequently.

Indeed, the first four years of the EMS witnessed an almost chaotic development, as several members pursued internal policy objectives with monetary stability being of second order of importance. France, particularly in the latter part of the 1979-83 period, followed an expansionist economic policy with relatively high inflation rates. This fostered exchange market tensions that led to several devaluations, amounting in total to about 30 per cent *vis-à-vis* the D-mark.

Other countries, like Denmark, Belgium, Ireland and Italy, pursued similar policies and had to devalue, too. It was a period of clearly non-convergent economic policies resulting in recurrent currency unrest and market pressure for exchange-rate adjustment. And realignments came.

Since 1983 things have changed decisively. Convergence became the dominating goal and improved substantially. This change of emphasis was not only based on the dismal experience of the years of 1979-83, but also on a common desire to pursue a stability-orientated economic policy. It was now widely recognized that convergence of fundamental economic performance was absolutely essential for the maintenance of the stability of the fixed exchange- rate system. This recognition found its expression in amendments to the system in 1987, the so-called Basle-Nyborg agreement.

Convergence was to be strengthened, in particular, through domestic economic policy measures, assisted by an elaborate system of surveillance and monitoring in various EC fora. For this purpose a set of economic indicators should be analysed for each country whereas disturbances in the exchange market should first and foremost be counteracted by exploiting "... the scope for a more active, flexible and concerted use of the instruments available, namely exchange rate movements within the fluctuation band, interest rates and interventions."

Exchange rate adjustments are also mentioned, but it is specifically stated that they should be "... infrequent and changes in central rates should be kept small ..." Thus, exchange rate adjustments could be avoided if convergent economic policy measures proved successful. As a matter of fact, it did. With the Maastricht Treaty blueprint for an economic and monetary union, the fixed-rate system gained in credibility and importance by the convergence criteria for entry, including the one requiring countries to observe — in the run-up to the third phase of the Emu — the normal fluctuation margins of the ERM, for at least two years, without devaluing. In the meantime, the Committee of Governors, in its annual report of April 1992, and in various written and oral presentations to the Ecofin Council, pointed out that convergence was not satisfactory. Markets were, however, convinced that the obligation to co-ordinate fundamentals among members was so strong that the fixed-rate system would be a safe stepping-stone to Emu.

In retrospect, it can be argued that market expectations were naïve or unrealistic, and did not appreciate the true differences in fundamentals. Moreover, it is a fact that the widespread credibility of the system led authorities to believe that adjustment of fundamentals could be postponed without serious risk. Looking at fundamentals, there is no doubt that over the past 3-4 years there have clearly been differences between the economic performance of the inner core group of countries, and developments in Italy, Spain and the United Kingdom. This applies to the balance of payments, public finance, inflation and competitiveness (as measured by some kind of real exchange rates). These differences had to be adjusted before entry into Emu, but it was assumed that there would be ample time to accomplish the adjustment.

The sequence of events leading to the explosion on September 16 was actually triggered by the Danish referendum in early June, polls on the French referendum during the summer and increasing difficulties with British ratification of the treaty. It started by increasing interventions in support of the Italian lira. But, in the process, credibility became gradually undermined and the blast in connection with the French referendum was not foreseen — neither was its powerfulness.

Even though much is known of how the crisis was handled, quite a lot is yet unknown. I am not in a position to add to what has been unveiled in the media or elsewhere, and I do not think it is so interesting to know who spoke what to whom. The sequence of events had a clear pattern. The first step was that the huge interventions at the margins in support of the Italian lira led the Germans to initiate negotiations between the two governments, as German monetary policy could be seriously imperilled by money creation on such a scale. The result was a devaluation of the lira versus the other currencies in the ERM by 7 per cent. However, tensions did not subside — markets were not convinced that this was enough.

Pressure increased and became explosive against sterling. Italy and the United Kingdom then decided to suspend intervention and leave the system temporarily. The French franc had to be supported strongly, even after the referendum. The pressure on the franc gained so much momentum that release of a common declaration between the two finance ministers and central bank governors was seen as being necessary. According to the declaration, fundamentals were such that exchange rate adjustment would not be justified. Also it is stated — somewhat cryptically — that both parties will act in accordance with the rules of the EMS.

Markets have since calmed down and the so-called inner core currencies remain intact. Reflows of capital to France, where the franc was under heavy pressure, and Denmark where the krone also had to be supported for a few days, have more than fully offset previous interventions.

Could the outcome have been prevented? Participants in the debate have already given answers — but quite different answers. Some say: It could have been prevented if countries with out-of-line currencies had, in time, devalued their currencies convincingly. Others say: Yes, if countries with out-of-line fundamentals had adjusted fundamentals, or had shown sufficient willingness to do so, markets would have been convinced. Finally, some say: Yes, if the system had functioned better. Let me comment briefly on these three attitudes.

The first group maintains that an exchange rate adjustment should have been accomplished earlier. It is true that an earlier adjustment would have prevented the September explosion, but it neglects the fact that the whole philosophy of the Basle-Nyborg agreement and the Maastricht Treaty was to avoid using the exchange rate as an instrument in the adjustment process. As noted previously, one of the treaty conditions for qualifying as a participant in the final stage of Emu is precisely that the country has not, over the preceding two years, actively devalued its currency.

The second group maintains that fundamentals should have been corrected earlier, but this disregards the fact that Italy — admittedly after some delay — had launched a comprehensive adjustment programme that was aimed at coming to grips with unsatisfactory fundamentals by abolishing indexation of wages, reducing transfer payments and limiting the public deficit. In the United Kingdom, fundamentals were deviating regarding the balance of payments. The public sector deficit was rising, but mainly due to the deepening of the recession, and inflation was clearly on a downward trend. Thus, a case might have been made for the argument that fundamentals would move in the right direction, but in the event the move was not sufficient to convince markets.

The explosion on September 16 was the outcome of a confrontation between markets and authorities. Markets — or more precisely the expectation of millions of economic agents — had gradually lost confidence in the determination of the authorities to defend the exchange rates. It is difficult to say exactly what should have been done, but it is a basic feature of a fixed-exchange rate system that authorities will lose if they do not show determination to defend the system. At the last moment the system was rescued by the Franco-German statement, indicating that support would be unconditional. This eventually convinced markets, and as I have mentioned, capital flows were reversed completely.

The third group maintains that the system should have functioned better. However, technical changes of the EMS cannot be a substitute for political determination to defend the system, which means that one should not try to find remedies in measures to improve the functioning of the system. The essence is that authorities miscalculated the degree of credibility that had developed and thought that there was ample time to undertake the necessary adjustments.

Suggestions have now been put forward that the disequilibrating capital flows should be analysed and that certain amendments or adjustments might be made to the EMS. Obviously we will analyse what has happened as we have been doing in the wake of previous crises. We will, in all probability, be able to learn from what has happened. In this connection, my own argument has always been that the major issue is the confrontation between market expectations and political determination to adhere to stability-orientated policies. A technical study cannot be expected to find answers to such complex issues.

Now, the second question from my introduction: How serious is the breakdown? There is no denying that the explosion of September 16 is a clear setback on the road towards Emu. An almost euphoric belief in the fixed-exchange rate system as a stepping-stone towards Emu has been shattered, but, as I have argued, markets had become over optimistic as the institutional framework of Emu was put in place. But, within this framework, realities turned out to be not so bright. Full convergence was not just around the corner, and not easy to acquire. The real problems would unquestionably have emerged later on, and it is not harmful that they are recognized now. In addition, it is reassuring that the inner core of the ERM has survived. I have mentioned that reflows have more than fully compen-sated for previous interventions in France and my own country. This means that the system functions appropriately. It would, however, be hiding the fact, not to mention the disagreement, which has come to the surface in several member countries as a consequence of the breakdown. A debate has begun and will continue on who has to adjust and whether the EMS rules should be amended. I am afraid that such a debate will open a Pandora's Box of intractable attitudes. It is quite natural that authorities in Italy and the United Kingdom feel that the system should have given them better protection. Likewise, the German authorities feel that monetary policy has been taken out of the hands of the Bundesbank by the flood of D-marks that have been created by those interventions. Even though there are un-derstandable misgivings about what happened in September, it is necessary to recognize that stability of the ERM requires that interventions are neces-sary only for a short period and that they are then reversed. This is a fun-damental rule of the game. The system has been impaired by recent events. The market's faith in the stability of the fixed-rate system was surprisingly strong but is now unreasonably low, as evidenced by capital flows of mag-nitudes never seen before, even in cases that are not warranted by funda-mentals. It needs a political effort to restore faith in the system.

Credibility is the essential requirement for the stability of the system and credibility has to be created at home. Under present circumstances it is the responsibility of national authorities and cannot be bought or imported. Not until Emu is established will credibility become a common responsibility.

Addendum (August 1993)

Events since this speech was held have demonstrated that the authorities have not succeeded in re-establishing sufficient credibility to the system. On 1 August, intervention margins were temporarily increased to +/- 15 per cent, which in reality suspended the ERM. This decision came after heavy interventions in support of the French franc and the Danish krone, in spite of the fact that economic fundamentals in both countries were to superior to Germany's.

Chapter 13

A German perspective

Professor Dr. Dr. h.c. Reimut Jochimsen
Member of the Central Bank Council of the Deutsche Bundesbank[1]

The Maastricht framework for Emu...

The economic and monetary union of Europe (Emu) is the most ambitious project yet of the endeavour started in 1952 to integrate Europe. This led to the signing of the Treaty of Maastricht and the establishment of a fully-fledged monetary union with the European Central Bank (ECB) and the European System of Central Banks (ESCB) managing the common currency: they are set up to be independent both of their national governments and the European political institutions. This is a unique and momentous project indeed. It is not the only bold move ahead in the Maastricht Treaty, which also provides for the establishment of European citizenship, the idea of evolving a common defence policy, and the idea of setting up co-operation in justice policies and on asylum seekers as well as migration in general. All these elements are important for the evolution of what the Maastricht Treaty named European Union. However, I intend to concentrate on economic and monetary union in Europe as such.

The case has been stated, both politically and on the basis of economic logic, that a common currency constitutes a necessary element for the completion of the single market. I disagree. It may be desirable, and it certainly presents important savings on transaction costs for all persons, firms and other economic agents in the event of its being successfully introduced, but it is not a necessary, and much less a sufficient, prerequisite for a single market. That makes it all the less probable that it can serve as the proponent, the promoter or even the engine for integration. This does not preclude that some degree of stability of exchange rates between the currencies

---

[1] *This contribution is based on a speech made at the Royal Institute of International Affairs, Chatham House, London on 2 February 1993*

of the economies merging into a single market may not only be desirable but even necessary, as I shall argue later. Nevertheless, concerning the text of the Treaty of Maastricht on Emu, I do not hesitate to say that, from my viewpoint as a central banker, this is on the whole a quite satisfactory institutional arrangement. This holds true in particular for the goal determination of the purpose of the common money, the primary objective of price level stabilization and thus protection of the internal value of currency.

...has price stability as a central aim

It is the first time that this important goal of monetary policy, namely the protection of the internal value of money, has been written into an international treaty. We have not had that before, for example, in the arrangements for the International Monetary Fund or for the other Bretton Woods institution, the World Bank. These were to be concerned about the stability of the exchange rate for achieving external balance both on current and on capital accounts. They were only pledged, to a lesser degree, to the maintenance of internal price stability.

If you go back to the second half of the 19th century, when the gold standard evolved as a universal monetary system, it was just the gold parity and, of course, instantaneous full convertibility which counted. National price levels had to adjust to the exigencies of this mechanism and consequently fluctuated considerably over time. Periods of deflation and of inflation thus alternated and movements in nominal wages — although these showed smaller oscillations — had to follow from the parities of the gold standard. After being restored in the 1920s, the gold standard broke down in the early-1930s only because different nation states refused to accept any longer the consequences which exchange rates, which had been fixed too ambitiously, inflicted upon employment, investment, wages and prices. Beggar-my-neighbour policies came to the surface as signs of a new economic nationalism refusing to obey any longer the rules of the game. Consequently, world trade collapsed, the Great Depression forged its inroads into pluralist democracy and free markets in many countries. Harry Dexter White and Lord Keynes, in the lessons they drew from the experience of the inter-war period agreed, at Bretton Woods in the autumn of 1944, that the deflationary, depression-deepening impact of competitive depreciations on economies staying the course — as well as trade wars and slumps — had to be avoided in the future but by means of stable-yet-adjustable exchange rates. Their prescriptions, though, were designed for a world in which the share of trade and other international exchange between nations were still on a relatively modest scale.

In a certain sense the Emu, treaty takes the lesson one step further than White and Keynes, namely by resolving not to repeat these deflationary effects on the price level, or to allow inflation to happen both which were judged to be economically and socially disastrous. The objective is now to develop an economic system which will make it possible for the national economies to perform so that each has a price level, neither on the inflationary, nor on the deflationary side, but with maximum long run stability.

There are a few concerns about the arrangements for the European Central Bank...

The Emu project sets up the institutional arrangement for the central banks in a reasonable way, but a few criticisms and quibbles still remain. The most important one concerns the ability to fix external exchange rates — of the common currency against the yen and the US dollar, for example — which, in my judgment, should not be a feature of the system. Indeed, it could very well put the objective of internal stability at risk. When negotiating a treaty with a very long life-span you might include this feature as an abstract possibility, but to enter into a fixed-exchange rate regime with external currencies or to have target zones for exchange rates with the US dollar and the Japanese yen is extremely risky and unrealistic.

Such regimes become even more dangerous if they are used as an instrument of industrial policy, even of competitive depreciation, of which we had enough in the thirties, or of other targets of structural policies alien to an international economic order where we should keep the monetary track as neutral as possible.

I also have some quibbles about the mandate for the national governors. The national governors are to be in office for a minimum of just five years. Their term can be renewed. I personally would say the best would be to give each and every member of the European Central Bank Council a fourteen year term, as the Federal Reserve Board offers.

...as well as other aspects of Emu

There are a number of missing elements in other aspects of the construction of Emu, besides the ECB and ESCB. I shall just mention the most important ones. One concerns the question of responsibility for actually following through the necessary stabilization policies on a sustained basis once you have entered into the currency union. In this respect, full recognition has not been given to the fact that it is not just the supranational monetary authority which runs the currency, but fiscal policy and collective bargaining over wages are also extremely important for the success of the stabilization policy of a reserve bank.

The treaty text appears to be clear on this. The primary objective of monetary stabilization is addressed to everyone in Europe who carries responsibility for economic and monetary policy. It is targeted at the heads of state and chiefs of government, at the national governments and all other state authorities, the Councils of Ministers, the European Commission, the European Parliament — they all will have to follow it. However, the instruments to implement this ruling are lacking and any sanctions envisaged if the law is flouted are only very weak, if indeed they are operational at all.

Judging from the German experience, it is not assured that you will easily, let alone automatically, obtain that climate of consensus-building in the cause of stability which will be needed for a successful monetary stabilization policy. The central bank alone can not effect this. It can execute monetary policy, of course, but it needs partners who in their attitudes and policies reckon with a similar rationale. The German experience demonstrates clearly that you need all these partners at the national and also, desirably, the regional level.

It is most important that the philosophy behind the policy of the central bank is deeply engraved onto society. This stability culture, has to evolve: the need for an assimilation or adjustment of attitudes and goals has to be understood and the costs of reaching this have to be weighed properly. This calls for a most thorough change in policy practice and for a new build-up of institutions in Europe to push the attitudes and values of an emerging European society, not just to register a statistical levelling of different national patterns and types of behaviour. In this respect the Maastricht Treaty leaves us with a *lex imperfecta*, a ruling without effective sanctions.

Further work is needed to complete the Maastricht Treaty

In addition, the Maastricht Treaty contains a *lex incompleta*, in that it does not write down all that is necessary to make monetary policy a success in terms of the stability of the value of the currency. Thank God, it does not create a Brussels superstate to run fiscal policy and to determine wages and incomes with a large part of Europe's gross domestic product collected for, and spent by, European institutions which would then provide the complementary fodder for an efficient monetary policy. On the other hand, it does not really put into place the institutional mechanisms which would enforce the minimum level of political co-ordination and co-operation necessary for the definition and execution of the objective of price stability. First of all, the new European union is still built on the community made up of single national states. There are no true European institutions, executive or legislative, in their own right which have a full foundation in the will of the European people. The ECB, apart from the European Court of Justice established in 1958, will be the only truly supranational authority of the Community. The ESCB and the ECB are to be founded by the twelve member states which in legal terms will forego their national sovereignty in this sphere for good. In contrast to the independence of the national central banks we know, like the Fed and the Bundesbank, the statute and status of the ECB and the ESCB cannot be changed by simple law, but only by identical decisions of all the member states. For all practical purposes this rules out any democratic accountability.

The longer such a state of affairs is allowed to persist, the more keenly this deficiency will be felt. What, on a European level, can bind together the national interests in fiscal policy and collective bargaining of income policies? Will a common currency suffice to bind these together effectively in a common stability effort? You may tie fiscal and incomes policy together, of course, to create compatible conditions from the point of view of the central bank, but this is only defined negatively, by means of the so-called convergence criteria. Only those countries satisfying these criteria can participate in the union, but this does not entail a fully developed, co-ordinated and consistent economic policy profile for the Community as a complement to the single monetary policy.

No doubt these convergence criteria describe the maximum deviations permissible and they point in the right direction, but negative criteria as such will not suffice. You need also a positive formulation, which goes beyond that, of the common economic and fiscal policies member governments will have to follow.

Is it realistic to have monetary union without political union?

It is our German understanding and experience, that you cannot have a common currency without a common state: this raises one of the main problems ahead of us in Europe. Let us assume, for argument's sake, that we are now starting the final stage of Emu and that we have member countries which are performing according to the criteria. They are all doing well, they are all stabilization-minded, there are no debt accumulators, there are no difficulties in terms of foreign exchange fluctuations: all are behaving very well and everything is going all right. I assume further that now an exogenous shock occurs, like an oil crisis. Will the solidarity of the member states be sufficient to deal with such a new burden without a properly functioning framework of common political background, determination of the common will and, of course, institutions which in times of stress and strain will guarantee mutual survival and adequate cohesion? You may wonder, how many shocks, like these may be expected in the future, now that the big split of Europe has been overcome. Will it not be possible or sensible in this context to suppose that peace and security are ahead of us? Institution building for the future always should be on the safe side, to anticipate the most difficult constellation and to prepare for the worst. Living in open societies and rapidly-evolving complex international patterns of co-existence you cannot but see that such shocks are no singular, rare exceptions. They have been a part of our experience in the years since 1973. Take Reaganomics, for instance: for Europe, it certainly was an exogenous shock of enormous consequence. There have been three oil price crises: 1973/74 and 1979/80 and then the reverse 1985/86. These hit all the industrialized economies, though their effects in individual countries varied according to their specific economic structures and oil dependency. We have experienced the fall of the Berlin Wall and the demise of the Soviet Union. The unification of Germany certainly was an exogenous shock to Germany and Europe which has not yet been fully digested but, more than that, it was asymmetrical and nationally differentiated in effect. The collapse of the dollar gold standard of Bretton Woods in the wake of the Vietnam War and the American inability to live up to its anchor quality also provided such a shock. The New York stock exchange crash in 1987 may have not been that exogenous after all, except for the new role of electronic programme trading which came as a surprise out of the dark.

Monetary union and regional disparities

The exigencies of protecting the common currency after the completion of Emu will also be tested in other contexts, especially if the single monetary policy leads to growing unemployment in the periphery. To introduce a common currency in a large economic area like the EEC lays open the differences in regional productivity as well as the disparities in wages, expressed in the common currency. This is likely to increase the pressures either to even out the disparities, or to have large movements of the factors of production. This will primarily mean migration, since interest rates will converge because of the single monetary policy, and it will not be possible to use interest rate differentials to induce capital movements.

There is nothing wrong with migration: the common and single market concepts are built on the free movement of all goods, services and factors of production including, of course, labour. The European union treaty, however, in its long catalogue of goals (see Article 3) implicitly stipulates that everyone should be able to find a job in the place or region or country, where he stems from, or where he likes to live, or where he finds his identity. The European single market makes migration possible, but not too much has occurred since 1958. The experience of the United States differs from this. But, before social insurance was established, not all the repercussions of these larger migrations were attractive. In any case, the culture and the language barrier in the US has not presented the same difficulties we have encountered in Europe. Despite this, many people have moved from the periphery to the preferred blue banana, the agglomeration band from

London and South East England, the Low Countries well into the Rhine-Ruhr, Rhine-Main and Neckar Valleys to Switzerland and to northern Italy, bringing with them pressures on infrastructure, jobs and houses.

With the illusion of a common money, the desire to share common standards of welfare might also arise which, to the extent that it is not fulfilled, will make it necessary to increase transfer payments. There is a taste of this in the European structural funds for regional and social policy, and the appetite is growing. A cohesion fund has been added to help strengthen the trans-national infrastructure for the social and economic cohesion of the single market. In a sense, it is an embodiment of the infrastructural prerequisites for a well functioning continent-wide market system, in that it is intended to set up and strengthen trans-national infrastructures in transportation, energy, telecommunication and the environment. Its purpose is not to equalize incomes in Europe, but to get the weaker regions off the ground, to assist them to participate more fully in the growth and development process. It would be a big mistake to confuse this microeconomic cohesion item and the structural regional disparity item with the convergence item of the macroeconomic performance criteria. The cohesion fund is providing the necessary complementary infrastructure for the proper functioning of the single market in peripheral member states, it only very indirectly contributes to better performances of fiscal policy etc.

If peripheral member states are to participate in effective market integration, such a trans-national infrastructure is particularly needed to bridge and to weld the market structures into a common one. The purposes of the cohesion fund as written down in the Maastricht Treaty very adequately describe this necessity. It has nothing *per se* to do with any specific objective of equalizing incomes.

There is a clear watershed that divides the world of an economic union based on market integration, leading ideally and ultimately to equal functional incomes for the production factors throughout the Community; and that of a political union which also encompasses the equality of income as a political objective for income redistribution. Incidentally, any intellectual laziness with these distinctions, which squashes these terms into one standard format, may prove to be very costly to the richer countries.

Some problems with the third stage of Emu

Intellectual honesty as well as political prudence should call here for utmost clarity. The difficulty arises when we start Emu's final stage without really complying with the criteria, or when we have to manage with exogenous shocks. Both kinds of situation might lend themselves readily to establishing transfer needs. Germany, since reunification, is living and suffering through exactly such a period, the end of which cannot yet be foreseen. In this case, the dynamics of the transfer mechanisms have their main compensation in the amalgamation into a welfare-orientated nation state with its elements of a fully-fledged, integrated federation. The European union is not to be such an integrated state, nor is there a consensus that it shall even become anything of that sort. The Maastricht Treaty does not contain these aspects, but it might have to develop into such a framework if it is not to break-up. Any premature, hasty move into the final stage might lead to a state of Emu, which after a few years either disintegrates, due to disillusionment and a lack of common political will, or due to the implementation of transfer mechanisms far beyond what we know today. We should reflect upon this perspective, and we should analyse why all the currency union schemes of the 19th century ultimately failed, except when they took place under a common structure of statehood. One must be fully aware of this logically apparent, but suppressed and hidden, link between a successful monetary union and the correspondent evolution of political integration and solidarity. From the point of view of the less-developed, usually more peripheral member states and regions, of course, there may be excellent reasons to follow such a course of joining the Emu and then generating the complementary transfer. And it may be a price the other partners are willing to pay, since integration, in fact, may be particularly useful to them. One must be aware, however, of the stress and strain this will place on these member states, a worthwhile effort only in the context of a long-term politically-structured community of solidarity as a lasting edifice with goals extending well beyond just economic integration.

We are, of course, not yet in a situation where we could successfully and fruitfully start with the final stage of Emu. At present, we are witnessing more growing divergences than in the late-1980s. Some are now proposing, for this very reason, to accelerate the process, inviting us to jump simply into the unknown as a remedy to this undesirable state. This would be sheer foolishness. It would aggravate all the problems I have tried to describe, it would not solve any one of them. Indeed, it might blow the final stage apart, right after its initiation. There is no way to get around the earnest fulfilment of the convergence criteria set, which are already softer and weaker than desirable.

In my judgement, it is absolutely essential to build Europe on solid foundations, and not to play any tricks. This holds true in particular for the monetary union since, here, the need for trust, trustworthiness, credibility and stability should forbid all adventurism. Fiddling with hopes that somehow monetary integration could be turned into, or serve as, an engine for further economic or political integration, unless based on firm grounds, could bring forth disintegration and re-nationalization, with extreme political effects.

Of course, there is a case for taking in as many partner states as possible on the strength of their achievements with converging performances. It is equally necessary to understand the exclusion of the others at least for some time. This could bring forth negative forces and breed ill feelings. But monetary matters are not suited to an unsound jump to obtain a quick fix, so to speak, where one can manœuvre. Already, the present political uncertainty is endangering the stability of the existing mechanisms of integration, the single market as well as the European monetary system (EMS).

Maastricht ratification and thereafter

It is out of this spirit that I convey to you my judgement that, though being a critic of much in the Maastricht Treaty, I am in favour of its ratification. This ratification, furthermore, should lead to further negotiations in order to improve and complement the text. I call for a conference of the member states soon after ratification. The national ratification debates have been so bitter, so divisive, and sometimes contradictory, that it is essential to redefine the finality of the European union, and to remedy some of the structural flaws in its texts. In France, for instance, both sides were fighting, so they said, for regaining national sovereignty. Those for the ratification of the treaty made the communization of the Deutschemark the centrepiece. The proponents argued that they would regain national sovereignty by gaining co-stewardship of the independent ECB and in the ESCB. The opponents argued that only refusal to ratify would lead to France retaining her sovereignty. I should like to assert here, in all clarity, that one has to understand that this national sovereignty has long eroded, that it will not be transferred by a definite legal act or, conversely, that a refusal to endorse that act will not preserve it. Much of the national sovereignty has already melted away as a result of internationally deregulated, liberal financial markets, in the interdependence and interpenetration of national economies and by European integration. The effects of such types of progress have redefined the national cause. There is no way back to former national sovereignty except at tremendous economic, social and political costs. So a repeal might indeed produce disintegration. The eastern European countries and the states of the former Soviet Union are just now learning about this kind of renationalization the hard way.

It is absolutely essential to clear up the finality of the union. This is necessary for the very viability of the monetary union project whether this includes political union or not. But even when political union is not included, at least the positive minimum co-ordination of the co-actors, so essential for the success of stabilization policy, has to be implemented. If this condition cannot be met it would be better to wait for firmer foundations to evolve. The haste with which some of the political institutions are now driving ahead is not helpful, it is even counter-productive. This certainly might be moving affairs in the opposite direction of the desired one, as we have learned from the negative effects of a positive and strict timetable for the further integration process.

Determination of the goals and the institutions of the EC

Let me come back to the other problem which is in the Maastricht Treaty and which is a systematic problem for European integration, namely the determination of the goals and the institutions, of the European Community (EC). In its legal name it will now omit the adjective 'economic'. As a matter of fact, this Community embraces far more European goals and common policies than the EEC Treaty has since 1958. There are now 20 instead of just 11 policies called for, the original ones have all been extended and made more ambitious than before. Likewise, these are not free of ambiguities and potential inconsistencies and even contradictions. The debate over the Commission's proposal of the financial package (Delors II) demonstrated this, as well as the wavering political will to progress that stridently.

The description of what you want also has to include a description of the transition process and it is this which is creating the biggest problems at the moment. When the Maastricht Treaty ratification appeared to be endangered after the Danish 'No' of June 1992 and a threatening French 'No' in late September 1992, markets began suddenly to re-appraisal, to re-evaluate their perspectives. The former belief of the markets that some kind of quasi-monetary union was already in existence, that would last unchanged until the start of the final stage, vanished rapidly. All of a sudden, because of political uncertainties, it became clear that this perspective had to be abandoned and that markets were simply wrong to assume that any realignment could be ruled out. Wishful thinking never makes for good business, so this reappraisal had to occur some day anyway. It was the political timetable itself which led to ante-dating that disillusion to the dates of the referendums.

The role and functioning of the European monetary system

This leads me to some remarks upon the role and the functioning of the European monetary system, and upon the necessity to keep it intact. This necessity poses itself irrespective of your predilection as to moving on to the final stage or not. It remains valid even if you definitely exclude the final stage. It would still be most essential to protect the European monetary system, to maintain it in place and keep it functioning. If it should break up, which I certainly hope will not happen, we would have to reinvent something similar in order to preserve the current process, of the single market completion, or just the present state of European integration. The European single market is not set up in the text of the Maastricht Treaty, but in the single European Act of 1986. This single market started at the beginning of 1993, but it has not yet been completed. It is not yet certain that we shall really succeed with it. It is very clear though, that without effective monetary co-operation between the member states, it will not be able to succeed ultimately.

Let me, for an underpinning of this thesis, go back a little bit into the history of European integration. In 1957, with the Rome Treaty and its establishment of the common market, the idea was to start a process of on-going economic integration which would be as deep and wide as possible, and which would be created as fast as would be feasible. In Rome, the monetary question, in effect, was excluded, because this was at that time managed by the Bretton Woods institutions. All EEC member states were members of the International Monetary Fund (IMF) and all the national currencies of the EEC member states were both fully convertible and tied to a fixed dollar rate (the two requirement for membership of the IMF). It was clear to everybody that the common market could not fruitfully start without such a clear monetary arrangement. By the end of 1958, the first year of the existence of the EEC, full convertibility on current account at least was achieved by the member economies. This was understood to be a *conditio sine qua non* for the success of the emerging common market. However, this achievement appeared endangered later by the very harsh experiences connected with the dollar. The Great Society, the debit financing of the Vietnam War and the inability of the American administration to defend the internal value of the dollar, produced the failure of American stabilization policy at home. This meant imported inflation for Western Europe, and for West Germany, in particular, which was committed to the Deutschemark's stability. Weaker and weaker dollars had to be purchased at the fixed rate by the Bundesbank against Deutschemarks because exports soared and imports did not keep pace. The Bundesbank consequently came under a kind of structural inflationary pressure from abroad. The US generated too much inflation, leading to strong imports which still failed to offset the soaring internal demand. Europe, in turn, had to import this inflation, and was destabilized.

Thus the end of the Bretton Woods fixed parities was inevitable. First, the US ended gold trading with central banks at the rate of US$35 per fine ounce of gold in 1971 and later disposed of the corresponding parity in 1973 altogether. The oil price shock following the Yom Kippur War later that year and ensuing economic crises did much to destroy any perspective of a return to the old regime. In Europe the 'snake' was created, later the 'snake in the tunnel', the purpose of which was to keep, at least in Western

Europe, exchange rates in touch with one another. This was understood to be a prerequisite of the further existence of the common market which had been 'completed' by 1969. You might recall that these different regimes were endured, constantly reinvented and improved, one of the most prominent parties vitally interested in this being the Common Agricultural Policy, which was built on the fixed-exchange rates between the member states. The interests of business and industry were even stronger. There was wide agreement that stable trade relations, direct investments and clear structures for deliveries, production and distribution, all leading to the tremendous growth in intra-EC trade and exchange, needed that as their basis.

I venture the thesis that the present state of European integration demonstrates the facts of mutual interlocking and interpenetration of an emerging European economy that already extends far beyond former patterns of trade dependency or mutual interdependence. Our economies of today are highly interlocked and interlinked. In Germany, 60 per cent of exports go to the common market, another 20-25 per cent to Efta. It is not any longer only a matter of big, multinational concerns and of trading companies to do business in Europe. Direct investment needs reliable orientation as to cost structures, market access, investment security. It is not only trade, direct investment and entrepreneurial endeavour. There are now joint companies everywhere and even small- and medium-sized firms set up branches in other countries. Thus, there are nowadays penetrating, omnipresent interests, embedded in the economic structure, which have a need of reliable and stable monetary relationships.

This linkage, based on the exchange rates in Europe, has long passed the point at which it is just a subject whose future can be decided by monetary policy-makers, or even politicians in general. The real foundations of the fully evolving spatial economic system in Europe call for its realization. Of course, you could — theoretically — renationalize all this. But at what cost? And with what kind of a future? And perspectives?

The political awareness in Europe right now is still seeking the priority goal we have to pursue, which is the realization and the completion of the internal market. Peter Sutherland, the former Irish EC Commissioner, has led, as chairman, a group which has issued a very readable and valuable study on the current state of the single market. It contains a rather pessimistic view: national governments all follow their own national interests and all want to exploit the single market to the benefit of these interests. There is, however, not enough identification with the common interest in the foundations and functioning of the single market. There is not even a full understanding that you need common policies on competition, the environment, regional disparities, trans-national infrastructures and social standards. Some say these are matters beyond the scope of mere market integration. They are interested in economic, not in social, environmental or regional aspects. Others have said that this presents them with the opportunity, based on the subsidiarity principle to withdraw, for example, from the common environmental policy. It is my firm conviction that the single market will not be a success, and will not be sustainable, if such common policies as well as some kind of stable-but-adjustable exchange rates are preserved. The alternative is to sacrifice these for an EC which is a type of enhanced and enlarged free trade area. Such a development would shake the very foundations of what we are committed to achieve in the early-1990s. The Euro-scepticism and Euro-pessimism of the early-1980s would reappear, and with it the ugly face of renewed economic nationalism.

In my view, the continuity, the confirmation and the strengthening of the monetary system should come in the top priority on the current agenda of integration policy. Its rules should not be changed, let alone weakened, but it is clear that the negation of eventual realignments and the blurring on the rules of the game since 1987 has to be put to rest. Moreover, we need a renewed effort to define the political and institutional foundations for the present and the future European integration process. The ratification of the Maastricht Treaty should be conducted in the sense that we reinforce the desire and the programme to move ahead together. If we do not do so now, this might well produce a disaster in terms of integration policy. There is no doubt on the other side that this ratification *per se* does not suffice to stabilize our common future. What we need is an additional effort to get the single market going and to keep the European monetary system fully functioning. In order to stabilize these perspectives further we need a prospect of what is ahead, which has to be built solidly and soberly on excellent foundations. These are so far only partially provided by the Maastricht Treaty, a *lex imperfecta et incompleta*.

Two important conclusions for the operation of the EMS

This analysis has two consequences.

First, one needs to go back to the origins, to the start of the EMS in 1978/79. The originators were clever men: Valery Giscard d'Estaing, Helmut Schmidt and Roy Jenkins. There were rules fixed calling for an early, gradual and smooth adjustability of exchange rates, when needed. These were forgotten during the second half of the 1980s, where one mistook the goal of keeping exchange rates stable as already constituting the result of actually holding them stable, without regard to the corresponding exigencies of adjusting domestic fiscal policies and collective bargaining accordingly.

And there is a second element to be criticized. It is now absolutely essential to de-politicize the fixing of exchange rates. I have hinted at that point already with my criticism of the Maastricht Treaty concerning the unworldly, unrealistic assumption about the short-run possibility for a fixed-exchange rate policy against the US dollar or the Japanese yen.

Markets nowadays are much too emancipated and too powerful for such an approach on the part of national governments. I say this with respect, and not really with much regret, since it underlines the need for more global co-operation in real, not symbolic, terms. It is a statement of fact that we have today a liberalization and a deregulation of financial markets, a globalization in an open-world economy, based on competition and exchange, ahead of the single market timetable, ahead of an effective international prudential supervision and common authority of control. I do not say that it was a mistake to move ahead that much and that fast. We should not undo it, but we should take notice of the new independence and even political-economic emancipation of the market structures. To contain them would call for much stronger and more sweeping precautions than just a return to the former 'normality' of pre-1973 with fixed-exchange rates for all industrialized economies and no full convertibility of capital movements, an avenue not open to us.

De-politicization is necessary in the sense that the fates of governments and of politicians should not be tied to specific exchange rates. Furthermore the independence of the individual national central banks, as stipulated in the Maastricht Treaty, should be granted now as well as the mandate to protect the internal value of money by achieving price level stability.

In addition the reserve banks should be given a say in exchange rate policy. So far, of all the central banks in the EC, only the Bundesbank has at least a say in this. We are not the ones to decide, regrettably, what happens with the exchange rate of the Deutschemark. However, at least we have a say in it: this after all was the overriding precondition for the Bundesbank, under its legal status and brief, to be able to enter into the agreement on the EMS. So far, most national central banks are still, in effect, the prolonged arms of their respective finance ministries. The EMS agreement was drafted and signed by the central banks, creating the illusion that they have a say in this system.

A large part of the turbulences of 1992 can be said to be a reflection of this unsatisfactory state of affairs. Now honesty calls for progress here. It was not very wise, after all, to tie exchange rates together into apparently irrevocably-fixed rates in the EMS without achieving simultaneous and full co-ordination with financial, social and incomes policies. It would be useful and essential, after the ratification of the Treaty of Maastricht, for the heads of state and government to talk about the finality of Europe and how to ensure that the foundations for the current European integration process are solid, clear and distinct.

There is no automaticity in social, political or economic life. There is never a kind of timetable, which is just automatically run down. All this always depends on the specific views of the acting personalities and whether the institutions actually do their job. In order to stay on track it would be a great help, as stated, if the national governments would decide now on altering the status and the mandate of their central banks to the provisions of the Maastricht Treaty. France has decided to do just that. The government and all the main parties agree to grant the Banque de France the legal status of independence from both the French government and parliament and to charge it with the mandate of primarily protecting the value of money. Other member states, like Belgium, Spain and Italy have already moved in that direction, as the Netherlands and Denmark have done in practice for many years.

In looking at these specific endeavours, it turns out, however, that one central problem is posed, but yet nowhere really solved: the essential prerequisite for the constitution of independence and stability orientation appears to be the selection of the personalities to argue and decide the monetary policy and to present the results to the public, organizing a feedback in a dialogue with business, politicians and the public. As our German experience shows, this interaction with the diverse strata of public opinion and the population is decisive. It is based on the plurality in the composition of the central bank council which, anyway, has to defend the policy decisions uniformly (even if reached with the slimmest of majorities). This appears to be the really decisive and principal foundation for the abiding credibility and specific autonomy of the Bundesbank and its lasting stability orientation. In the Bundesbank constitution the diverse, and sometimes even controversial, nomination procedures of the states of the Federal Republic sending a larger number of members than the Federal Government, guarantees in effect that many groups in the societal spectrum find themselves represented in the council.

An EMS enhanced by independent, stability-geared central banks as well as de-politicized, stable-but-adjustable exchange rates might be a better guarantor. In order to enhance the integration process the three elements of Emu, EMS and the single market are intricately tied together in the sense, that in order to preserve the perspective for the single market we have to retain a functioning EMS. Only then can we get the opportunity to create a European monetary union — this is merely a chance, not an assurance. Maastricht does not yet contain the full textbook for the story ahead. This *lex imperfecta et incompleta* will have to be mended and amended. But, furthermore, there is the irreplaceable need for a very wide, genuine and sweeping convergence, not only in the performances of the economies, but also with respect to goal determination and policy formation.

Chapter 14

An Irish perspective

Bertie Ahern TD
Minister for Finance, Republic of Ireland

With the benefit of hindsight, the currency crisis within the European monetary system should not have been allowed to happen. There were ample warning signs. It was evident that some currencies were overvalued and that inadequate progress was being made by some countries to meet the Emu convergence criteria. The improving track record of the EMS, and the enthusiasm for greater integration following Maastricht, blinded us to the reality that there were serious imbalances which required urgent attention. The markets indeed began to treat the ERM as a quasi-monetary union. Therefore, the situation was open to shocks. The Danish referendum in June 1992 provided the first shock. There was still time for an ordered response from the monetary authorities, but little was done. The last opportunity to take co-ordinated action was the meeting of finance ministers early in September at Bath but this meeting was wasted in futile rhetoric and recrimination.

As with all crises that are let out of control, there was overreaction. The speculators ruled the day in a manner that, at best, can only be described as a severe embarrassment for the authorities. In turn, this generated a kind of panic reaction among investors in general and any suspect currency came under attack regardless of underlying economic conditions. The Irish pound fitted into this category because of the perceived close relationship with sterling. Following on the chaos of Black Wednesday, the Irish currency came under immediate pressure. Overseas investors in Irish government bonds began to withdraw from the market in the expectation of an early devaluation of our currency and there was also considerable speculative activity. Our response was to demonstrate, in every way that we could, that it was our full intention to maintain the currency at its parities within the ERM.

It is well to reflect on Ireland's position at the beginning of the crisis. Ireland had been a member of the narrow band of the ERM since its inception in 1979. This meant that when sterling strengthened in 1979, we had to break our one-for-one link with it: this link had existed since the foundation of the State in 1922. The break was a sea-change for us. It took some years for us to come to terms with the new disciplines of the exchange rate regime. However, since 1986, we had been successfully overcoming our budgetary deficit problem, which is now under control. Inflation, too, had fallen to levels which were among the lowest in the Community and we enjoyed a substantial balance of payments surplus. Since the 1970s, trade with the UK had declined significantly as a percentage of our total trade, as European markets became more and more important for us.

In addition to this, we had supported the moves to Emu. The Irish electorate had, by an overwhelming majority, supported the Maastricht Treaty in a referendum in June. Policy in Ireland was (and still is) based on being in a position to join Emu and be part of a single currency from the earliest date. This aim, and our ERM membership, had the support of both the trade union and the business sector. As a very small unit, in international terms, the Irish currency needs an anchor. For several years, this anchor had been provided through membership of the exchange rate mechanism of the EMS. Our clear and unequivocal policy was to maintain a stable position within the narrow band of the mechanism. Therefore, when the crisis erupted in September 1992, our policies could not be abandoned; nor did we believe that they should be. No group domestically sought to change that policy in September.

This stability is vitally important for us. It is reasonable that we should expect protection from a system embracing much larger currencies when we conform to the spirit and the letter of the rules. The upheaval in September 1992 was a traumatic experience. It was not of our making and there was nothing that we could do unilaterally to protect our position adequately. Membership of the EMS seemed to become a liability rather than an advantage as the currency speculators focused their attention on the system. Perhaps the most disappointing aspect was the sheer inability of the Community to respond in an adequate way. It was evident from the outset that the EMS was in real danger of disintegration. The markets needed some demonstration of Community solidarity to persuade them that things might return quickly to normal. The October summit in Birmingham, however, confirmed the markets' worst suspicions that the Community did not have the ability, due to internal dissensions, to find a prompt solution. And so it was essentially the case that each member had to look after its own interests. There was considerable rumour at the time about plans being laid for a two-speed approach to monetary union. There was no basis in reality for such rumour. It did, however, create additional problems for Ireland as the markets speculated that the impact of sterling devaluation would force the Irish pound out of the first category in any two-tier structure.

The initial classic reaction to pressure on the currency is to raise interest rates. Irish official rates were raised quickly by three percentage points, from 10 3/4 to 13 3/4 per cent. This was followed by increases of the same order in retail rates generally, including mortgage rates. This was particularly painful for mortgage-holders in Ireland, since almost all mortgages are at variable-rates. In addition, industry was faced with increases in its cost of capital. As the crisis continued, the government, having regard to the need to protect employment, established a temporary market development fund of IR£50m to assist small businesses which were under immediate market pressure as a consequence of the currency changes. This facility had the approval of the European Commission and it was quite effective in providing protection for some vulnerable firms.

Central to the markets' perception of the Irish pound at that time was the belief that the Irish pound could not survive a sterling devaluation. At the beginning of September 1992, the Irish pound was trading at 94.7 pence sterling; by 5th October it was touching £1.10 sterling, an increase of 16 per cent in five weeks.

The markets disregarded the gains made in competitiveness over the UK prior to the crisis because of low inflation and lower wage costs in the period since 1987. Despite our best efforts, there appeared no way to break this perception of dependency on sterling at the pre-crisis levels. Sterling movements, of course, are an influence on our situation but, contrary to the widespread perception, this influence is limited and has been declining in recent years. Something less than one third of our total trade is with the UK, but this is not the full picture because a substantial proportion of our exports to the UK is insulated from sterling fluctuations, being traded in US dollars, for example. The markets were convinced from an early stage, however, that we were much more dependent on the UK and this conviction was fortified by the high profile given to threatened job losses in some sectors of the economy.

By mid-October, the UK base rate was down to 8 per cent while the corresponding Irish rate was nearly 6 percentage points higher. The initial consensus in Ireland against devaluation was beginning to weaken.

There was a general expectation at the time that the crisis would be over by end-1992, even though there was no hard evidence for this. Reductions in German interest rates were seen as the key to unlocking the grand solution and there were persistent reports that such reductions were imminent. The general feeling was that the markets had overreacted and that sterling and the lira would regain some ground after 'overshooting', and also as new policies began to take effect. As time marched on, however, it became increasingly clear that prospects of an early solution were diminishing. In

November, the Spanish and Portuguese currencies were devalued — this was the second devaluation of the peseta in weeks — and the spotlight now turned very much on the Irish pound. Even if we had chosen the option of devaluation at that time, there was no prospect that our Community partners would have agreed to a figure of 10 per cent, but would rather have insisted on a smaller change. This, in retrospect, could have increased pressure on us to devalue a second time in January, when sterling again weakened sharply.

We were supported by our partners in making a stand against devaluation. Apart from other considerations, they saw an issue of principle in our case. By reference to the standard economic criteria of inflation, balance of payments and fiscal position, devaluation of the Irish pound was not warranted. We were fulfilling the requirements for convergence and there was no case for devaluation on these measures. For the first time, a currency in the narrow band of the exchange rate mechanism was under severe attack. The other side of the coin was the prolonged market pressure which led to excessively high interest rates, which were unsustainable. On a few occasions, the overnight lending rate of the central bank was 100 per cent.

In the middle of the crisis, we were faced with a difficult dilemma. Under European Community law, we were required to remove all remaining exchange controls from 1 January 1993. (Contrary to some reports at the time, we did not introduce new controls in September 1992, but simply enforced the controls that were then in existence.) There were predictions that full compliance with Community law on 1 January would result in immediate and massive outflows of funds. We never at any time, however, entertained the option of seeking a further derogation and we gave our Community partners repeated assurances on this. The controls were terminated on schedule and our position was vindicated. There were no immediate outflows as a consequence, and the ending of controls was recognized by the markets as a very positive demonstration of our commitment to Community obligations.

By the end of January 1993, we were eventually forced into devaluation due to a combination of factors. An unexpected reduction in official rates in the UK led to a sharp fall in sterling and consequent further pressure on Irish interest rates. Substantial increases in retail rates, including mortgage rates, were going to be unavoidable, despite efforts at devising a subsidy scheme. Employment was under imminent threat in a number of firms in the labour-intensive sectors of the economy. Despite expressions of support for our position, it was evident that the Community was not in a position to take initiatives on our behalf. Opinions at home were strongly divided. In a survey of prominent economists and commentators conducted by a newspaper on the eve of devaluation, a small majority recommended that the Irish pound should not be devalued. The decision was taken by the Irish authorities to realign downwards the Irish pound by 10 per cent against our central rates within the ERM narrow band. At the time, some of the partners argued that devaluation by a lesser amount would be more appropriate. It was our expectation that a 10 per cent depreciation in central rates for the Irish pound would lead to a 7-8 per cent depreciation in our market rate. In our opinion, only a change on this scale would satisfy the market and eliminate the pressure on the currency. We took this step reluctantly because we believed that sterling would strengthen again after a time and this subsequently happened.

Within a few days of the devaluation of the Irish pound, the Danish krone and the French franc were put under extreme pressure. There was co-ordinated central bank intervention to support the currencies and the reduction in German interest rates, which had been awaited for months, would appear to have enabled these two currencies to avoid realignment or devaluation. This table of events led some to conclude at the time that the German authorities drew a clear line between the Irish and French and Danish currencies. Their assessment was that the Irish currency did not belong to the inner circle, perhaps because of our high unemployment and of Community transfers to us. Obviously I cannot disprove absolutely this view about the German authorities' stance. I have no evidence, however, that they were waiting for devaluation of the Irish pound. On the contrary, I am satisfied from my regular contacts with them that they fully shared the view that our economic and financial conditions did not warrant devaluation. They reduced interest rates in their own time for reasons that had to do with domestic German conditions, rather than the fate of other European currencies. This priority was clearly demonstrated in the final phase of the crisis when they were unable to reduce Deutschemark rates sufficiently to rescue the French franc.

I should also put on record that we never considered the option of following the example of Italy and the UK by suspending our obligations under the exchange rate mechanism. This would have been an entirely backward step for us that might have had unwelcome consequences for the longer term. The argument put forward that it would lead to a rapid reduction in interest rates was superficial to say the least. In any event, this approach would have amounted in effect to free float and, in today's world, this can be very risky for a small currency.

The devaluation of the Irish pound was a blow to the EMS out of proportion to the significance of our currency, in volume terms, in the system. A currency in the narrow band was forced to yield to market pressures against the considered opinion of the Community authorities that devaluation was unwarranted. This was a clear reflection of the inability of the authorities to take concerted action after several months of indecision. There were eleventh-hour proposals for multilateral intervention but we were forced to the conclusion that these had come too late to be of advantage to us.

Since devaluation, there has been a remarkable turnaround in a very short period, way beyond our best expectations, with interest rates at their lowest levels since the 1970s and external reserves at record levels due to large reflows of funds. This improvement is due to a combination of factors but it reflects very definitely a renewed confidence in our currency. The markets have put a positive interpretation on our efforts to hold the exchange rate over an extended period in the face of intense pressures.

The Irish pound was not affected during the final phase of the crisis. The markets recognized that our strong position in the ERM band was appropriate to the circumstances. The scale of speculative activity against ERM currencies was overwhelming. The German and French authorities had different priorities on interest rate policies. Decoupling of interest rates was not possible and the ERM lost credibility because it could not provide stability. While a variety of possible solutions were put forward which would preserve the mechanism more or less intact, realistically the only options were to abandon the mechanism entirely, or to minimize the intervention obligation. The sheer scale of market speculation had demonstrated that, while unlimited intervention might be workable in theory, it was no longer practicable when the orders of magnitude became so great. Ultimately intervention can only buy time for other changes of policy, if such changes are needed.

Much has been said, and written, in recent months about the lessons to be learned from the crisis. At the end of the day, we find that there are no new solutions. The EMS crisis was not, fundamentally, a consequence of 'fault lines' or technical inadequacies. It was a consequence of serious imbalances of substance which had created some false exchange rate levels. For several years, we have been carried forward by the euphoria of the single market and, more recently, the prospect of economic and monetary union. There is nothing wrong with this; on the contrary, ambitious targets are a necessary ingredient of real progress. We all agreed, of course, that progress should be monitored carefully through elaborate surveillance procedures and convergence programmes. However, the monitoring process has fallen far short of what is really needed and it might not be unfair to say that multilateral surveillance and convergence programmes have yet to show a real impact. If there is any lesson to be learned from the crisis, it is that we must be under no illusions about the importance of proper surveillance procedures and the necessity to enforce changes where these are clearly necessary. There must be a more effective early warning system and the authorities are aware of this. The start of Stage II of economic and monetary union, which is scheduled for 1 January 1994, provides the ideal opportunity for introducing improved procedures.

German unification intensified the problems arising from lack of convergence. The pressures imposed by unification on the German economy sent shockwaves throughout the Community. The dominant economic partner felt obliged to pursue monetary policies which were inconsistent with the needs of other member states. As a consequence, countries with strong economic fundamentals were locked into a high interest rate policy at a time when the priority was to generate increased economic activity and employment. The ERM offered no solution to this dilemma.

It has been freely acknowledged that the pressure which led to the effective suspension of intervention arrangements was not warranted on economic terms. It was generated by the markets who have the strength, it seems, at the moment to determine ultimately whether a currency should change its parity. This calls into question the relationship between the authorities and the markets ,and the degree to which deregulation should be allowed. It is a question that must be addressed at Community level, and also at world level, with the US and Japan.

The EMS has been heavily battered by the events of the past year. The Community countries must now re-group quickly to re-establish an effective alliance based on mutual obligations. Whether this should be within the framework of the EMS, precisely as we have known it, or whether changes and some new structures are needed, is a matter for debate. Monetary co-operation is essential if we are to exploit properly the advantages of a single market. I believe that the political will to achieve greater integration is as strong as before. It is now the responsibility of the monetary authorities to devise appropriate arrangements.

When the Irish pound was under pressure, our situation was monitored in great detail in the financial media. It was noticeable that some reports and comments emanating from non-Irish sources tended to be ill-informed and often tendentious. It was very difficult to correct misreporting and to retrieve a situation once a false report had then circulated. One positive outcome has been the much clearer appreciation, of the international media and the markets, of the separate identity of the Irish pound.

In the past few months, there has been a very significant change of outlook in Europe. Employment has now become the priority. For a long time, Ireland was a lone voice campaigning in Europe for a much greater focus on the problem of unemployment. Now, as unemployment figures rise inexorably across the Community, there is a sense of urgency in looking for solutions. The initiatives taken at Edinburgh and Copenhagen by the European Council are a recognition of the problem. These initiatives are no more than a first step and much more will be needed if we are to make an adequate response. The alternative is rising unemployment and consequent demoralization; if this is the future, then it is time to question fundamentally the values of the Community.

The European economy is becoming increasingly interwoven. It is in relatively poor shape at the moment and the future is hedged with all kinds of uncertainties. There may be a temptation to depart from the orthodox budget and financial policies in attempting to find solutions. This, in my opinion, would be a mistake. Solutions must come through structural reforms, incomes policies and a renewed effort towards genuine progress on convergence. The momentum for economic and monetary union must be sustained.

Chapter 15

A Dutch perspective

Professor Dr. A. Szász
Executive Director, De Nederlandsche Bank

Introduction

In the period of currency turbulence that started in September 1992, the Dutch guilder was always close to the central rate with the German mark — and usually somewhat above it — while money market interest rates were consistently below German levels. Thus, during the repeated bouts of severe speculation, the Netherlands Bank was obliged to support the currencies under pressure in the ERM, on balance increasing its foreign exchange reserves by about one third (gross interventions were roughly twice that amount, but a considerable part has since been repaid in guilders). The Bank was therefore in a position comparable to that of the Bundesbank, but on a more modest scale, and it was spared the criticism of which its German counterpart so often was on the receiving end. The guilder was in fact often seen as a mark substitute, lacking the German market's size, but also the consequences of unification. Investors seemed to agree with Bundesbank President Schlesinger who once paid the Dutch currency the highest compliment of which a German is capable: "The guilder is the best D-mark!".

Background

The Netherlands has been the first country in the European Community to pursue a 'hard currency policy' by linking its currency to the German mark. Being a relatively small, open economy, the Dutch authorities were aware of its dependence on developments abroad, in particular in Germany, and of the resulting limits of their monetary sovereignty. They realized the potential benefits of financial discipline emanating from international exchange rate arrangements based on pegged-but-adjustable exchange rates. When the global Bretton Woods system broke down in 1973 the Netherlands hoped that maintaining a stable exchange rate with the German mark would provide it with the advantages that a system of stable exchange rates can offer. This was not only because Germany is Holland's principal trading partner, accounting for almost 30 per cent of its imports and exports on average. Even more importantly, the Bundesbank is the world's most independent central bank, and its stability-orientated policies enjoy widespread support from the public and the political parties. By linking the guilder to the German currency, the Dutch authorities hoped to use the mark as an anchor of stability. Initially, this policy was controversial, leading to periodic debates in the press and sometimes in Parliament. The debate was stimulated by the fact that the Netherlands' competitive position deteriorated during the seventies. This was often blamed on the exchange rate policy, although there was also at the time a debate about the extent to which the export of natural gas was causing what was often referred to as the 'Dutch disease'. Gradually, it was realized that the deterioration of the competitive position was caused neither by the exchange rate, nor by gas exports, but rather by the increase in real wages exceeding productivity increases year after year, thus eroding corporate profits. There was little the central bank could do against this continuing cost-push inflation. A strict control of the money supply is difficult to achieve in a small open economy anyway, but it certainly was so in view of the large current account surpluses arising partly from gas exports. Finally, it was more or less generally

Figure 15.1   International money market rates (3-mth. euro-deposit rate, monthly average)

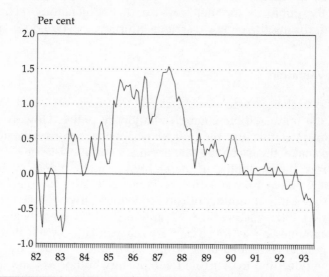

Figure 15.2   Interest rate differential: Netherlands - Germany

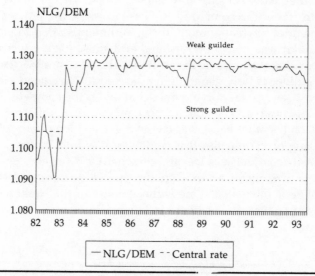

Figure 15.3   Exchange rate: Dutch guilder / Deutschemark

accepted that the fundamental cause underlying this process was the rapid growth of the public sector (not least due to the generous social security system) and, during the eighties, serious efforts were started to curb its expansion.

The last devaluation

Keeping the exchange rate stable against the mark provided the central bank with the only credible counter-inflationary policy. However, the stability was only relative and the guilder was, on occasions, adjusted downward in the snake, the exchange rate arrangement in existence since 1973. It was only from the beginning of the eighties that the monetary authorities signalled their intent to maintain the central rate with the mark. That the market accepted this commitment can be deduced from the fact that Dutch money market interest rates in 1982 and early 1983 were below German rates — sometimes by as much as 75 basis points — while the exchange rate of the guilder continued to be strong (see Figures 1.1 to 1.3).

The cabinet decision to overrule the monetary authorities and to devalue the guilder by two per cent against the mark in the realignment of March 21, 1983, came as a shock to the market[1]. Its impact on confidence can be surmised from the fact that, since that time until 1992, Dutch money market interest rates were hardly ever lower than German interest rates. In fact, for many years, they were considerably higher and whenever the central bank allowed them to decline compared to German rates, the guilder started to weaken. Soon after the realignment, the government started to make it clear that this decision was not to be repeated and subsequent governments left no doubt that this was also their position. The March 1983 decision concerning the guilder is now generally considered to have been a mistake. In so far as there was any favourable impact at all on the competitive position, it is hardly discernible. The impact on confidence as reflected in relative interest rates, on the other hand, was considerable and long-lasting. It was only at the beginning of the nineties that credibility was fully restored. This illustrates how easily confidence is lost and how hard it is to gain.

Two sets of circumstances explain the guilder's strong position during the events of September 1992. One is the stability of the Netherlands' economy compared to that of Germany: inflation is moderate, the stabilization

---

[1] *According to the 1978 Exchange Rate Law, the government decides on the exchange rate after having obtained the central bank's advice which the government then has to send to Parliament. In the advice given by the bank in 1983 and subsequently published by the government, the bank insisted on keeping the central rate with the mark unchanged. Dr. Ruding, the minister of finance, later acknowledged in public comments that he had agreed with the bank but was overruled in the cabinet.*

programme of public finances, to date, is more or less on track and the current account of the balance of payments is in surplus. The Netherlands' underlying position, therefore, is consistent with its exchange rate policy. This, however, was also the case in EC countries which, in contrast to the Netherlands, did suffer speculative attacks. There must have been, therefore, an additional reason for the guilder's strength. This is the credibility of the exchange rate policy. I believe that the Netherlands Bank's consistent hard-currency policy has been a major factor in establishing this credibility, though, I admit that there I may be biased. Oddly enough, the government's 1983 mistake may also have helped: the disadvantages of the alternative to present Dutch exchange rate policies have been so convincingly demonstrated that the market does not believe any government could afford to repeat the experiment.

The events of September 1992

In September 1992, and during its aftermath, the exchange rate mechanism of the European monetary system was faced with a shock in confidence comparable with the one the Dutch government caused nearly a decade earlier, but on a considerably larger scale. Both the lira and sterling rapidly depreciated in the order of 10-15 per cent, preceded by the Swedish currency which was unilaterally linked to the Ecu and followed by several other ERM currencies. Those taking positions against these currencies made heavy gains. Those who trusted the authorities lost heavily; how could they explain themselves to those whose money they lost if they continued their trust regardless and lost again? This, rather than any conspiracy to topple one remaining ERM currency after the other to multiply speculative profits — as some senior politicians seemed to believe — explains the continued currency turbulence in the aftermath of September[1].

Some have concluded that a system of stable exchange rates cannot work in a world with increasingly integrated financial markets — and in the absence of exchange restrictions — unless one accepts constraints on policies that would cripple the economies concerned. The Dutch experience is different. It does, however, demonstrate how essential credibility is. Credibility requires the acceptance of constraints, and the costs these imply should

---

[1] *On the basis of a series of interviews with market participants conducted in preparation of a Group of Ten report on capital movements published in April 1993, it can be concluded that a majority did not regard the pressures as "...a vicious game of 'parity busting' by speculators, fuelled by earlier profits." (International Capital Movements and Foreign Exchange Markets, par. 26). The turbulence, at least in its early phases, rather reflected defensive action by investors trying to hedge against exchange risk.*

be weighed against the disadvantages of floating which, for medium-sized closely-integrated economies are considerable.

The rules of the game

Experience in the first ten years of the EMS' existence has demonstrated that certain rules have to be respected if the system is to function well. First of all, exchange rates have to reflect competitive positions. If they do not, they have to be adjusted. If they do, they have to be defended. Failure to do either endangers the credibility, not only of the policy of the country concerned, but of the system as a whole. Until September 1992, the main problem was the failure to adjust exchange rates in time. Thereafter, the question became how to defend exchange rates that were reflecting fundamentals but, for whatever reason, were not trusted by the market.

The Basle-Nyborg agreement, reached in 1987, contains three rules essential for the defence of exchange rates. First, if they come under pressure, they should be defended by interest rate increases at an early stage and not as a last resort. Once markets perceive that interventions are considerable and continuing, speculation is bound to develop. At that stage, measures to defend the currency have to be far more drastic than if taken at an early stage. Second, interest rate action has to be supported by a proper use of the fluctuation band with the aim of creating a two-way risk within the band. Third, in case where a devaluation is justified, its size should be limited so that it should wholly or largely be absorbed in the band and the actual exchange rate should not necessarily change.

These rules mean that markets should realize that speculation against ERM currencies is costly in terms of interest rates, risky in terms of exchange rate movements within the band, and not profitable even if the expected devaluation occurs. Once markets are convinced that these rules of the game are being applied, speculation is likely to become stabilizing rather than destabilizing.

This implies that interest rates, not interventions, are the main instrument for defending exchange rates. The authorities have to convince markets that the exchange rate, not lower interest rates, are their objective. In this, they have failed.

The July crisis

During the crisis of July 1993, the guilder's position was similar to that in the September 1992 crisis. The guilder was at the top of the fluctuation band — slightly above the Deutschemark — until, in the terminal stage, the French franc was allowed to sink to the bottom where intervention became obligatory; at that point, the guilder was joined at the top by the Deutschemark. Interventions by the Netherlands Bank in Danish kroner and, in the final stage, in French francs, were considerable.

The Dutch representatives entered the talks, at the end of July and the first days of August, with two objectives. The first was to keep unchanged the existing relations between the guilder and the Deutschemark, including mutual intervention obligations. The second was to help save as much of the exchange rate mechanism as possible under the circumstances. Since the outcome of the negotiations was a generalized widening of all participating countries' fluctuation bands to 15 per cent on either side of the central rate, the first objective could only be realized on the basis of a bilateral arrangement between the German and Dutch authorities.

In its advice — given in accordance with the Exchange Rate Law — the bank stated that it regarded these very wide margins as an emergency measure. The significance of preserving the system in this form is that, by doing so, participating countries indicate their intention to return to a more effective exchange rate mechanism when circumstances allow this. Continuation of the Deutschemark-guilder relationship provides the markets with a maximum of certainty in so far as Dutch policies are concerned in an international monetary environment characterized by uncertainty. This is of great importance for the Dutch economy. In addition, maintenance of this part of earlier exchange rate relations can be seen as a contribution to the return to more orderly conditions in the EMS in the future.

Prospects for Emu

What are the prospects for a return to a system of stable exchange rates? Confidence in such a system is shaken and it will not be easy to restore the credibility on which it has to be based. At the same time, the fact remains that at least the continental EC countries have pursued stable exchange rates among themselves for many years, not only for political reasons, but also — and perhaps even more so — because all have open economies and close mutual ties. They cannot afford free floating rates, they need managed rates, and in that management, mutual obligations — if credible — can be a great help.

What are the prospects for Emu? Clearly, they have not improved. However, the motives to move to Emu are mainly political, and they have not changed. Whether it will turn out to be realistic depends on the success member countries have in restoring orderly conditions in the EMS, as well as on their success in getting public finances under control. Both are necessary with or without the objective of Emu. If they succeed, prospects for Emu may brighten once again.

Chapter 16

A Portuguese perspective

Vítor Bento and Vítor Gaspar
Banco de Portugal[1]

Introduction

Traditionally, the frequency of realignments has been used as a criterion to identify stages in the EMS experience. According to such a criterion, we would have entered a new stage in the Summer of 1992. Since then, there have been five realignments — involving four currencies — and two central banks suspended their intervention obligations under the ERM, meaning that their currencies are technically floating. There is no precedent in ERM experience of either five realignments in less than one year, or of previous ERM members' currencies floating.

The Portuguese escudo joined the ERM on April 1992. The joining of the escudo was preceded by a period of limited floating that started on October 1990. In fact, during this period from October 1990 until April 1992, the escudo appreciated against most currencies, including the Deutschemark. The escudo had been following a managed-exchange rate regime, more precisely, a 'crawling peg' since 1977. As experience in exchange rate management under such regime accumulated, the accuracy in implementation of the exchange rate targets increased, strengthening the credibility of the Banco de Portugal as shown by a sizeable capital inflow, in particular since 1988.

This note discusses the recent ERM tensions from the viewpoint of the Portuguese escudo. As already mentioned, there have been five realignments in the last eleven months and the Portuguese escudo has seen its central parity devalued twice, on 22 November 1992 and 13 May 1993.

---

[1] *The views expressed in this article are those of the authors and do not necessarily represent those of the Banco de Portugal.*

A number of interesting features may be highlighted concerning the Portuguese case. Firstly, the Portuguese escudo was the last currency to join the ERM before the crisis, having entered the mechanism in April 1992. Secondly, the realignments were not provoked or initiated (or desired) by the Portuguese authorities. In fact, both in November 1992 and May 1993, the Portuguese escudo was not under particularly strong speculative pressure. Nevertheless, the coming devaluation of the Spanish peseta changed the environment in which the choice of the central parity of the escudo had to be made. Thirdly, the time schedule for full capital liberalization (full convertibility of the escudo) was announced in August 1992 — before the occurrence of the exchange market crisis — and was carried out within the prescribed dates, ensuring that full capital liberalization was in place before the end of 1992.

This paper is organized in two sections. The first section describes the reaction of the Portuguese authorities to speculative attacks on the exchange markets. The September episode will be used as an example since it is probably the closest to the notion of speculative attack. The second section of the paper discusses the role of capital controls during the September crisis, and the process towards full capital liberalization in Portugal.

Instruments for the defence of the central parity

From a theoretical viewpoint, the unilateral defence of any central parity is always possible if that is the single goal of monetary policy. The unconditional acceptance of the exchange rate target as the guide for monetary policy implies the non-existence of any explicit or implicit ceiling on the interest rate. In other words, the interest rate instrument is to be totally available for the defence of the currency's parity. This suggests that interest rates are the decisive instrument in countering incipient speculative pressures on a currency.

If the defence of a central parity is the prime objective of monetary policy, then the Basle-Nyborg agreement provides the necessary panoply of instruments to ensure the desired results. As is well known, the policy recommendation was to attain a better balance amongst exchange rate fluctuation inside the ERM currency bands, exchange market intervention, and adjustments in interest rates.

Short-term policy dilemmas may emerge given conflicting requirements from external balance (that is, the exchange rate target) and internal balance. The conflict is more likely when there is high and rising unemployment, unsustainable budgetary policies and current account imbalances.

The Banco de Portugal has acted according to the Basle-Nyborg consensus in the defence of the stability of the escudo. The most significant episode in this regard is probably the September crisis. In fact, it was the only instance in which one can identify a sudden intense speculative attack directed to the escudo. Most of the remainder of this section will be devoted to its presentation from the viewpoint of the Portuguese escudo. Other relevant episodes will be covered in the final subsection.

Background developments to the September crisis

In spite of some decline against the narrow band currencies (the 'core' of the ERM) following the result of the Danish referendum, the Portuguese escudo had to be kept within its ERM margins by means of frequent purchases of foreign currencies by the Banco de Portugal, up to mid-August. Most of the decline of the escudo (and also of the peseta) against the core ERM currencies during this period resulted from the weakening of sterling, which was at the bottom of the system. However, net capital inflows into the escudo remained strong.

On 13 August, the Portuguese authorities announced the decision to lift all the remaining capital and exchange controls before the end of the year. The completion of this liberalization process was to be implemented in three steps: immediate free access of residents to external borrowing with maturities not less than one year; lifting of the ban on non-resident purchase of domestic floating-rate debt in escudos, by end October; scrapping of all the remaining controls — basically the access of non-residents to the domestic money market — by year-end. Note that residents had already been allowed, without restriction, to hold domestic accounts in foreign currencies, and to freely invest in foreign securities of any maturity.

The Banco the Portugal accompanied that announcement with a sharp reduction of its key interest rates — between 1.25 per cent and 1.75 per cent — so as to force a quick adjustment of market rates to a 'post-liberalization' equilibrium level, and to prevent the mounting of undesired and disturbing capital inflows during the adjustment process.

The market underwent what seems to have been an over-adjustment, with an overshooting of domestic interest rates (see Figure 16.1). Together with the growing uncertainties surrounding Emu and the exchange markets[1], this development led non-residents to start liquidating their positions in escudos and the Banco the Portugal began to purchase sizeable amounts of escudos on the exchange market, for the first time in years. This intervention, however, was mostly aimed at providing liquidity for a smooth

---

[1] *Recall that on, 21 August, a group of central banks tried to restrain the US dollar fall by means of a concerted intervention. This intervention did not provide much success and the US dollar depreciated sharply with the consequent strengthening of the Deutschemark seems to have marked the acceleration of the exchange crisis which reached a climax by mid-September.*

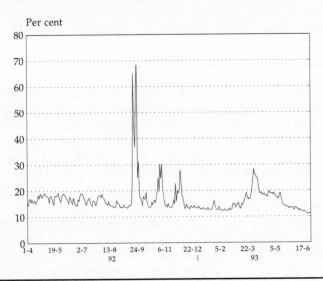

Figure 16.1   Escudo O/N domestic rate, April 1992-June 1993

operation of the exchange market, rather than at sustaining any specific level of the escudo exchange rate.

The capital outflows, and the ensuing purchases of escudos on the exchange markets, were very beneficial from the point of view of domestic monetary policy, since they contributed to the long-pursued goal of containing domestic liquidity. Indeed, short-term capital inflows had been the most disturbing factor of Portuguese monetary policy in recent years, as they were responsible for the overshooting of the monetary targets. The intervention to accommodate capital outflows, in turn, drained excess liquidity out of the system. The 'consumption' of foreign exchange reserves posed no problem, since the total stock could be considered excessive relative to the size of the economy. Moreover, such liquidity draining would also be very helpful to counter the overshooting of market interest rates.

Development of tensions

The pressure on the Portuguese escudo mounted, from early September onward, when the likelihood of an ERM realignment increased in view of the growing difficulties which some countries were having in following the tight German monetary policy, especially if their determination was to be tested by the markets. The escudo was then associated with the currencies facing those difficulties, in spite of the different economic performance and cyclical position of the Portuguese economy — balanced current account, positive direct investment flows, 'over-employment' and higher growth than the EC average — and the clear intent of the Banco de Portugal to set interest rates at the level required to sustain a stable exchange rate.

Such pressure was particularly strong on September 16 — developing as a typical speculative attack — when the British pound, the Italian lira and the Spanish peseta were also under severe attack, which led the first two currencies to withdraw from the ERM and the third one to be devalued by 5 per cent.

The reaction of the Portuguese authorities

The reaction of the Portuguese authorities comprised a combination of the three instruments recommended by the Basle-Nyborg agreement — use of the band width, exchange market intervention and an increase in interest rates — together with the activation of the existing exchange controls[1].

■ *Fluctuation inside the currency band*
As a first reaction, the escudo was allowed to weaken significantly inside the band, although it was decided not to use the full width of the band. In fact, it was considered that letting the escudo reach its lower margin risked being perceived as a sign of extreme weakness under the circumstances. Furthermore, given that the escudo participates in the ERM with a wide band, the full use of the margin is not necessary to induce significant exchange rate risk. However, when the penalty cost on short positions forced short covering, the escudo was allowed to appreciate significantly — almost to its upper limit.

■ *Intervention in the exchange markets*
Intervention in the exchange markets was particularly strong between September 15 and 18, with large sales of foreign exchange reserves. The amount of these interventions, most of which was ultimately purchased by non-residents against escudos, more than exhausted all the liquidity available in the euroescudo market, triggering a significant rise in its interest rates[2] (see Figure 16.2).

---

[1] *The remaining outflow controls, although still in force, had become a non-active restriction, since all the pressure in the last couple of years had been exerted by the huge capital inflows into the Portuguese economy.*

[2] *It should be recalled that by then and due to the existing capital controls, domestic and euroescudo money markets were still (partly) segmented.*

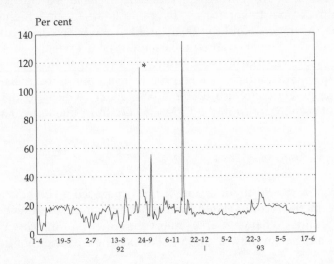

Per cent

*) Accurate data not available for this period. However, on 18 & 21 September, rates exceeded 1000%

Figure 16.2   Euroescudo T/N rate, April 1992-June 1993

Besides the effect on the euroescudo market, those exchange market interventions strongly reduced the domestic monetary base. In fact, the amount of exchange intervention between those two days of September was a significant portion of the required bank reserves (the major item of the monetary base), creating an immediate shortage of liquidity and pressing domestic rates upwards.

■ *Activation of existing exchange controls*
In view of the feeble communication between the domestic money market and the euroescudo market, the exhaustion of liquidity on the latter was expected to press strongly for illegal forms of non-resident financing in escudos. This was mostly because regulations on capital outflows had not been active restrictions for some years and therefore no strict control was exercised on their enforcement. The overdrafts in the (correspondent) accounts held by non-residents with resident banks were likely to be the most obvious last resort of financing for short escudo positions[1].

---

[1] *These overdrafts were not allowed under the exchange regulations still in force, without previous authorization from the central bank, except when resulting from transitory and unintentional payment problems (wrong payment orders, delays in the circulation of those orders, etc.).*

Therefore, the Banco de Portugal immediately — on September 17 — reminded the banks of the existing regulation, under which all overdrafts in escudo accounts held by non-residents required prior authorization from the central bank.

Nevertheless, the Banco de Portugal was deeply concerned that the existing regulations should not create problems to the proper working of the payments system. In particular, the central bank envisaged that the regulations should not force anybody to default on obligations incurred in escudos. For that purpose, the central bank avoided any 'administrative' enforcement of the regulations, and resorted to price measures to attain its objectives.

■ *Increase in interest rates*
The existing (incomplete) segmentation between the domestic market and the euroescudo market allowed the former to be protected against the costs (high interest rates) necessary to fight exchange rate speculation, if the latter springs from non-residents.

In order to prevent blockages in the payments systems, the central bank supplied liquidity directly to the euroescudo market through foreign currency swaps. Such liquidity was supplied at discouraging rates, which rose with the amount demanded by the market. Having started to supply liquidity at 50 per cent, the Banco de Portugal ended its money market intervention in the euroescudo market at 1000 per cent. However, all market liquidity requirements were met. Short-term euroescudo interest rates reached more than 2000 per cent.

At the same time, the Banco the Portugal decided to authorize all the overdrafts in escudo accounts held by non-residents. For the aim of limiting this facility to a last-resort form of financing and of eliminating any interest by domestic banks in favouring those overdrafts, the Banco the Portugal subjected the authorization of the overdrafts to their financing by the central bank. Commercial banks had then to borrow from the central bank the amount of overdrafts in their non-resident accounts, at a rate set daily at around twice the euroescudo rate. Again, it was made sure that all the liquidity required to meet incurred obligations would be supplied, albeit at penalty costs[1].

The high cost faced by non-residents to finance short escudo positions created during the major speculative attack — 15-17 September — led them

---

[1] *Note that non-spot sales or purchases of escudos were not allowed (except if connected to a commercial transaction). This means that short escudo positions (besides intra-day) could not be covered on the foreign exchange market, for the same value date.*

to cover those positions quickly. This reaction, in turn, led the exchange rate to appreciate sharply on 21 September, when it gained more than 5 per cent against the Deutschemark, before returning to the previous level, on the following days (see Figures 16.3, 16.4 & 16.5).

It is interesting to note that, as the Banco de Portugal refrained from intervening in the exchange market during this reaction, the escudos bought by non-residents were sold by the non-bank domestic sector[1]. This sector became then an important source of downward pressure on the escudo, particularly as of that date.

Since there were virtually no barriers to investment by Portuguese residents in foreign currency assets, potential sales of escudos from this source was thus almost unlimited. Therefore, the segmentation of money markets would not have provided enough defence to counter potential speculation against the escudo. Domestic rates had also to be allowed to rise so as to discourage any 'speculation' by residents.

Thus, in order to keep the domestic money market tight, the central bank suspended its usual way of intervening in the money market[2]. Instead, it started to supply liquidity by doing repos in fixed amounts with rates determined by auction. The central bank then resorted to daily auctions of relatively small amounts so as to keep the market short of reserves until the end of each reserve period.

The result was that domestic rates soared up to 180 per cent on 18 September (end of the first reserve period to be affected). Up to the end of September, the Banco de Portugal held several auctions of liquidity, at average rates ranging from 26 per cent to 58 per cent.

■ Conclusion

The combination of the four instruments used by the Banco de Portugal seems to have proved adequate to counter the speculation, particularly during its most active stage. Besides its direct effect in support of the exchange rate, exchange market intervention — because it was not sterilized — was also very effective as a money market instrument. Indeed, the purchase of escudos by the Banco de Portugal was instrumental in forcing the immediate adjustment in interest rates and was very useful in mopping-up a substantial part of the liquidity overhang on the market, which hampered the pursuance of monetary policy objectives.

---

[1] *In some cases these sales came from forward hedging of commercial transactions.*

[2] *Usually, the central bank would supply all the liquidity required by the banks, for the duration of each reserve requirement period, at a fixed rate.*

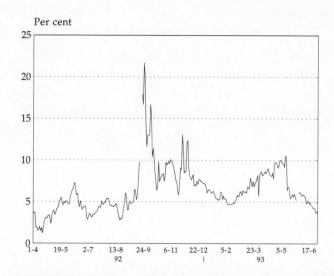

Figure 16.3   Escudo/Deutschemark interest rate differential (3-month bid rates), April 1992-June 1993

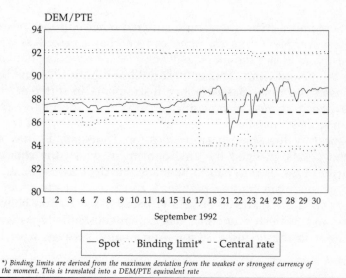

*) Binding limits are derived from the maximum deviation from the weakest or strongest currency of the moment. This is translated into a DEM/PTE equivalent rate

Figure 16.4   Deutschemark/escudo hourly quotations, 1-30 September 1992

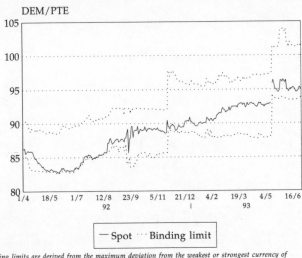

Figure 16.5   Deutschemark/escudo daily official quotations, April 1992-June 1993

Other episodes

After the September crisis, the escudo suffered other episodes of exchange market pressure. Nevertheless, none can be characterized as a sudden speculative attack. In fact, the subsequent episodes were weaker, but lingering.

During the period from October 1992 until mid-May 1993, the Banco de Portugal used the three Basle-Nyborg instruments in different combinations. The policy seemed to be sufficient to contain speculative pressures within manageable limits.

The request by the Spanish authorities (on Thursday, 13 May 1993) to devalue the peseta changed the environment in which the choice of the central parity of the escudo had to be made. Firstly, because Spain has become one of our main trading partners[1], and is one of our main trading competitors in third markets. Secondly, because integration between the Portuguese and Spanish economies has grown substantially, as is particularly apparent in the financial sector. And finally, because since Portugal

---

[1] *Portugal's main trading partner is still Germany although the gap relative to Spain has been narrowing.*

and Spain acceded the Community at the same time there is the (debatable) perception that the two economies face similar adjustment processes.

Therefore, the Portuguese escudo has seen its central parity devalued twice, on 22 November 1992 (by 6 per cent) and 13 May 1993 (by 6.5 per cent). The realignments were not provoked, or initiated (or desired) by the Portuguese authorities. In fact, both in November 1992 and May 1993, the Portuguese escudo was not under particularly strong speculative pressure.

The role of capital controls and interest rates

In the long run, capital controls are not only ineffective means of insulating the domestic capital market of open economies ,but are even detrimental for an efficient allocation of resources. Nevertheless, if capital controls are in place, they may prove effective in the short run as a means of control for a sudden speculative attack pressures. This is illustrated by the Portuguese experience in September 1992.

Capital controls allow smaller interest rate costs on the domestic market from fighting exchange rate speculation. However, the key response lies in the ability to use the interest rate. In fact, the present crisis seems to have shown that sound fundamentals may not be enough protection against a speculative attack on the exchange rate. The market assessment of the ability of a country to sacrifice temporarily the domestic objective in favour of the external one — that is to say, the freedom to assign the interest rate to stabilize the exchange rate — was determinant in triggering or stopping the attacks.

Without capital controls, the domestic authorities are unable to impose differentiated costs on the domestic and euromarkets. Given the existence of capital controls, that will tend to increase the size of the interest rate adjustment required in the domestic market. But it is also true, in the case in point, that the determination shown by the central bank in using this instrument is essential to ensure the credibility of the exchange rate. For this purpose, it may not be necessary to keep extremely high interest rates for too long, if they are raised in a timely manner and the market perceives the authorities determination in the move. It is true that this sort of action may cause painful short-term costs, but it may prove most beneficial in the long run.

It should not be forgotten that the central bank inevitably plays a destabilizing role, in the case of huge exchange rate speculation, if it tries to keep stable interest rates while defending the exchange rate. In fact, as it tries to stabilize the interest rate, the central bank supplies the market with the (cheap) liquidity necessary to purchase the foreign currency reserves which it has, in turn, sold to defend the exchange rate.

Full capital liberalization and full convertibility of the escudo are extremely important benchmarks in the transition of the Portuguese economy to a modern, open and market-based economy. In particular, there are direct efficiency gains from improved access to the international financial markets. There are further benefits coming from the strengthening of the incentives for sound and stable macroeconomic policies. These arguments were decisive in the decision by the Portuguese authorities not to request the continuation of the derogation under the 1988 Council Directive on the freedom of movements of capital.

Chapter 17

A Spanish perspective

The official view of the Bank of Spain

Introduction

1992 marked the end of a long phase of stability in the ERM. From January 1987 to mid-1992, the ERM enjoyed its period of greatest stability, maintaining its parity grid without major tensions. The stability of nominal exchange rates in this period was especially significant if three factors are also taken into account: first, the incorporation of three new currencies into the ERM; second, specific international political and economic events, which might have adversely affected foreign exchange stability in the ERM; and third, substantial headway in the liberalization of capital movements in many member countries.

One of the most noteworthy features of the ERM from 1987 to mid-1992 was the virtual absence of forex-market agents' expectations about imminent realignments. Evidently, this does not mean there were no moments of tension. However, such tensions were temporary and did not become so intense that the then-prevailing parity grid was called into question. Accordingly, these tensions could be sufficiently countered using the instruments recommended in the Basle-Nyborg agreement in mixes appropriate to each situation. As a result, these agreements seemed adequately to safeguard exchange rate stability against a background of untrammelled capital movements.

The absence of expectations about a realignment, particularly from the start of 1990, was largely due to the initial effects of German reunification and the move towards European economic and monetary union. At first, German reunification caused a change in market sentiment regarding the Deutschemark, which weakened within the ERM, markedly so in 1990, and for much of 1991. The successive steps towards Emu made a notable impact on expectation as the market accorded greater credibility to the 'strong currency' policies pursued by certain countries so as to further their convergence towards the economic results of the more stable countries (in short, exchange rate adjustments would be less necessary and frequent if more telling headway were made with economic adjustments). It was precisely the subsequent course of these two factors which was pivotal to the radical change in expectations that prompted the turmoil in the ERM in the last part of 1992 and its continuation in 1993.

The Danish 'No' vote in the referendum on the ratification of the Maastricht Treaty on 2 June 1992 saw the start of a period of instability marking what is no doubt the most serious crisis to afflict the EMS since its creation in March 1979. The stability that had prevailed in the ERM since January 1987 was abruptly interrupted. Since September 1992, five realignments have occurred; two currencies have withdrawn; central bank interventions have been on a hitherto unprecedented scale; interest rates have fluctuated intensely; and, finally, fluctuation margins for currencies in the ERM have had to be widened appreciably.

Once the initial impact of German reunification gradually abated, the result of the Danish referendum put into question the process that had reinforced the confidence in the maintenance of the grid, thus producing a sudden and radical change in foreign exchange market expectations about ERM currencies.

The source of the ERM crisis lies in a series of varied and complex problems. But if the main determinants are to be highlighted, a predominant role would have to be attributed to cyclical divergences and the attendant economic policy dilemmas in a setting of foreign exchange expectations highly influenced by the vagaries of the monetary union project. Differences in the cyclical positions of the European economies and the policy mix adopted by Germany to meet unification-induced problems gave rise to divergences in economic policy priorities. The persistence of macroeconomic disequilibria in several countries, together with the high and rising unemployment in some members' economies, were reflected in increasing difficulties with maintaining foreign exchange stability. Consequently, difficulties in co-ordinating economic policies emerged which, exacerbated by insufficient nominal convergence and a sudden change in monetary union expectations, ultimately generated serious foreign exchange tensions.

The behaviour of the Spanish peseta in the ERM up to mid-1992

From the time it joined the ERM until the crisis that began in September 1992, the peseta traded almost exclusively in the upper part of its fluctuation band *vis-à-vis* the other currencies in the system. The strength of the peseta was such that, at certain times, it reached its fluctuation ceiling against another currency. However, it was possible to counter these pressures without excessive difficulties via interventions on the foreign exchange market and interest rate cuts (as provided for under the

Basle-Nyborg Agreements). In short, although the peseta evidenced a certain upward tendency, ERM membership curtailed this appreciatory process. Specifically, the upper limit of its band acted on many occasions as a stabilizer, due to the absence of expectations about the revaluation of its central parity.

Although the entry of the peseta in the ERM in 1989 tended to increase the credibility of the Spanish monetary policy, its effectiveness to counter inflationary pressures has been conditioned by the relatively expansionary stance of fiscal policy and by the insufficient restraint in wages growth. This economic policy mix has been behind the relative strength of the peseta during this period of time.

The variability of the nominal exchange rate of the peseta had tended to diminish until the ERM crisis broke. Most significantly, this greater exchange rate stability had been achieved just as the Banco de España's volume of gross interventions (buying or selling) on foreign exchange markets was falling. Also, the greater stability of the peseta had not translated into an increase in the variability of interest rates. Running in train with this heightened exchange rate stability was a progressive liberalization of capital movements.

At the end of 1991 and for much of 1992, the peseta found itself in a new position due to the weakness of sterling. The essential difference compared with previous occasions on which the peseta had been at the edge of its ceiling against another currency was that sterling, like the peseta, had a wide fluctuation band. Thus, the peseta, though close to its maximum appreciation ceiling with sterling, began to depreciate against the ERM narrow-band currencies, driven by the downward course of sterling. This complex situation left exchange rate policy with virtually no room for manœuvre: had it been sought to avoid the depreciation of the peseta against the narrow-band countries via currency-selling interventions and/or official interest rate rises, the peseta would have rapidly hit its ceiling against sterling and the Banco de España would have been compelled to pursue an exchange rate policy in the opposite direction. The ERM crisis in September 1992 broke when the peseta was in this difficult position.

The prelude to the ERM crisis

After the Danish 'No' vote in the referendum on the Maastricht Treaty on 2 June 1992, market expectations changed radically (as indicated above). The consequences of the Danish referendum for interest and exchange rates were immediate. The risk premiums increased on currencies which had benefited to a greater extent from the counter-inflationary credibility bestowed by the ERM and which were furthest from meeting the convergence criteria. The day after the Danish referendum, almost all ERM currencies depreciated against the Deutschemark. The convergence of interest rates ceased and, in some cases, differentials *vis-à-vis* the Deutschemark began to widen. The foreign exchange markets, which had largely disregarded the fundamentals of ERM members, became more responsive to certain countries' macroeconomic disequilibria and their possibilities of converging within the stipulated terms. Among the narrow-band currencies, the lira was most affected as rumours of devaluation connected with growing doubts about the possibility of macroeconomic imbalances being corrected spread throughout the market.

The peseta was likewise adversely affected by the Danish referendum, given the deterioration taking place in macroeconomic expectations. But also influential, to a certain extent, were a knock-on effect from the Italian situation — due to the market tendency to equate, not always justifiably, the two countries — and the drag on the peseta by sterling, against which the peseta was close to its appreciation ceiling. Like the other wide-band currencies, the peseta began to depreciate against the stronger narrow-band currencies, although it held in the upper part of its fluctuation band against them. From 2 June to 31 August 1992, the peseta depreciated by 4.1 per cent against the Deutschemark. Concurrently, money market interest rates rose notably, and the Banco de España decided to raise the interest rate on repos on Banco de España certificates from 12.4 per cent to 13 per cent on 24 July. Long-term interest rates surged, driven in part by non-residents' sales of government debt. At the same time, the Banco de España had to intervene quite heavily, selling foreign currency. However, this would prove to be far below the interventions it would be compelled to make in the period between September and November.

In the first half of August, the further weakening of sterling placed the peseta at its ceiling against the British currency, and the Banco de España had to intervene buying sterling. Subsequently, with the depreciation of the dollar and the renewed strength of the Deutschemark combining with growing uncertainty over the result of the French referendum on the Maastricht Treaty, the peseta once more slipped against the ERM narrow-band currencies and drew close to its central rate against the Deutschemark, then at Pta 65 per Deutschemark. The peseta edged away from its upper limit *vis-à-vis* sterling, though it remained 5.8 per cent above its central rate against the pound until mid-September. The room for manœuvre of Spanish exchange rate policy was thus enormously cramped.

The ERM crisis between September and November 1992 and the first two devaluations of the peseta

In early September, the position of the ERM currencies within the bands reflected the instability prevailing and the lack of confidence in the grid.

Adding to this was the growing uncertainty in the run-up to the French referendum arising from the opinion polls on its likely outcome, which acted as a catalyst for the launching of speculative attacks, providing them with a fixed date. Besides, the foreign exchange difficulties facing the Nordic currencies, which were unilaterally linked to the Ecu, and particularly the announcement by the Finnish authorities that they were decoupling from the Ecu, fuelled realignment expectations (their negative impact on the ERM currencies would, from that point on, be a constant throughout the crisis).

In this context, the downward pressure against the lira mounted, despite the surge in Italian interest rates, so that recourse was made of heavy marginal interventions in support of the Italian currency. But the situation finally became untenable and, on 13 September, the lira was devalued by 6.76 per cent. This decision was accompanied, the following day, by a slight cut in German official rates.

After the above two decisions, tensions seemed to subside the following day and most ERM currencies appreciated *vis-à-vis* the Deutschemark (for instance, the peseta strengthened by 0.4 per cent against the German currency). But tensions heightened again on 15-16 September. The market considered that the decisions taken were insufficient, their view no doubt influenced by statements by the authorities of several countries which suggested differences in opinion as to the extent of the realignment made. Unprecedented speculative capital movements occurred against sterling, the lira and, to a lesser extent, the peseta. On 16 September, the fiercest speculative attack in the history of the ERM was unleashed. After heavily intervening on 15 September, the Banco de España let the market find a new level for the peseta in its then prevailing bands. In the course of a that single day (16 September), the Spanish currency depreciated by 3.4 per cent.

Once the British and Italian authorities had communicated their decision to allow their respective currencies to float outside the ERM, following the EC Monetary Committee meeting in the early hours of the morning of the 17th, the Spanish authorities requested the devaluation of the central rate of the peseta by 5 per cent, which was agreed with the other members. The decision was based on the Spanish authorities' wish to uphold ERM commitments, and on their conviction that, otherwise, speculative attacks on the peseta would become intolerably intense making it most difficult to combat them with any success.

The Spanish authorities' strategy was aimed at keeping the peseta in the ERM, convinced as they were that this was the most appropriate alternative from the Spanish economic policy standpoint and with regard to the continuity and effectiveness of the ERM. Indeed, from the Spanish authorities point of view it would be highly desirable, with a view to the future, to preserve the ERM, the centrepiece of EC economic policy co-ordination and a key tool for the convergence of macroeconomic performance.

In the following days, in the run-up to the French referendum, the pressure on several currencies heightened notably. The peseta was positioned in the lower part of its ERM band, but some way off its floor. It held there with virtually no need for intervention on the foreign exchange markets. But after the close outcome of the French referendum, the tensions in the ERM spread to the peseta, which slipped within its fluctuation bands despite heavy intervention by the Banco de España. Hence, in order to ensure compliance with their ERM undertakings, the Spanish authorities decided to introduce measures penalizing speculative transactions by non-residents. This was done via Banco de España Circular 16 dated 23 September 1992. The measures were subsequently relaxed to some degree pursuant to Circular 17 dated 5 October 1992. The contents and operation of the circulars are explained in an annex to this article. Their aim was to raise considerably the cost of the financing (via residents' swaps or forward operations, following the flexibility introduced with the second of the two circulars) of the new speculative positions taken by non-residents against the peseta. To some extent, the measures were tantamount to a tax on these operations, aimed at deterring agents from resorting to them.

Initially, the markets seemed to over-react to the measures pursuant to Circular 16. The peseta duly appreciated considerably. At the same time, there was some disengagement by non-residents from the Spanish secondary markets for government bonds and equities, and this was reflected by the prices on these markets. Euromarket/domestic market interest rate differentials widened considerably. This initial reaction was due to relative confusion about the scope of the measures. But once this confusion cleared, the government bond, equities and currency markets resumed their normal course, and euromarket/domestic market interest rate differentials narrowed to the point of virtually disappearing in the longer-dated maturities. The peseta, then, moved gradually downward and once more traded at between 71 and 71.6 per Deutschemark, remaining there until 20 November (prior to the second devaluation of the peseta).

As stated, and in view of the turmoil prevailing on European financial markets, the Spanish authorities decided to introduce measures penalizing the most blatantly speculative operations so as to defend the peseta's new position in its bands. The aim of these measures was to deter short-selling of pesetas by penalizing the basic instrument of very short-dated speculation, i.e. financing obtained via swaps. That penalization implied, obviously, higher financing costs for speculators. The same goal may be obtained through sharp increases in interest rates, recourse to which was made by some other monetary authorities facing downward pressure on their currencies. Which of the two option could be more appropriate in dis-

couraging speculative operations is an ι teresting question that is open to
debate. Under the circumstances of the   pisode of foreign exchange crisis
between September and November 199. the Banco de España tended to
prefer the alternative of introducing oblię ıtory non-interest-earning deposits, since it was thought to be a more sele ːtive and a less disruptive — for
financial markets and operators — way oι sharply increasing the position-
taking costs for speculators.

As to the effectiveness of these measures, a conclusive assessment seems
rather difficult to be made, especially given the relative short period of time
in which they were in effect. On the one hand, they had an initial negative
impact on financial markets, reflected by a considerable decline in non-residents' outright holdings of government debt — largely related to forward
repurchases of such debt — and, to a lesser extent, by sales of variable-yield
securities. On the other hand, the measures proved, with the passage of
time, relatively effective in fulfilling their stated objectives. In October and
early November, tensions abated in the ERM; however, pursuant to Circular 17 allowed, at times of tension, for the differentials between euromarket
and domestic market interest rates to widen notably. This no doubt reduced
the volume of currency-selling interventions in favour of the peseta and,
therefore, helped stabilize the exchange rate of the peseta during this period, despite the widespread market expectations about the inevitability of
a further devaluation of the peseta.

Events in the third week of November confirmed that tensions had not disappeared. The new crisis of the Swedish krona translated into fresh pressure
on the most vulnerable ERM currencies at that time. The market pressures on
the peseta, given the strong devaluation expectations, once more required
heavy intervention in its defence. In view of the situation, the authorities requested the 6 per cent devaluation of the central parity of the peseta, which
was agreed at the EC Monetary Committee meeting on 21 November.

In the wake of the second devaluation of the peseta, The Banco de España
decided to raise its money market intervention rates. At the same time, it announced the lifting of the measures in Circular 17/92. The rise in interest rates
had the purpose of sending an unequivocal signal to the markets that monetary stringency would be maintained to combat inflation. The authorities also
wished to demonstrate their resolve to keep the peseta within its new bands.
The lifting of the measures applied via Circular 17 was, meanwhile, fully consistent with their exceptional and temporary nature. This second devaluation
of the peseta thus brought its market onto a normal footing.

The evolution of the peseta up to mid-February 1993

The subsequent course of the peseta apparently confirmed the normaliza-
tion of its market and that expectations stabilized, as was the authorities'

objective. Indeed, from the end of November to the end of January, the peseta trended very gradually but continuously upwards. Hence, despite the devaluation of its central parity, the market exchange rate of the peseta at end-January stood at 1.2 per cent above its value before the second devaluation. That points out to the fact that the speculative position-takings against the peseta were hardly profitable on this concrete episode of turbulence. The relative strength of the peseta was all the more significant if regard is had to the fact that during this period the Banco de España made numerous foreign currency buying transactions. These allowed a portion of the foreign reserves lost from September to November to be recouped. With the exchange rate firm, the authorities decided on 22 January to shave 0.5 points off the thrice-monthly intervention rate, which was further reduced by 0.25 percentage points to 13 per cent on 12 February.

The scale of the adjustment of the central parity of the peseta after the two devaluations amounted to 10.7 per cent, which meant that the new bands even overlapped slightly the bands with which the peseta joined the ERM. The market price of the peseta had depreciated at the end of January 1993 by about 10.5 per cent from its value at the start of 1992. The two successive devaluations of the peseta seemed to had placed it in a position more attuned to an appropriate level of competitiveness for the Spanish economy.

The November realignment restored stability for the wide-band currencies, but not so for some of the narrow-band currencies. In a climate marked by a lack of confidence in the grid then prevailing, several speculative attacks against the Irish pound, the Danish krone and the French franc were launched in December, January and early February. Following the devaluation of the Irish pound and the successful defence of the Danish krone, the ERM entered a phase spanning the February-May period where stability gradually resumed for the narrow-band countries and tensions once more flared around the two wide-band currencies (the peseta and the escudo).

The third devaluation of the Spanish peseta

The source of the weakness of the peseta in the period February-May 1993, apparently lay in the increasing sluggishness of economic activity and the political uncertainty fuelled by the calling of elections. In mid-February the peseta, which had remained untouched by the turbulence besetting the narrow-band currencies in December and January, was subjected to fresh selling pressure. The trigger on this occasion was apparently the release of figures disclosing a sharp fall in employment in the last quarter of 1992 as well as comments from EC official sources about the likelihood of a multispeed Emu. To counter this speculative pressure the Banco de España made a comprehensive recourse to all the Basle-Nyborg instruments. Firstly, it used the flexibility provided by the width of the band, letting the exchange rate of the peseta depreciate substantially. At the same time, the monetary authority intervened heavily on foreign exchange markets, while in turn allowing short-term rates to rise, on occasion, to between 16 per cent and 18 per cent. The use of these two latter instruments in a quite comprehensive manner produced a reversal in the exchange rate movement. Over the course of March the tensions seemed to abate, and the peseta once more settled as the strongest-positioned ERM currency. At the same time, interbank interest rates once more dipped to 13 per cent-14 per cent.

However, the calling of elections for June on 12 April unleashed fresh pressure against the peseta, necessitating new foreign exchange market interventions and a new rise in very-short-dated interest rates. Again, the Banco de España used the flexibility provided by the width of the band and allowed a gradual depreciation of the peseta. Following the intervention, in concert by the central banks of the ERM narrow-band countries, in favour of the peseta on 23 April, the Spanish currency tended to stabilize in the lower part of its band, albeit supported by interventions by the Banco de España.

In these circumstances, the growing evidence of a rapid slowdown in economic activity meant very firm expectations became embedded about a cut in interest rates, which the markets deemed incompatible with the parity of the peseta then prevailing. The severe pressure on the peseta mounted on the second week of May, and as it was likely to last for a long period owing to increasing political uncertainties surrounding the possible outcome of the general election — and its consequence for the Spanish economic policy — the Spanish authorities requested and obtained a third devaluation of the peseta, this time by 8 per cent on 13 May. The following day, the Banco de España reduced the benchmark official ten-day repo rate by 1.5 percentage points to 11.5 per cent.

Although all the three devaluations of the peseta have been decided under severe market pressures, the last one seems to be hardly justifiable on economic terms, being the consequence of the great political uncertainties produced by the call of advanced general elections in Spain. As stated previously, the second devaluation placed the Spanish economy in what seemed to be an appropriate level of competitiveness, as the impressive improvement in the Spanish trade balance appears to show. Furthermore, the Spanish interest rates high levels was a consequence of the efforts to defend the ERM parity of the peseta against the strong speculative attack, as the significant rate reductions following the third realignment tend to prove. Therefore, the decision of the Spanish authorities to request a third devaluation was forced by the high economic costs induced by the attempt to maintain the parity of the peseta in an scenario of strong political uncertainties. The strong commitments of the Spanish authorities towards the ERM were again proved on this occasion.

After the realignment, the peseta's exchange rate tended to stabilize in the upper half of its new ERM band, which enabled the Banco de España to make some intervention purchases to replenish its reserves and to reduce further the official interest rate on two successive occasions by 0.25 percentage point each, on 25 May and on 2 July, to 11 per cent. Nevertheless, two episodes of downward pressure on the Spanish currency have reappeared. The first one occurred at the end of May in connection with the approaching of the general elections and the pressures subsided immediately after the outcome of those elections was known. The second episode is related with the reappearance of renewed tensions in the whole ERM on July. On both occasions, the Banco de España allowed its currency to weaken substantially within its band without intervening or letting money market interest rates increase significantly. At mid-July, the peseta had depreciated by about 21 per cent *vis-à-vis* the Deutschemark from its value at the start of 1992.

For the devaluations to be effective in resolving the imbalances still in place in the Spanish economy, it is crucial that the resulting recovery in

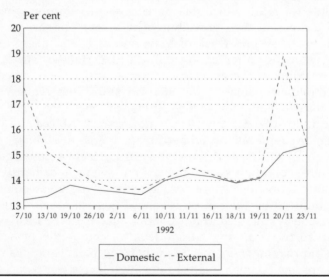

Figure 17.1   Internal and external swap rates — 1 day

competitiveness should not be rapidly cancelled out by inflation. This requires a balanced policy mix based on cost control and productivity gains which provides for lasting improvements in competitiveness.

The monetary storm has underscored the vulnerability of the ERM to speculative movements, which may acquire towering proportions. The expansion of financial markets in recent years and the entry into force of free capital movements have made a system of pegged-but-adjustable exchange rate, such as the ERM, more unstable. One of the main lessons of the recent crisis is that when the exchange rates of ERM currencies are misaligned in relation to their fundamentals, mechanisms must be established to provide for the readjustment of the grid of parities. If, by contrast, the grid is considered to be in step with fundamentals, the ERM should have defence mechanisms. Any such defence will normally require co-ordination among the member states on a greater scale than that witnessed during the crisis. In any event, the monetary storm has highlighted the problems inherent to the transition towards monetary union, problems which are all the greater the more uncertain the plans and timetable for union are. Resolving the ERM crisis is thus inextricably linked to negotiating the obstacles to monetary union. To do so, a degree of stability within the ERM must be restored.

Appendix

With the issue of Circulars 16 and 17, dated 22 September and 5 October 1992, respectively, the Banco de España adopted temporary and exceptional measures geared to penalizing very short-term peseta lending to non-residents.

Since the contents of Circular 16/92 remained essentially unchanged — except for technical improvements and simplifications — in Circular 17/92, only the details and working of this second Circular will be analysed here. Circular 17/92 made it obligatory for banks and savings institutions to make a non-interest-earning deposit with the Banco de España, at terms to be set by the Banco de España, for an amount equal to the full peseta value of three items: 1) same day value sales of pesetas against foreign currencies to non-residents; 2) increments registered in net sales (i.e. sales less purchases) of pesetas against foreign currencies to non-residents value 'next day' *vis-à-vis* the net peseta-selling position of each entity on the date of the circular's enactment; and 3) the increase in positions involving the forward sale of foreign currency against pesetas to non-residents *vis-à-vis* the position of each entity on the working day of the foreign exchange market prior to the day on which the circular went into force.

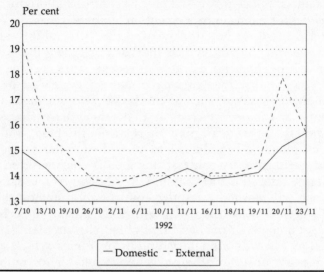

Figure 17.2   Internal and external swap rates — 1 week

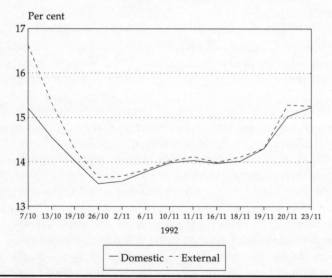

Figure 17.3   Internal and external swap rates — average of 1, 3 and 6 months

The Circular was inevitably expressed in routine foreign exchange market terms (which, like any other technical jargon, are difficult for outsiders to understand), but its essential message was that non-residents would not be able to borrow pesetas via swaps (i.e. through repurchase agreements involving cash purchases and forward sales of pesetas against foreign currencies) except at a very high cost.

Circular 17/92 was accompanied by a recommendation to Spanish credit institutions not to increase their peseta-denominated credit balances *vis-à-vis* non-residents, without such recommendation infringing on banks' regular balance-sheet lending (foreign trade financing, working capital, mortgage loans, etc.).

The measure was 'incremental' in the sense that it did not penalize previous non-resident borrowing positions via swaps, but only punished increases with respect to positions existing when the circular went into effect. The purpose was to halt any further flow, but not to punish loans via swaps already granted. It is worth noting, also, that the measure did not penalize the hedging operations of residents — transactions with residents were entirely excluded from the circular — and therefore, hedges related to balance of payments current or capital accounts were not affected.

It did, however, affect forward hedges that non-residents wished to make with Spanish banks. The reason was technical and was, of course, one of the drawbacks of the Circular: since longer-dated swaps could easily be converted into shorter-dated swaps, for the Circular to be effective, all non-resident swap financing transactions had to be penalized at all terms, thus creating obstacles for non-resident forward hedges unrelated to speculative operations.

The non-interest-earning deposit at the Banco de España led to a very strong increase in the effective interest rate on peseta loans via swap, and since it only affected loans via this channel between resident and non-resident entities, it was the same as establishing a differential between the interest rate of the 'domestic' peseta and the 'external' peseta.

Operations between residents were able to continue at rates similar to those on the interbank market, whereas operations with non-residents had to pay the 'quasi-tax' in the form of the obligatory non-interest-earning deposit with the Banco de España. However, to the surprise of many market players, during the nearly two month when Circular 17/92 was in effect, differentials between domestic and external rates occurred almost only in shorter-dated swaps (between one day and one week) and were much less, or even nil, in longer-dated swaps.

The explanation lays in the fact that residents in Spain still had full freedom to offer their funds abroad and, given the opportunity of lending pesetas at very high interest rates outside Spain, a large volume of pesetas shifted from the domestic to the foreign market. This strong transfer of

lendable pesetas abroad meant that external interest rates remained unchanged at terms for which there was no particularly strong speculative
demand. Thus, the measures worked well in the sense that they penalized
the shortest-dated swaps (whether or not related to speculative borrowing
against the peseta) but had few ill effects on longer-dated transactions
which they had not sought to penalize.

Figures 17.1-17.3 present interest rate trends at different terms for 'domestic' swaps (i.e. between residents) and 'external' swaps (i.e. between
residents and non-residents or between non-residents). The figures clearly
show that the differentials between both series of interest rates were larger
for shorter-dated swaps than at longer dates, and also reflects how these
differentials remained very small except at times of tension, when they
tended to increase abruptly at all terms (for example, during the first two
weeks after the measure was adopted, and in the days prior to the second
realignment of the peseta). Altogether, this seems to indicate that the full
freedom (at no time curtailed) of residents in Spain to redeploy deposits,
thus increasing the supply of pesetas available for loans abroad, considerably softened the measures' impact at terms where there was much less
speculative tension, i.e. longer terms. Similarly, even at times of great tension (in the days leading up to the second realignment, for example), the
differentials between the longer-dated swaps were comparatively very
small, and this, in turn, is a clear indication that very short-dated swaps,
between two days and one week, are the basic vehicle of the speculative
tension against a currency whose origin is solely exchange-related, so to
speak, as distinguished from the tension that arises in transactions related
to current or capital accounts.

As earlier indicated, Circular 17/92 established that the Banco de España
should set weekly the term of obligatory deposits. This clearly meant that
the impact of the 'tax' could progressively diminish via de reduction of the
term of the deposit. The initial term was one year, being reduced to six
months on 9 October.

Lastly, the measures established pursuant to Circular 17 were eliminated
on 24 November after the second devaluation of the peseta, in keeping with
the rationale underpinning their initial implementation. All told, Circular
17/92 may be said to have worked well and to have fulfilled its stated aims.

PART V

Perspectives on the crisis — European countries with floating-exchange rates

Chapter 18

An Italian perspective

Carlo Santini
Banca d'Italia

In the second half of 1992, the European monetary system experienced a phase of violent turbulence, after five years of relative stability with no re-alignments. In the course of those five years, the pound, the peseta and the escudo had entered the exchange rate mechanism, opting for the wide, 6 per cent fluctuation band. In January 1990 the lira had entered the narrow 2.25 per cent band, and in May of that year Italy had completed the liberalization of capital movements.

Yet, only few months after the signing of the Maastricht Treaty had brought the prospect of economic and monetary union into the realm of practical policy by establishing a programme and timetable for its implementation, the EMS was shaken by a deep crisis. Between September 1992 and May 1993, there were five realignments. The participation of the pound and the lira in the ERM was suspended. Renewed criticism from within and outside the EC was directed at the system of fixed-exchange rates as unsuitable in a Community whose members retained monetary policy independence. In some quarters it was seriously debated whether the programme of economic and monetary integration outlined in the Maastricht Treaty could be realized, at least as scheduled.

This paper traces the course of events with special reference to the lira and offers a tentative assessment of the effects of the currency crisis on the EMS and on the prospects for economic and monetary union.

When the first signs of tensions within the EMS emerged, immediately following the Danish referendum rejecting ratification of the Maastricht Treaty, the lira's central rate *vis-à-vis* the D-mark was 748.217; it had been set when Italy adopted the narrow fluctuation band of 2.25 per cent in January 1990. The market exchange rate was about 755 lire to the D-mark.

In the five years from 1987 through 1991, the annual inflation differential between Italy and the other EC member countries narrowed to an average of 1 percentage point, compared with 5 points at the inception of the EMS in 1979. Over the same five years, Italy's international competitiveness deteriorated by 4 per cent in terms of producer prices and by 11 per cent on the basis of unit labour costs. The steady real appreciation of the lira within the EMS was an essential part of Italian foreign exchange policy. It helped bring Italian inflation down towards the European average and spurred firms and unions to conclude agreements that safeguarded competitiveness by containing costs and raising productivity. The practicability of this exchange rate policy was questioned by the failure to control the domestic causes of inflation and, once capital movements had been completely liberalized, by the government's loss of credibility owing to failure to restore sound public finances.

From 1986 on, Italy ran a growing external current account deficit, due not to the trade balance but to the balance on services and transfers, first and foremost interest payments to non-residents. Until 1990, growing net capital inflows offset the current account deficit and produced an increase in the official reserves. In 1991 the net inflow of capital diminished, no longer compensating the current payments deficit.

	1st half	3rd qtr.	4th qtr.	Year
Current account balances	**-18,498**	**-7678**	**-6558**	**-32,734**
- Goods	-5157	4118	4092	3053
- Services, income and unrequited transfers	-13,341	-11,796	-10,650	-35,787
Capital flows	**13,382**	**-32,536**	**30,936**	**11,782**
- Total non-bank capital	-28,258	-15,322	30,059	-13,521
- Foreign capital	18,001	1862	7184	27,047
- Italian capital	-46,259	-17,184	22,875	-40,568
- Bank capital	41,640	-17,214	877	25,303
Errors and omissions	**-8965**	**-4718**	**2087**	**-11,596**
Change in official reserves (- = increase in reserves)	**14,081**	**44,932**	**-26,465**	**32,548**

Figure 18.1   Italy's balance of payments, 1992 (ITL billion)

The completion of foreign exchange liberalization, in 1990, stimulated very substantial portfolio adjustments on the part of residents. Inflows of capital from abroad peaked in that year, thanks to the high level of interest rates in Italy and widespread confidence in the stability of the lira. The situation began to change in 1991 and, in 1992, there was a progressive deterioration until the September crisis.

	1987	1988	1989	1990	1991	1992
Current account balances	-2066	-7623	-15,142	-17,782	-26,598	-32,734
- Goods	-392	-1501	-2956	431	-923	3053
- Services, income and unrequited transfers	-1674	-6122	-12,186	-18,213	-25,675	-35,787
Capital flows	11,203	21,653	34,177	52,143	28,775	11,782
- Total non-bank capital	5630	11,429	19,198	29,167	-10,594	-13,521
- Foreign capital	15,023	29,054	40,699	71,628	37,745	27,047
- Italian capital	-9393	-17,625	-21,501	-42,461	-48,339	-40,568
- Bank capital	5573	10,224	14,979	22,976	39,369	25,303
Errors and omissions	-2362	-3124	-3649	-19,205	-10,748	-11,596
Change in official reserves (- = increase in reserves)	-6775	-10,906	-15,386	-15,156	8571	32,548

Figure 18.2   Italy's balance of payments, 1987-1992 (ITL billion)

The reversal of the expectations of exchange rate stability was gradual at first but swift and decisive in the summer of 1992. The causes were both domestic and international. The domestic causes included the growing importance attached to the problem of the public finances, and in particular the weakness of governmental resolve in carrying out an adjustment programme to halt the rise of the public debt in proportion to GDP. The government's failure, year after year, to achieve its own budgetary targets recurrently intensified the doubts concerning the sustainability of the debt and fuelled rumours of extraordinary measures capable of triggering a rush to sell off government securities. The state of the public finances thus came to symbolize a much broader crisis affecting the entire Italian political system. As the governor of the Bank of Italy recalled in his concluding remarks to the Ordinary General Meeting of shareholders on 31 May 1993, in the spring of 1992 "...the Italian economy was in a weakened state owing to delay in implementing economic policy measures. The 'management of the economy' had become an urgent issue. ...As awareness of these failings spread, the unfavourable assessment by economic agents was reinforced and radicalized to the point where it became a blanket judgment on the country as a whole."

Most prominent among the international causes of the crisis was the result of the Danish referendum, which fostered the conviction that convergence, pursuant to the Maastricht Treaty, would be deferred and that, consequently, the central rates of the currencies of countries which had not yet achieved a satisfactory degree of price stability or were affected by severe public finance difficulties had become unsustainable. The 20th of September, the date of the French referendum on the Maastricht Treaty, thus became a point of reference for a general realignment within the EMS. The reversal of the optimistic expectations concerning Emu made for an unsustainable conflict between domestic and external objectives within the Community. Especially in the countries that had been most successful in curbing inflation, the interest rates required to maintain the EMS central rates conflicted more and more sharply with the need to combat the protracted economic downturn. The debate focused on German economic policy after unification, and specifically on the Bundesbank's tightening of monetary conditions in response to the worsening budget deficit and the inflationary impulse generated by excessive wage increases.

To counter the increasing pressure on the lira from the beginning of June, the Bank of Italy made full use of the instruments provided for in the Basle-Nyborg agreement, namely interest rate variations, exchange market interventions and movements of the lira within the fluctuation band.

On 4 June the Bank of Italy raised the rate on fixed-term advances by half a point; conditions in the money market tightened. The rate on central bank repurchase agreements rose from just over 12 to 14.5 per cent and the overnight rate to more than 15 per cent (see Figure 18.3). During the month the Bank's interventions in the foreign exchange market amounted to the equivalent of $5.6bn. The progressive weakening of the lira within the narrow band since March grew more pronounced and the lira's differential *vis-à-vis* the strongest ERM currency widened to 1.49 percentage points (see Figure 18.7).

On 4 July, the new government, formed after the April general election, was fully empowered by a parliamentary vote of confidence. Its programme reaffirmed the policy of stability of the lira within the EMS as instrumental to bring inflation down to the rates found in the lowest-inflation countries of the Community.

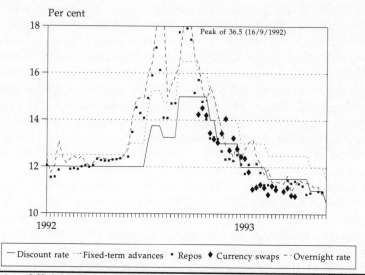

Figure 18.3   Official Italian interest rates and money market rates
Data: End of week for discount rate and fixed-term advances; average of marginal rates effected during the week for repos and swaps; weekly average of bid-ask prices for overnight rates

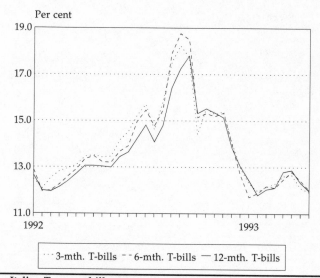

Figure 18.4   Italian Treasury bill rates
Data: Twice monthly average tender rates gross of withholding tax

However, the pressures in the foreign exchange market did not abate and, on 5 July, as the government began considering measures to redress the public finances, the Bank of Italy raised both the discount rate and the rate on fixed-term advances by 1.5 percentage point to respectively 13 and 14.5 per cent. On 16 July official rates were raised by a further 0.75 points, following an analogous increase decided by the Bundesbank. The Bank of Italy tightened its control of liquidity, with the result that the overnight rate recorded highs of close to 19 per cent. Between the 1st and 20th of July the Bank carried out foreign exchange market sales totalling $8bn but the lira weakened further, falling close to its ERM floor.

A period of relative calm in the foreign exchange markets followed, that lasted about a month, until 24 August. A contributory factor was the important agreement on the cost of labour that the trade unions and Confindustria (the Italian Confederation of industry) reached on 31 July, with the government's mediation. The centerpiece of the accord was the definitive and complete abolition of all forms of wage indexation. At once, and even more so in the months following the devaluation of the lira, the agreement proved to be of fundamental importance in preventing the eruption of a wage-price spiral and keeping the domestic causes of inflation under control. Measures adopted by the government at the same time to contain the 1992 budget deficit helped calm conditions in the foreign exchange and fi-

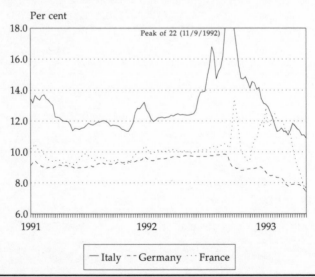

Figure 18.5   Three-month interbank rates in Italy, France and Germany
Data: Weekly average of daily rates

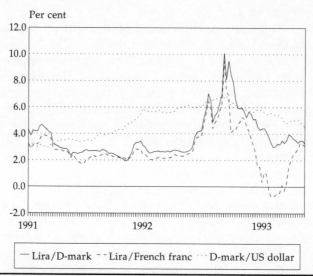

Figure 18.6   Interest rate differentials
Data: Weekly average of daily rates based on the difference between the 3-month interbank rate and the equivalent foreign rate except in the case of the the dollar rate, which is for 3-month T-bills

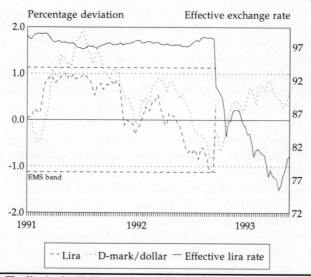

Figure 18.7   The lira in the EMS
Data: The nominal effective exchange rate of the lira is vis-à-vis the currencies of Italy's 14 leading trading partners (1987=100); the lira rate rate is percentage deviation from the centre of the EMS band; the Deutschemark/dollar rate is the deviation from the average for the first week of January 1991

nancial markets, inducing the Bank of Italy to lower the official discount rate by half a point on 4 August.

The 24th of August marked the onset of the most acute phase of turbulence in the EMS and of pressures against the lira. "The succession of opinion polls in France showing stronger-than-expected opposition to the Maastricht Treaty fuelled international speculation. The delays accumulated by the Italian economy in the convergence process and particularly the persistent imbalances in the public finances exposed the lira more than other currencies to expectations of depreciation focusing on the date of the French referendum (20 September), which was crucial for European construction" (Statement by the governor of the Bank of Italy to the Senate of the Republic, 24 September 1992).

On 28 August, after interventions to support the lira that amounted to around $5bn in just a few days, the Bank of Italy allowed the lira to fall to its ERM floor. On 4 September, official rates were raised by 1.75 points; refinancing through open market operations became more costly, with rates rising to more than 20 per cent in early September. Liquidity control was more stringent: the overnight rate soared to over 30 per cent on 11 September, while the 3-month interbank rate rose above 20 per cent. The Italian authorities refrained from adopting exchange controls in any form, confirming the irreversibility of Italy's strategic option in favour of the market and European openness.

In their contacts within the Community, the Italian authorities argued that what was under attack was not a single currency, the lira, but the entire European monetary system. In his statement of 24 September to the Senate, Governor Ciampi observed: "The speculation was aimed against the system. Two aspects were interrelated: the inconsistency of relative interest rates and the inconsistency of the exchange rates. For the response to be valid and credible, it had to be made jointly from the whole system; whether the adjustment should concentrate on the former inconsistency or the latter was the issue that had to be decided". No decision was taken, quite evidently also to avoid actions that could have negatively affected the result of the imminent French referendum. On 28 August, and again on 5 September, the Ecofin Council concluded, and made the conclusion publicly known, that changes in the central rates would not be an appropriate response to the tensions of the moment.

The interventions to support the lira became very large; the Bundesbank soon came to consider its purchases of lire at the compulsory intervention margin as incompatible with the objective of domestic monetary management.

In these circumstances, over the weekend of 12-13 September the Italian and German authorities agreed to propose a general realignment of the EMS central rates, to be accompanied by a reduction in German interest rates. The Italian authorities repeatedly requested a meeting of the EC Monetary Committee to conduct a thorough examination of the situation of the EMS and provide appropriate indications concerning the extent of the realignment. The majority of the other countries did not accede to this request; it was decided by telephone that only the lira would be devalued by 3.5 per cent and that all the other currencies would be revalued in equal measure. The reduction in German official rates was small.

The flow of funds back into the lira only lasted one day, the 14th of September. Speculation immediately intensified against sterling; subsequently it resumed its attacks on the lira. Notwithstanding massive Bank of England intervention, a 2-point increase in the UK discount rate to 12 per cent and the announcement of a further increase to 15 per cent with effect from the following day, on 16 September the United Kingdom asked that the EC Monetary Committee convene to decide on a realignment but, before the meeting began, announced its intention of suspending sterling from the ERM. Inevitably, the Italian authorities were obliged to take a similar decision concerning the lira, which had been supported by very large interventions on 15 and 16 September, despite the extreme tightness of liquidity in the money market, which had driven the overnight rate to above 36 per cent.

In the face of general expectations of an imminent devaluation, eliminating the speculators' expected gains would have necessitated raising interest rates by hundreds of percentage points. Such a decision is always difficult and, in Italy, it was impracticable, since it would have threatened to destabilize the government securities market in a context characterized by a large public debt with relatively short maturity. Moreover, tensions had already grown acute in the secondary market in government securities, where the price of 10-year Treasury bonds had fallen from between 98 and 99 at the end of May to 92 at the beginning of September and would reach a low of 86.5 at the turn of October.

Once the lira was allowed to float, it followed a downward path, with wide fluctuations, and reached its maximum depreciation at the beginning of April 1993, when it traded at around 1000 to the D-mark. Subsequently the exchange rate gradually returned to less abnormal levels, with the lira/Deutschemark exchange rate situated at around 905 at the beginning of July. At these levels, the real effective depreciation of the lira from the beginning of September 1992 was 15 per cent *vis-à-vis* all the leading currencies and 13 per cent *vis-à-vis* those of the Community. The loss in competitiveness since the realignment of January 1987 had been completely offset; indeed, thanks also to the limited rise in costs and prices, Italy's productive system now shows a gain in competitiveness of around 10 per cent compared with the beginning of 1987. Italy's enhanced competitiveness is reflected in the balance of trade: in the first quarter of 1993 exports to non-

Community countries grew by 20 per cent and those to Community countries by 9 per cent; Italy's trade balance with these two groups improved by, respectively, 2.7 and 6.7 trillion lire compared with the results a year earlier.

Since withdrawal from the ERM, Italian monetary policy has tightened its control of money supply, in particular M2, as an important factor in the process of bringing down inflation and restoring stability in the foreign exchange market. Official rates have been reduced gradually (at the beginning of July, the discount rate stood at 9 per cent and the rate on fixed-term advances at 10 per cent), taking advantage of similar movements elsewhere in Europe, of the slowdown in inflation (the twelve-month rise in the cost-of-living index was 4.2 per cent in June 1993, as against 5.7 per cent in May 1992) and of the recovery of confidence, thanks primarily to the government's determination to carry on the work of rehabilitating the public finances and to the historic agreement on wage determination, reached at the beginning of July of this year, which has consolidated the one established on the previous July and set wage bargaining on a new and sounder basis.

The Italian authorities remain committed to the lira's re-entry into the exchange rate mechanism, in keeping with Italy's fundamental decision to participate fully in the process of European economic and political integration. For an open and integrated economy such as Italy's, an exchange rate objective constitutes a useful anchor for the control of inflation and inflationary expectations. But return to the ERM depends on certain domestic and external preconditions. The former include continuing disinflation and achievement of the objectives that the government has set for redressing the public finances. Only with full restoration of credibility can the lira safely face the test of the markets.

At the international and particularly the Community level, the reflection on the events that have occurred in the EMS since June 1992 and on the project of European integration set forth in the Maastricht Treaty must continue.

Lasting exchange rate stability among the ERM currencies depends on the convergence of economic conditions in the member countries. It is the prime responsibility of each of them to implement economic policies that are consistent with the objective of convergence. It is also necessary to reinforce the 'systemic' aspects of the EMS with a view to consolidating the achievements already made in the construction of the single market and continuing progress towards economic and monetary union.

Upon its institution the EMS was assigned the function of creating an area of monetary stability in Europe, in response to the disappointing performance of the floating-exchange rate regime that followed the collapse of the Bretton Woods system. The countries with relatively high rates of inflation accepted the discipline implicit in *de facto* anchoring of their currencies to the D-mark, the system's most stable currency. Now, however, this conception of the EMS must be transcended. With the gradual formation and consolidation of a group of countries distinguished by stability, monetary policy coordination must be strengthened and made operative.

In this light, the EMS should be considered a 'Community good' and it must increasingly be managed at the Community level. The European Monetary Institute, whose inception the Maastricht Treaty sets for 1 January 1994, is the body through which such coordination must be effected. Precisely because determining the right central rate for any currency is difficult and in large part discretionary, this task must be carried out jointly by the national authorities. This exercise will prepare the way for any agreed realignment, still possible as economies continue to converge, or for the common defence of exchange rates that are fundamentally appropriate but nonetheless come under speculative pressure. The successful joint defence of the French franc and the Danish krone in late-1992 and early-1993, despite the violence of the speculative attacks suggests that the current rules of the EMS provide ample scope for action to preserve the system's stability.

The characteristics of the second stage of Emu make it potentially unstable and difficult to manage. The recognition of national authorities' autonomy in the conduct of monetary policy, if rigidly interpreted, conflicts with progress in the coordination of economic policies, which the treaty also provides for. This dilemma can be resolved either by recognizing the *de facto* hegemony of one country, to whose monetary policy the others adapt, or by enhancing the Community dimension of national decisions.

The first solution is in contrast with the principle of equality between member countries, on which the European Community has always been based. The value of this principle remains intact and in fact can only be reinforced by the prospect of an enlargement of the Community.

The search for a solution to the potential conflict outlined above that is consistent with the 'Community spirit' can start from the provisions of the Maastricht Treaty itself. As a first step, the role of the EMI in co-ordinating monetary policies, especially among the countries that have made the most progress towards convergence, should be emphasized. This will tend to produce a core group of countries that will prepare for transition to the third stage of Emu according to the timetable laid down in the treaty and that can serve as a pole of attraction for the others. Gradual participation in the final stage of the union is in fact in accordance with the Maastricht Treaty, which lays down the relevant criteria in Articles 109j and 109k.

The crux of the question is not actually the acceptability of what has been termed a 'two-speed Europe', which is, to repeat, already provided for in the treaty. Rather, it is the creation of the political and economic conditions necessary for the Emu project to proceed and for participation in the third stage to be achieved by all. The crisis of the second half of 1992, which involved not only the exchange rate structure within the Community but the very credibility of economic and monetary union (as of August 1993, the ratification of the Maastricht Treaty has not yet been completed), must be overcome by the vigorous reaffirmation of the political commitment to the project of European integration.

If the current treaty appears unbalanced, with a developed and ambitious component dealing with economic and monetary union and provisions on political union that are still uncertain in scope and features, it is not by weakening the former that an equilibrium compatible with the reinforcement of European integration can be attained. And if the present institutional arrangements of economic co-operation in Europe appear inadequate to deal with unforeseen shocks, whatever their origin (German unification, to name one), or to impart a powerful impetus to the economic restructuring and modernization needed for sustained growth in output and employment, it is not by retreating towards independent national policies that the Community can overcome the present delicate phase of cyclical difficulties and those that may follow in the future.

The European Council, in Copenhagen on 21-22 June 1993, concluded that the favourable outcome of the Danish referendum "... should mark the ending of a prolonged period of uncertainty on the Community's direction". It is to be hoped that, in the future, this meeting will be seen as giving renewed momentum to the drive towards economic and monetary union.

Chapter 19

A Finnish perspective

Markku Pulli
Central Bank Policy Department, Bank of Finland

Finland has a long history of trend-wise currency depreciation within a fixed-exchange rate regime. In the decades following the Second World War, economic policies were strongly geared towards growth. As the economy was also highly sensitive to fluctuations in world-market prices of forest-based products, and wages and other costs of production were sticky downwards, it developed a distinct proneness to inflation. From time to time, the export sector experienced crises generated by excessive cost pressures, which often culminated in a devaluation of the currency.

Since the beginning of the 1970s, one of the prime goals of economic policy has been to break this trend in order to eliminate expectations of currency depreciation and the premium in interest rates that is associated with a weak currency in a market environment. Finland seemed to make considerable progress in this area in the 1980s; the exchange rate was fairly stable and, in fact, even appreciated somewhat. The last few years have, however, demonstrated just how difficult this task is, especially if confidence building coincides with external shocks.

Exchange rate policy prior to autumn 1992

From the beginning of the 1970s, the Finnish markka was pegged to a trade-weighted currency basket, first unofficially and formally from the late-1970s. This basket was replaced by the Ecu basket in June 1991, when the markka was unilaterally linked to the Ecu. As regards the composition of the basket, the change was of only minor significance as the currencies making up the Ecu basket or directly pegged to it had a weight of more than four-fifths in the Bank of Finland's trade-weighted index at the time.

Rather, Finland's decision to peg to the Ecu was motivated primarily by integration considerations. By establishing the Ecu as an anchor for economic policy, the authorities wished to emphasize that the aim of economic policy was to achieve convergence with the economic policies pursued by member states of the European Community. The economic policy interpretation of the previous trade-weighted index was somewhat different, as the trade-weighted index can be regarded as more competitiveness-orientated.

Finland's decision to peg to the Ecu was preceded by a similar decision by Sweden. Sweden's decision triggered expectations in the Finnish foreign exchange market that Finland would follow suit. At the same time, there were vehement demands that the markka should be devalued in connection with the link to the Ecu. Given Finland's history of periodic exchange rate adjustments, this provoked a strong reaction in the foreign exchange market. Market uncertainty developed into a full-blown currency crisis. In the event, the markka was linked to the Ecu at the prevailing exchange rate and the nervousness was dispelled, but only for a few months.

By pegging the markka to the Ecu — and particularly without any change in the fixed parity — the authorities sought to reinforce Finland's commitment to a stable exchange rate. The need for a stronger commitment had been underlined in spring 1991 when a strike by transport workers and dockers threatened to bring Finland's export trade to a halt. It demonstrated that devaluation behaviour was very firmly entrenched in the labour market; at the same time as the profitability of the export industries was weakening it was already being endeavoured to share out the perceived gains from devaluation.

When the peg to the Ecu was made, it was clear that a unilateral link would not offer the same degree of credibility that membership of the ERM would bring. It was therefore judged that the decision needed to be backed up by a wide-ranging economic programme, especially considering the worsening problems that loomed before the economy. Such a programme would have included a tightening of fiscal policy and measures to reduce costs, particularly in industry. But in the end it proved impossible to implement these measures.

In fiscal policy, a major stumbling block was posed by existing legislation, which made the passage of measures through Parliament dependent on their receiving a qualified majority. This meant, for example, that the government could not force through decisions providing for cuts in government spending without the support of at least part of the opposition. The legislative procedure was changed in this respect in 1992, which was an essential condition for the subsequent shift in the course of economic policy. Another problem was that at the time of the peg to the Ecu there was not wide awareness in society of the scale of the crisis. The extent of the adjustment process needed was not recognized, and consequently it proved difficult to obtain the support of the unions and Parliament for the required measures.

In the absence of fiscal policy measures, in autumn 1991 the focus in economic policy shifted to achieving an incomes agreement aimed at cutting costs in the economy. Against a background of renewed unrest in the foreign exchange market, a serious attempt was made to lower nominal wages through a centralized pay settlement. But in the event the proposal failed to gain adequate support from the unions and this fuelled heavy speculation against the markka. The Bank of Finland had to abandon its attempts to keep the markka within its fluctuation band, and on the following day new limits for the band were fixed, which implied an effective devaluation of 12.3 per cent.

The devaluation was the first since the deregulation of capital movements and its effects differed considerably from those of previous devaluations. Uncertainty continued to prevail in the markets and long-term interest rates moved higher. In addition, particularly companies in the domestic sector suffered heavy exchange rate losses as a result of the rise in the markka values of foreign debt accumulated in the late-1980s and in interest payments thereon. The devaluation boosted the competitiveness of the export sector, but it also accelerated the decline in domestic demand. Because of weak domestic demand, the devaluation did not lead to significant price increases, and so the rise in nominal interest rates entailed a sharp increase in real interest rates, which compounded the debt problem and deepened the slump in investment activity.

After the November 1991 devaluation, Finland's exchange rate policy found itself between two regimes — flexible interest rate policy and fixed-exchange rate policy. Hence it was only four months later, in March 1992, that the new exchange rate came under attack. On this occasion the markka was defended through a combination of sharply higher interest rates and the announcement of spending cuts by the government. In addition, the Bank of Finland entered into swap agreements with certain other central banks. These steps succeeded in staunching the capital outflow but interest rates remained at a high level.

Finland's experiences of the rapidly recurring attacks against the currency in the wake of the 1991 devaluation closely resemble the experiences of several ERM countries that devalued their currencies in 1992-93. In the current market conditions it is extremely difficult to achieve credibility for the new exchange rate after a devaluation. There is no immediate improvement in the economy after devaluation as both the 'J-curve' effect and unfavourable effects in the financial markets reduce aggregate demand. As, moreover, it has just been demonstrated to the markets that an exchange rate adjustment is an option available to the authorities, uncertainty in the foreign exchange markets quickly starts to mount again. Restoring the credibility of exchange rate policy after a devaluation calls for far-reaching measures in other areas of economic policy but all too often both politicians and the public at large believe that the exchange rate change, as such, will remedy the economy's ills.

The decision to float the markka

In contrast to most other European countries, interest rates were at a high level in Finland from spring 1992 onwards. Towards the end of the summer the pressure on the markka began to mount again after tensions within the ERM had intensified and the Swedish krona had come under attack. Expectations of a realignment within the ERM triggered speculation against the markka as it was suspected that Finland might follow any downward adjustment of currencies within the ERM. This was a new situation since there had not been any realignment within the ERM during the time the markka had been pegged to the Ecu.

The Bank of Finland's response to the unrest in the foreign exchange market was to allow interest rates to move higher in the latter part of August 1992. The three-month Helibor rate climbed to 17 per cent, opening up a gap of some seven percentage points in relation to the corresponding rate for the Deutschemark. In spite of this, the Bank had to intervene continually in the markets to support the markka's exchange rate. The markets were, of course, aware that the official reserves were being depleted even though much of the intervention took place in the forward market. In an effort to reduce uncertainty the Bank of Finland resorted to swap arrangements in order to replenish the reserves.

In the first week of September, however, the currency outflow gathered pace in the run-up to the French referendum on the Maastricht Treaty. Finally, the markka was allowed to float on 8 September. The exchange rate immediately weakened by about 10 per cent in relation to the Deutschemark but then quickly stabilized.

The decision to float the markka was made with reluctance. A contributory factor was that the bolstering of the foreign exchange reserves would have required further recourse to swap arrangements. The basic reasons for the decision were, however, connected with the overall state of affairs in economic policy. In particular, there was not judged to be any scope, politically, in fiscal policy for any further actions that would have quickly led to a significant improvement in the government's difficult financial position. In fact, the government's budget proposal for 1993, which had only just been presented to Parliament, already implied a substantial tightening of fiscal stance.

The situation in the labour market was quiet in the autumn. Notwithstanding this, there did not seem to be any prospect of a breakthrough in pay negotiations that would have calmed the foreign exchange market. Moreover, there was broad agreement in the country that price competitiveness in manufacturing was at a satisfactory level, so this consideration was not a major factor underlying the uncertainty about the exchange rate. It seems that the basic problem was simply the loss of credibility of fixed-exchange rate policy.

Currency movements in the autumn largely reflected hedging operations by firms operating in the domestic market that had foreign-currency debts. Many of these firms had suffered exchange rate losses in connection with the 1992 devaluation and, because of the slump in the domestic market, were in a poor position to bear any further losses. Especially in situations like this the interest rate weapon is very much a two-edged sword.

Changing the limits of the markka's band and setting a new fixed parity for the currency no longer represented a viable alternative to floating. The events in the early part of the year had demonstrated that the fixing of a new fixed-exchange rate would soon have led to the re-emergence of uncertainty. And as the fixed-exchange rate policy had effectively been abandoned as a result of exchange rate changes, not even exchange rate policy considerations justified the setting of a new parity.

When the crisis in European currency markets came to a head two weeks later it proved that the decision to float had been the right one under the circumstances. The markka simply would not have been able to withstand the forces that would have been unleashed against it in that connection. Of course, the crisis could not have been foreseen but the direction in which events were developing on the eve of the French referendum was evident to everyone.

Developments in the foreign exchange market during the markka's float

Although conditions in the foreign exchange market in Finland calmed down immediately after the markka was floated, interest rates remained at a high level in autumn 1992 during the turmoil in the ERM. The interest rate differential between the markka and the Deutschemark did not start to narrow until after a fiscal policy package had been announced and a pay settlement had been reached. In October the government published a medium-term programme and associated measures for the consolidation of central government finances in the period 1993-1995. In the labour market unions and employers reached an agreement in November which kept negotiated wages unchanged for the second year in succession.

After the markka was floated its exchange rate remained fairly stable until December 1992. The unrest in foreign exchange markets in Sweden and Norway did not have any significant impact on the Finnish foreign exchange market although it was reflected in the relatively high level of market interest rates. Towards the end of the year the markka started to weaken on the news that the performance of the economy had been poorer than expected; the Swedish krona also started to weaken. Towards the end of March 1993, the downward trend in the markka's value came to a halt and the markka started to appreciate.

The turmoil in currency markets last winter had a major effect on capital flows related to repayments of the private sector's foreign currency debts. Several factors have been at work here. The basic problem stems, of course, from the fact that during the boom of the late-1980s companies raised foreign currency loans on the international markets to finance investments the return on which has turned out to be poorer than expected. Now companies are adjusting their debt levels to their changed income expectations. Furthermore, the markka's float may to some extent have created a need to reduce the amount of foreign currency debt held by companies; the optimal amount of foreign currency debt has decreased if companies perceive that exchange rate uncertainty has increased. It is also evident that companies have found it difficult to renew their maturing foreign currency loans on the same terms as before and that Finnish banks have endeavoured to reduce the amount of foreign currency loans that they raise for their customers in the international markets. But, in addition to these reasons, the capital flow has probably intensified as result of the exchange rate losses caused by the markka's depreciation. Companies' sensitivity to exchange rate risks has increased.

As monetary policy now lacks the anchor provided by a fixed-exchange rate, price stability has assumed greater importance than before as an explicit goal of monetary policy. The Bank of Finland has set specific guidelines for its monetary policy over the next few years by announcing that its goal is to bring down the rate of inflation permanently to the level of two per cent by 1995. It is based on assumptions about the likely path of economic developments in Finland and the rest of Europe in the medium-term. The target allows for a rise in the price level slightly in excess of two per cent in 1993-1994, when the markka's depreciation and the planned VAT reform in 1994 will generate exceptional pressures for price increases. However, the purpose of the inflation target is to demonstrate that the aim of economic policy is to keep domestic inflationary pressures in check.

The low inflation target has been criticized on the grounds that the rise in consumer prices in recent times has been rather subdued. Unfortunately, this criticism is somewhat misdirected: there exists a danger in the current situation both in Finland and in many other European countries that incipient economic growth will be cut short by a resurgence of inflation over the next few years. Nevertheless there are reasons why Finland's inflation target can be regarded as realistic. The most important is that the exchange rate is floating — it has not been devalued as was customary in the past.

The setting of prices in markets, both in companies and in the labour market, is based on prevailing demand conditions and expectations about inflation. When, during the era of financial market regulation, the exchange rate was adjusted in a step-wise fashion as a means of solving cost crises in industry, it was inevitable that the adjustment would be passed through into prices after an interval of some years. When a currency is floating a weakening in the exchange rate will not necessarily lead to expectations of accelerating inflation if it is believed that the exchange rate could be strengthening when price pressures emerge. Moreover, demand is likely to remain subdued in Finland over the next few years.

After the first few months of the markka's float, short-term market interest rates in Finland have been at roughly the same level as Ecu interest rates. As this has been accompanied by slow inflation, real interest rates have been exceptionally high in Finland. Under these circumstances the primary constraint in the conduct of interest rate policy has not been inflationary pressures but rather the country's external debt. It has been possible to bring down the level of interest rates only to the extent that there has been sufficient interest in holding foreign debt. Heavy borrowing abroad by the central government has eased the situation somewhat. The current level of interest rates is nevertheless rather high in relation to inflation and the inflation target.

Developments in the Finnish bond market

The Finnish bond market is now developing at a rapid pace. The financing needs of the central government have increased the importance of the market, and its development has been aided by certain institutional changes. The bond market remained in a very underdeveloped state for a long time, partly due to the central government's modest borrowing requirements.

In 1992, a primary dealer system was launched in Finland, which provided a framework for market making in government debt instruments. Moreover, the taxation of capital income has been changed; since the beginning of 1992, all capital income has been taxed at the rate of 25 per cent. This has increased households' interest in investing in taxable interest-bearing instruments and shares. Another important change as a regards a well-functioning share market was the removal of restrictions on share ownership by foreigners at the beginning of 1993.

Foreigners' portfolio investments in Finland have, however, remained relatively modest. This probably reflects uncertainty regarding exchange rates. It has been estimated that, at the end of April 1993, foreigners' holdings of markka-denominated debt instruments amounted to FM 23bn and their holdings of Finnish shares to FM 10bn. Raising the level of such holdings is a key objective of economic policy, as it would facilitate the government's debt financing operations and help ensure an adequate supply of risk financing for investment when the economy begins to grow and investment needs increase.

Re-establishment of exchange rate stability in Finland

Currently, the prime objective of Finland's economic policy is to restore economic stability and create the conditions for moving the economy back on to a path of balanced growth over the next few years. This would also pave the way for stability in the currency market.

Ultimately, the results will be greatly influenced by international developments. A deepening of the recession in Europe would exacerbate Finland's adjustment problems, for the weaker is demand in Finnish export markets, the deeper is the slump in domestic demand because of the current account constraint. Despite the sharp increase in Finnish exports to non-European markets, Europe's share in Finnish exports continues to be dominant. Moreover, Finland's foreign exchange market is closely linked to the European markets, so that continued instability in the latter would have a direct impact on conditions in Finland.

Finland's objectives regarding integration have not changed as a result of recent developments but have instead assumed more tangible form. Finland has applied for EC membership and accepted the Maastricht treaty as the basis for membership. It is thus clear that Finland aims to participate in the future in Europe's common exchange rate policy, provided that efforts to achieve closer monetary policy co-ordination in Europe are successful.

But, whatever happens with respect to the integration process, a natural long-run objective for Finland is to return to a fixed-exchange rate regime at some point in the future. In a small country that is dependent on foreign trade, a fixed-exchange rate reduces the uncertainty attached to firms' decision making and thus provides a favourable environment for investment. It also provides an anchor for economic policy that is clearly visible to the public. However, a prequisite for these favourable effects is that the fixed-exchange rate must be credible.

Following the decision to float in autumn 1992, it became apparent that, because of the economic situation in Finland and the turbulence in the European currency markets, a quick return to a fixed-exchange regime policy was impossible. It was further judged by the authorities that such a return to a fixed parity would require at least the following:

- a substantial improvement in the economic fundamentals and in expectations concerning economic developments;
- fixing the exchange at a realistic level;
- adequate exchange reserves (i.e. much larger than the previous 'normal level');
- a clarification of conditions in the European foreign exchange markets.

There have been some favourable developments in Finland's economic situation although, up to summer 1993, these changes have been more evident in economic policy than in the state of the economy. It is clear that last winter the markka's external value dropped below its equilibrium level. Fixing the exchange rate at too low a level always involves the risk that inflation will start to accelerate and jeopardize the prospects for balanced growth. The overshooting of the markka's depreciation is illustrated by the fact that the price competitiveness of Finnish industry rose to an exceptionally high level by historical standards. But the results of the adjustment process under way in the economy are only gradually starting to become evident. In spring 1993 unemployment was still rising and the current account was still in deficit, albeit clearly improving. A dominant opinion among the Finnish authorities was that probably, once the adjustment process had moved further ahead, it would be easier to decide what exchange rate would be reasonable in the longer term.

A quick return to the Ecu peg would also have been ill-advised because of the unstable conditions within the ERM. The turbulence within the ERM would probably also have aroused expectations regarding the exchange rate in Finland, had the markka not been floating at the time.

Frequent realignments of ERM exchange rates give rise to fundamental problems in regard to pegging the markka to the Ecu. Recent developments within the ERM clearly demonstrate that there are significant differences in economic policy stance between participating countries. This causes problems because the purpose of linking one's exchange rate is to use the economic policy of the other country (or countries) as an anchor for one's own policy. If the policies pursued by the anchor countries differ, the signal given by the link concerning economic policy objectives becomes obscured.

A change in the role of the ERM affects, of course, primarily the EC countries. But it also affects the outlook for exchange rate policy in Finland and the other countries involved in EC membership negotiations. Up until last year, many people in these countries saw participation in the ERM as a means to automatically rid themselves of the problems connected with exchange rate policy. Now that prospect seems much more unlikely.

If exchange rate flexibility becomes an established feature of ERM operations, there is the danger that the ERM will not necessarily provide a good basis for exchange rate stability, especially in the periphery countries. Experiences gained in recent years from the unrest in the exchange rate markets indicate that serious problems attach to the 'fixed-but-adjustable-peg'. It is extremely difficult to prevent the emergence of devaluation expectations by flexibly adjusting exchange rates. Market participants inevitably begin to anticipate these adjustments as they endeavour to hedge themselves against exchange rate changes. This can lead to a situation where the weak currencies are expected to go on weakening and the strong currencies to go on strengthening. Thus it is possible that the system is unstable and that equilibrium cannot be achieved until the 'fixed-but-adjustable-peg' becomes a floating-rate system. This is an old argument, but one which is much more seldom heard these days than it was a few years ago.

Moreover, there is the problem that the flexible adjustment of exchange rates might delay the convergence of economic policies. This could lead to even greater differences between countries or at least slow the closing of the gaps between them. The arrangement could then become frozen irrevocably into a two-tier system: strong countries with low interest rates and better growth prospects and weak countries with high interest rates and poorer growth prospects. On the other hand, it is clear that no exchange rate regime can guarantee convergence; rather the key to this lies in each country's own economic policy.

The situation in Finland with respect to exchange rate policy is very similar to that in Sweden. Norway also shares the same problems to some extent, although its economy is somewhat stronger at the moment. All these countries are currently negotiating for EC membership. Each country, however, negotiates and makes decisions independently. As these negotiations are of central importance with respect to exchange rate policy, there are limits to how far these countries can go in formulating a common strategy on exchange rate policy questions.

Finland and Emu

Finland's position regarding Emu and the timetable for its implementation has not been clearly defined yet, as the negotiations for EC membership are still in progress. However, it seems natural that Finland should, in principle, take a positive attitude to the Emu process. Especially from the viewpoint of a small country, a single currency and single exchange rate policy are associated with positive features. Small countries are more likely to experience disturbances in their foreign exchange markets and thus their interest rates are more likely to include a risk premium, which weakens their longer-term prospects for economic growth.

The prime objective of Finland's economic policy is in any case the restoration of balance to the economy. If success is achieved here, Finland will be well placed to participate in more extensive monetary integration. Though the goals of Finland's economic policy are based on domestic considerations, their fulfilment would mean that Finland would meet the Emu criteria in the latter half of the decade.

The central government budget deficit is estimated to amount to some 6 per cent of GDP in 1993. (This takes into account the adjustment in the definition of the central government sector required to bring it into line with EC practice.) According to estimates of the effects of the government's fiscal policy package, the 3 per cent criterion will be met by 1996. Finland's public debt had long been at a low level by international standards, but in recent years it has grown rapidly. The medium-term objective is for the ratio of central government debt to GDP to amount to no more than 70 per cent in 1997; for the general government sector, the objective is 80 per cent after that. These debt ratios should fall towards the end of the decade according to information currently available.

Inflation has been subdued in recent years in Finland; in fact, it has been among the lowest in Europe. But this is partly a result of the deepness of the recession. It is the aim of monetary policy to keep inflation in check also when the economy starts to recover. This would also enable Finland to meet the Emu inflation criterion. In that case, it is likely that fulfilling the criterion on long-term interest rates would not pose a problem either. Finland may not be able to squeeze the risk premium down to zero, owing to her small size and remote location, but the stabilization of inflation at a low level would probably keep the long-term interest rate differential below the upper limit set by the criterion.

In conclusion

Events in recent years in Finland, as elsewhere in Europe, have demonstrated that the effective conduct of exchange rate policy depends crucially on the underlying state of the economy as well as on the other areas of economic policy. But the relationship runs the other way as well, since exchange rate policy affects economic developments. Despite the abruptness and magnitude of recent events, it is important to retain a longer-term perspective in setting objectives for exchange rate policy.

Beginning in the 1980s, one of the priorities of Finnish economic policy has been to break the devaluation cycle and to bring about behavioural and structural changes that would strengthen the economy's competitiveness and enhance its ability to adjust to open international competition. The fixed-exchange rate regime had an important role to play in these endeavours; it was a key instrument of economic policy.

The adjustment needs facing the Finnish economy have been exceptionally great, on account of both domestic factors and external shocks. This has led to a change in the exchange rate regime. The regime shift will be of crucial importance for putting the economy back on a balanced growth path. But it is equally important that the regime shift is not used — in Finland or in other countries that are currently floating their currencies — as a disguise for an attempt to address the current economic crisis as a demand management problem. Structural changes are needed even more than ever.

Adjusting to European integration is an additional challenge to Finland. Deepening of co-operation in exchange rate policy in Europe would help Finland to make the necessary economic adjustment, regardless of its own exchange rate policy. And at least in the slightly longer term, participation in European exchange rate co-operation has clear advantages for Finland.

Chapter 20

A Norwegian perspective

Harald Bøhn
Market Operations Department, Norges Bank

The linking of the Norwegian krone to a currency basket

From 1978 to 1990, the krone exchange rate was linked to a trade-weighted basket of currencies. However, the krone exchange rate was adjusted on a number of occasions, the last time on 11 May 1986, when the krone was devalued.

The weights in the currency index were chosen with a view to stabilizing the competitiveness of Norwegian exports of manufactured goods. In principle, the export industry's competitiveness would not be affected by international currency fluctuations if the krone exchange rate was kept stable as measured by the index. If the krone appreciated against one of the basket currencies, Norwegian exporters' competitiveness would weaken in relation to producers in that country.

The exchange rate regime ensured that the krone at the same time depreciated against the other basket currencies so that, on average, competitiveness would be maintained provided that price and cost inflation did not exceed that of the basket countries.

In the two years following the devaluation in 1986, Norges Bank generally intervened in the foreign exchange market only when the exchange rate index neared the diversions limits. Since mid-1988, however, Norges Bank smoothed exchange rate fluctuations to an even further extent. There were several reasons for this:

- Norwegian banks had scaled down their activity in the foreign exchange market. Small transactions could therefore have a major impact on the exchange rate index and cause unrest in the market.
- The credibility of the fixed-exchange rate policy had been strengthened, making it easier for Norges Bank to stabilize the exchange rate index also within the diversion limits.

- Fewer interventions were required to prevent exchange rate movements which could entail dramatic effects.
- Exchange rate stability would reduce the currency risk attached to the Norwegian krone, making it easier to keep interest rates at a low level.

In order to produce a liquidity and interest rate effect through its exchange market interventions, Norges Bank has generally intervened by buying and selling foreign exchange in the spot market. Thanks to a more active intervention strategy the krone exchange rate, as measured by the currency basket, remained very stable in the period from early 1989 to October 1990, when the krone exchange rate was linked to the Ecu.

During most of the 1980s, Norway still had substantial foreign exchange regulations. In the first part of the decade, the regulations were mainly used to keep the interest rate above international rates by regulating capital inflows. After the oil price fall and devaluation in 1986 the regulations were geared towards restricting capital outflows. However, in Norway — as in other countries — the foreign exchange regulations were gradually losing their effect. This necessitated an adjustment of short rates to a level that would produce a balance in the exchange market. The realization that the foreign exchange regulations were becoming less effective ultimately led to their dismantling. After 1 July 1990, only a few regulations remained for the purpose of tax control and current account statistics. However, they are of little or no significance in relation to monetary policy.

The dismantling of the foreign exchange regulations did not give rise to any problems in terms of implementing monetary policy. The exchange rate remained stable even after the deregulation in the summer of 1990, without any significant change in the frequency of interventions.

In the period from the autumn of 1986 up to the linkage of the krone to the Ecu, the interest rate differential against the basket currencies, as well as against the Ecu and the Deutschemark, narrowed. The interest rate differential against the basket currencies hovered around half a percentage point for the three-month rate for most of 1990, while the differential against the Deutschemark was in the order of 1.5-2.0 percentage points.

The linking of the Norwegian krone to the Ecu

On 19 October 1990, the government decided to link the international value of the krone to the Ecu. The central rate was chosen with a view to avoiding an immediate change in the value of the krone. The fluctuation margins around the central rate were kept at 2.25 per cent, i.e. the same as under the previous basket system.

By stabilizing the krone against the Ecu, Norway also linked its currency to a group of currencies farther removed from its trade pattern than was the case under the previous basket. As a result, the krone could periodically fluctuate widely against those non-Ecu currencies which are important for our competitiveness. The difference between the previous basket and the Ecu was, however, limited. Taking into account that the Swedish krona and the Finnish markka were linked to similar currency baskets, and that some basket currencies shadowed the Deutschemark, the Ecu currencies' share of the basket was 74 per cent.

When the exchange rate regime was revised, Norges Bank particularly emphasized that a credible fixed-exchange rate policy requires that price and cost inflation in Norway be aligned with the level in the countries to which we peg our currency. Higher price and cost inflation would weaken Norway's competitiveness against EC countries. By linking the Norwegian krone to the Ecu, Norway was also linking the krone to the currencies of a group of countries with price stability as a long-term objective of economic policy. On average, price inflation in Ecu countries was lower than in the basket countries. It was therefore assumed that the new exchange rate regime would place additional constraints on price and cost inflation in Norway than under the previous basket system.

The decision must be seen in terms of the Norwegian authorities' attempts to achieve associate membership in EMS co-operation during the year prior to the linkage. Through the Ecu linkage the government wanted to emphasize its desire for closer co-operation with the EC.

The government's decision of 19 October 1990, to link the krone to the Ecu, was followed up by bilateral swap agreements between Norges Bank and Community central banks for a total amount of Ecu 2bn. It was also agreed that Norges Bank would undertake its intervention policy in the spirit of the fundamental objectives and intentions of the EMS and that Norges Bank and Community central banks would co-operate in response to excessive fluctuations between third-country currencies, EMS currencies, the dollar and other major currencies.

Norges Bank can only draw on the swap credit once its ordinary instruments have been used. This normally means that Norges Bank stabilizes the krone by buying kroner using its own foreign exchange reserves and adjusts the interest rate level with a view to stabilizing the krone exchange rate. The swap credit is as such not a first-line reserve that can be used before other means have been applied.

The purpose of the agreements is to have sufficient funds available in order to support the krone exchange rate. Furthermore, it was generally perceived that when the swap agreements were made public, their existence would in itself enhance confidence in the authorities' ability to stabilize the exchange rate.

Implementation of policy under the Ecu link

October 1990 to August 1992

Norges Bank's intervention policy, aimed at stabilizing the exchange rate with only small deviations from the central rate, was also applied after the Ecu linkage. During the period when the krone was linked to the Ecu, the krone exchange rate remained within an interval of 0.10 to 0.50 percentage point below, or weaker than, the central rate. The krone exchange rate largely remained within 0.20-0.30 percentage point below the central rate, and thus fluctuated very little within the maximum margins of 2.25 per cent against the Ecu.

The use of intervention currencies changed after the introduction of the new regime, with an increase in the use of Deutschemark and private Ecu, and less need for US dollars. There were several reasons for this. With a more stable relationship between the krone and the Ecu the banks were more inclined to take positions in Deutschemark instead of US dollars. The Deutschemark also figured more prominently as a transactions and reserve currency in this period.

From October 1990 to July 1992 the interest rate differential between the three-month eurokrone rate and the average three-month rate in the EC fell from 1 percentage point to 0.4 percentage point. This may have indicated greater confidence in the fixed-exchange rate policy.

The Norwegian interest rate was lower than the EC rate in the period from March-July 1992. The differential between the Norwegian and German three-month rate in the same period declined from 2.8 percentage points in October 1990 to about 1 percentage point in July 1992.

Long-term government bond rates in Norway were somewhat higher than the average rate in the EC in 1992, mostly at about 1/4 percentage point. The interest rate differential against German government bonds was about 1 1/2 percentage points.

Inasmuch as the exchange rate system and exchange rate policy resulted in a stable krone exchange rate against the Ecu, it was reasonable to expect a decline in the interest rate differential between Norway and EC countries.

August to December 1992.

The turbulence in international currency markets spread to Norway in the beginning of July 1992. After Norges Bank sold foreign exchange for Nkr 2.3bn in the first half of the month, the market unrest subsided despite the increase in key rates in a number of European countries on 16 July. However, at the beginning of August the krone came under renewed pressure and, during August and the first week of September, Norges Bank sold foreign exchange equivalent to Nkr 10.5bn. At the same time, money market rates moved on a rising trend. Against this background, the interest rate on central bank overnight lending to banks was raised from 10 to 11 per cent, and the deposit rate for banks from 9 to 11 per cent, with effect from 7 September.

The Bank of Finland's decision on 8 September to suspend the fixed-exchange rate policy for an indefinite period, the increase in Swedish money market rates, tensions within the ERM combined with US dollar weakness led to further unrest on the Norwegian foreign exchange market in September. Norges Bank responded to the turbulence by intervening heavily in support of the krone, accompanied by a tight liquidity policy. Three-month money market rates varied between 15 and 20 per cent during most of this month. This stabilized the foreign exchange market and, in the latter half of the month, Norges Bank bought foreign exchange. Norges Bank's net purchases of kroner in September came to Nkr 8.3bn, which was relatively modest compared with interventions in other European countries. During the turbulence in September non-resident customers generally accounted for the currency outflow, whereas Norwegian operators mainly contributed to a currency inflow.

The krone regained strength in October. Norges Bank repurchased foreign exchange and interest rates fell. At the beginning of November, Norges Bank's foreign currency purchases were higher than the outflow in August and September. At the beginning of November, Norges Bank lowered the overnight lending rate in two steps down to 10 per cent. Money market rates were then lower than they were prior to the turbulence.

When the Swedish central bank signalled higher lending rates on the morning of 19 November, the Norwegian foreign exchange market also became nervous. After it was announced that the Swedish krone would be allowed to float, Norges Bank sold foreign exchange equivalent to Nkr 14bn in the course of one hour. The central bank's overnight lending rate was raised from 10 to 17 per cent on 20 November and daily limits were imposed on the banks' borrowing facility in the central bank. The pressure on the krone persisted that day and foreign exchange sales to support the krone came to Nkr 36.8bn, the largest intervention amount ever in Norway. The bulk of the transactions was effected by Norwegian residents who directly converted krone funds to foreign exchange on 19 and 20 November.

The central bank's overnight lending rate was raised to 25 per cent with effect from 23 November. On the same day, there was a currency inflow, and Norges Bank's net purchases of foreign exchange were equivalent to Nkr 13.9bn. Over the course of the following days, currency flows went both ways and, in the period from 24 to 27 November, Norges Bank's net foreign exchange purchases corresponded to Nkr 4.2bn. Against this background, it was decided to lower the overnight lending rate to 17 per cent with effect from 30 November. The foreign exchange market was relatively stable from 30 November to 4 December, but with a net currency outflow of Nkr 3.1bn. The overnight lending rate was reduced by an additional percentage point to 16 per cent with effect from 7 December.

In November, Norges Bank made use for the first time of the swap agreements entered into with Community central banks after the Ecu linkage.

During the period of turbulence in the foreign exchange market, Norges Bank supplied liquidity by purchasing CDs and issuing fixed-rate loans with short maturities. The overall liquidity supply was constantly adjusted, so that some banks had to draw on the overnight lending facility in excess of the daily limits. These banks had to pay penalty rates which contributed to keeping marginal money market rates at a high level. In most of the period from 20 November to 10 December the three-month money market rates were well above 20 per cent.

The foreign exchange situation changed after 7 December, among other things as a result of expectations of exchange rate realignments in the ERM following the EC summit in Edinburgh in mid-December. Norges Bank's net sales of foreign exchange were equivalent to Nkr 12.1bn in the days to 10 December.

Following consultations with Norges Bank, the Ministry of Finance suspended the central bank's obligation to buy and sell kroner within the established fluctuation margins against the Ecu on 10 December. The decision was taken following a three-week period involving considerable net foreign exchange sales to support the krone. Monetary policy measures initially helped to stabilize the foreign exchange market, but attempts to ease liquidity policy again resulted in a currency outflow which showed no signs of abating. It was also stressed that mounting tensions within the ERM, with a high interest rate level and expectations of exchange rate realignments, would result in problems for Norway's fixed-exchange rate policy. The decision to suspend the intervention obligation was accompanied by a reduction in the central bank overnight lending rate from 16 to 11 per cent and the removal of restrictions on the overnight borrowing facility.

The pressure against the krone in August and September can largely be ascribed to expectations of exchange rate realignments within the ERM. Such realignments would lead to a depreciation of the Norwegian krone against the stronger ERM currencies. When the Italian lira was devalued by 7 per cent, and subsequently floated along with pound sterling, the krone depreciated against the Deutschemark by about 2.5 per cent, with the krone held constant against the Ecu. The pressure against the krone was thus partly due to technical factors.

In November 1992, the turbulence was triggered by Sweden's decision to abandon its fixed-exchange rate policy on 19 November. That decision had an immediate spillover effect on the Norwegian foreign exchange market. Confidence in Norway's ability to maintain the value of the krone against the Ecu deteriorated after Finland and Sweden had to abandon their Ecu link, and their currencies depreciated considerably.

Floating-exchange rate regime

The minister of finance gave an account of the situation in the foreign exchange market to the Storting (Norwegian Parliament) on 11 December 1992 and drew up guidelines for the conduct of monetary policy in the period ahead. He emphasized that monetary policy must be geared to allowing Norges Bank to recover some of the foreign exchange that was sold during the currency crisis. Moreover, Norges Bank was to attach importance to establishing a new fixed-exchange rate level for the krone as soon as international circumstances permitted.

The minister of finance underlined in his statement that the floating-exchange rate did not entail that interest rates could be set solely on the basis of domestic considerations. Interest rates would continue to be dependent on international rates and exchange rate expectations. A distinct Norwegian monetary policy aimed at low interest rates would lead to a depreciation of the krone and thereby to higher price inflation.

In the period after the krone was floated, Norges Bank has operated on the basis of these guidelines. In the days immediately following the decision, the krone exchange rate fell by almost 6 per cent. Since then, the krone exchange rate has gradually appreciated. Money market rates fell rapidly in the first days after the float, but remained at a high level up to the beginning of January 1993. As the krone appreciated against the Ecu, however, interest rates were gradually lowered. Norges Bank used this opportunity to purchase foreign exchange. From the time the krone was floated up to mid-May, Norges Bank purchased foreign exchange amounting to Nkr 47.8bn. By end-April, Norges Bank's international reserves had reached Nkr 121bn.

Both short and long rates have declined more rapidly in Norway than in the rest of Europe. At the beginning of 1993, the interest rate differential against the Ecu and Deutschemark was 1.9 and 3.4 percentage points, respectively, for three-month rates. At the end of April, the Norwegian rates were lower than both the Ecu and Deutschemark rates, with a differential at -0.9 and -0.1 percentage point. For 10-year government bonds the differential against the Ecu fell from 0.7 to -0.6 percentage point in the same period and, against the Deutschemark, from 1.9 to 0.4 percentage point.

Norges Bank has thus not been confronted with any substantial problems in implementing the floating-exchange rate policy. This is probably due to a relatively strong Norwegian economy measured on the basis of a number of traditional criteria. The current account is running a surplus, price inflation is moderate and the central government's financial position is healthy, despite sizeable deficits in recent years. This has contributed to strengthening market confidence in the Norwegian krone, despite the importance of petroleum revenues in the external account and government finances. Not only have the economic fundamentals been positive, but interest rates have been lowered consistently when the krone has been strong, thereby establishing confidence in Norges Bank's determination to maintain a stable krone exchange rate under the floating system.

After Norges Bank lowered the rate on overnight lending to banks from 16.0 to 11.0 per cent on 10 December, the overnight lending rate was cut in twelve steps to 7.50 per cent at the end of May.

Summary

Figures 20.1 to 20.6 provide a summary of the developments in the money and foreign exchange markets after January 1990. Figure 20.1 shows changes in the krone exchange rate in relation to the trade-weighted index and indexed Ecu. The trade-weighted index is constructed based on approximately the same principles as the exchange rate index used by Norges Bank up to October 1990. This index was therefore very stable during this period whereas, since then, it has varied more. In the first part of the period this was mainly due to changes in the US dollar/Deutschemark exchange rate. After the Finnish markka, the Italian lira, pound sterling and the Swedish krona were allowed to float, changes in these exchange rates against ERM currencies also had an effect on the exchange rate index. When the Norwegian krone was floated, both the trade-weighted index and Ecu index fell by about 6 per cent, and then rose again. The trade-weighted index has generally shown larger day-to-day variations than the Ecu index during this period.

Figures 20.2 & 20.3 show the magnitude and frequency of exchange market interventions. For the period as a whole, Norges Bank intervened on about half of the working days. The frequency of interventions was at its lowest in early 1991 (directly following the Ecu linkage) and in the first half of 1992. It also fell slightly right after the floating of the krone, but in the period February-April 1993, Norges Bank intervened frequently to purchase foreign exchange. The intervention amounts were largest in the autumn of 1992 and spring of 1993. In 1990 Norges Bank was a net purchaser of foreign exchange, but in both 1991 and 1992 sales exceeded purchases.

Figures 20.4 & 20.5 show the interest rate differential against the Ecu, Deutschemark and currencies in the trade-weighted index. During most of the period in 1992, Norwegian money market rates were marginally higher than Ecu rates, but also lower for brief periods. In the autumn of 1992 the differential widened and, in December, averaged 4.4 percentage points. The

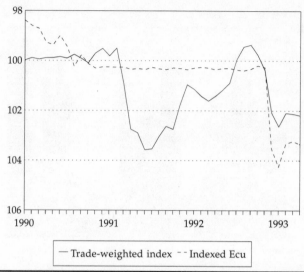

Figure 20.1   Norwegian krone exchange rate measured by the trade-weighted index and indexed Ecu, January 1990-April 1993

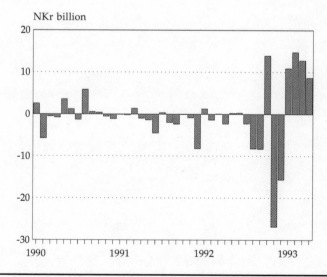

Figure 20.2   Net currency interventions per month in billions of kroner

Per cent of working days

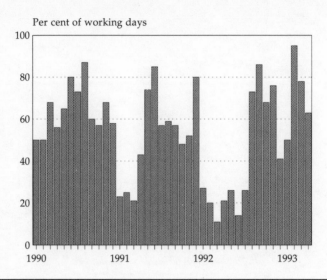

Figure 20.3   **Interventions: Percentage share of working days per month, January 1990-April 1993**

Per cent

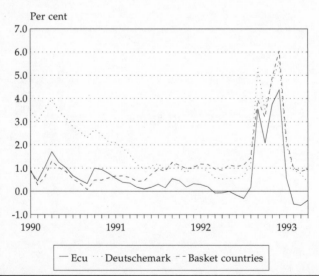

Figure 20.4   **Interest rate differentials NKr-Ecu, NKr-Dm, NKr-basket countries. Three-month euro-rates, January 1990-April 1993**

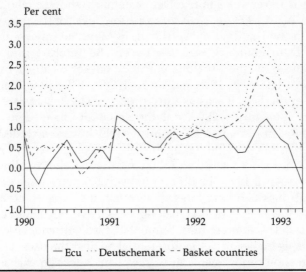

Figure 20.5   **Interest rate differentials NKr-Ecu, NKr-Dm, NKr-basket countries. Five-year bond rates, January 1990-April 1993**

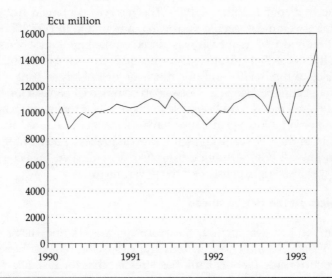

Figure 20.6   **Norge Bank's foreign exchange reserves in millions of Ecu, January 1990-April 1993**

differential then narrowed and has been negative during most of 1993. The interest rate differential against Deutschemark showed about the same trend and, in April 1993, reached a record low level of 0.4 percentage point on average. In the last days of April and, in May, the interest rate differential against Deutschemark was negative. The interest rate differential against currencies in the previous currency basket declined markedly between the devaluation in 1986 and up to 1990. At the time Norway linked its currency to the Ecu, it was slightly positive. The basket rate was higher than the Ecu rate during 1990, but the situation changed in 1991, when interest rates fell in some non-EC countries which were included in the basket. The interest rate differential against the basket currencies rose in 1991 and 1992, but has since narrowed following the decision to allow the krone to float. At end-April 1993, the differential was 0.5 percentage point.

Differentials between long rates show much the same trend as short-rate differentials. However, Norwegian long rates have not fallen below Deutschemark rates. The interest rate differential for Deutschemark, unlike that for short rates, is higher than the differential against the basket.

Figure 20.6 shows movements in Norges Bank's foreign exchange reserves up to April 1993. Changes in reserves reflect central bank intervention operations in the foreign exchange market, with a decrease in autumn 1992 and a rise in the spring of 1993. Moreover, central government foreign debt has increased since autumn 1991, by a total of Nkr 27bn in 1991 and 1992, and Nkr 3.2bn in the first four months of 1993. The reserves continued rising in May, when central government foreign borrowing, amounting to Nkr 10bn, was disbursed. In 1991 and 1992, emphasis was placed on the importance of contingency reserves in the event that private banks were suddenly unable to obtain foreign funding. Since autumn 1991 and, for much of 1992, Norges Bank has had to provide foreign currency loans to Norwegian commercial banks. However, since December 1992, all banks have been able to finance their foreign exchange operations in the market. Norwegian banks have substantially reduced their foreign currency debt in the last years. Foreign borrowing relieved some of the upward pressure on interest rates stemming from Nkr-denominated financing. Borrowing abroad was also less expensive for the government.

Policy choices in the period ahead

Throughout the post-war period, the Norwegian authorities have chosen to define the krone exchange rate in terms of a specific relationship to one or more other currencies. Norges Bank has stressed that for a small, open economy like Norway, stable exchange rates are an important precondition for economic stability. In a letter dated 6 May 1993 to the Ministry of Finance, Norges Bank highlighted the following reasons for resuming a fixed-exchange rate policy when circumstances permit:

- Exchange rate changes have a major impact on the price level because of the high share of imports in domestic demand.
- Exchange rate stability of the krone provides exposed industries with the degree of currency stability which is feasible in a global economy, where currencies tend to fluctuate.
- During income settlements, it is important that the social partners take due account of Norway's external competitiveness and do not expect this issue to be resolved through exchange rate adjustments.
- Uncertainty about the krone exchange rate results in higher real interest rates, because of the risk premium involved. Calculations in Norges Bank indicate that the real interest rate in periods when exchange rate adjustments were used frequently was 12 percentage points higher than it could have been if we had maintained a stable exchange rate.

Experience from a number of countries shows that monetary policy should be formulated with the objective of avoiding price inflation. Otherwise, the expectations generated by a more expansionary monetary policy will be built into price and wage formation. Inflation is thereby amplified without having achieved sustainable positive effects on the real economy.

As an EC applicant, it is difficult for Norway to envisage another alternative than linking the krone to European currencies. Developments over the past year have clearly demonstrated the drawbacks of a unilateral Ecu link, which Norway was forced to abandon, despite fairly sound economic fundamentals. A unilateral link will obviously require a better functioning EMS. A more attractive alternative seems to be to participate on an equal footing with EC countries in their exchange rate co-operation. However, so far, the signals indicate that this can not take place until membership negotiations have been concluded, or Norway accedes to the EC.

International conditions may also necessitate the retention of the present floating-exchange rate regime over a relatively long period. In this period, it is important to implement monetary policy with the aim of keeping price and cost inflation under control. Otherwise, the real economic costs required to regain stability may be considerable.

References

This article is, to a large extent, based on the following publications from Norges Bank:

- Christiansen, Anne Berit (1990): *The New Exchange Rate System, Economic Bulletin 1990/4*, p. 262-265

- Norges Bank (1989): *Foreign Exchange Market, Economic Bulletin 1989/3*, p. 163-169

- Norges Bank (1993): *Norges Bank, Annual Report 1992*, p. 5-9

- Spildrejorde, Trygve (1992): *Norway's exchange rate system after linking the krone to the Ecu in October 1990, Economic Bulletin* 1992/4, p. 261-270.

Chapter 21

A Swedish perspective

Thomas Franzén, Deputy Governor & Kerstin Mitlid, Senior Economist
Sveriges Riksbank

Introduction

In November 1992, after nearly 60 years with various versions of fixed-exchange rate systems, the Central Bank of Sweden — the Riksbank — was forced to pursue a floating-exchange rate policy.

The objective of monetary policy during the period of fixed-exchange rates was to achieve price stability, and the fixed rate thus served as an intermediate objective. The prerequisite, if a fixed-exchange rate is to result in price stability, is that there is broad political support for the objective of the exchange rate. If market agents are confident that such support exists, the awareness that excessively high wage and price increases inevitably lead to unemployment have a restraining effect on price formation. If, in contrast, there is a lack of confidence in the durability of the exchange rate policy, the adjustment to balanced price development must occur through increased unemployment.

Developments in Sweden and the rest of Europe last autumn showed, however, that it was impossible to maintain confidence in a fixed-exchange rate regime when the adjustment requirements had been allowed to become too great. Political support for the fixed-exchange rate system did not suffice, since the system had not been linked to an economic policy compatible with a fixed-exchange rate. In an internationalized world with deregulated markets that function efficiently, and in which the agents often have large currency exposures, lack of confidence in a currency quickly leads to massive pressure.

Developments during the 1980s

When the Riksbank was forced to abandon the fixed-exchange rate system in November 1992, no adjustments in exchange rates had been made for ten years. Up to May 1991, the Swedish krona was tied to a trade-weighted basket of currencies, and was allowed to fluctuate within a band of +/- 1.5 per cent. On 17 May 1991, the krona was linked unilaterally to the European currency unit (Ecu), with no change in exchange rates or the fluctuation band. The link with the Ecu was motivated by Sweden's desire for a closer relationship with the European Community, manifested by the application for membership some weeks later.

The large devaluation of the krona in October 1982 was intended as the starting point for the krona as a hard currency. This devaluation followed a devaluation in the preceding year, and in combination these amounted to a devaluation of slightly more than 25 per cent. The underlying strategy was to transfer resources from the sheltered sector of the economy to the sector exposed to competition.

As a consequence of Sweden's long history of devaluations, inflationary expectations were high. Thus, it was of great importance to demonstrate clearly and unambiguously that there was political support for the exchange rate objective. This was done in part though the introduction of the so-called 'foreign borrowing norm' which did not allow the State to increase its borrowing in foreign currencies — accordingly a balance of payments deficit, for example, had to be financed by the private sector. Expectations of high inflation were therefore quickly reflected in interest-rate levels in Sweden as the private market sector sought compensation for the greater risk of devaluation. The concept was that when fiscal policy was excessively expansive it would result in higher interest rates, the latter development acting as a restraint on the national budget.

The sharp increase in prices, wages and salaries during the 1980s, and the consequent decreases in competitiveness, show that this strategy failed. Expectations of high inflation, coupled with the expansion of credit following deregulation of the credit market, caused inflation to rise steeply. The price increases in equity shares and the real estate market were especially notable. The timing of financial deregulation was determined mainly by the fact that innovations in the financial markets had reduced the effectiveness of controls. When the credit market was deregulated the prevailing tax system was structured in such a way that it favoured accumulation of debt. This was because interest expense was fully deducible for tax purposes while the marginal tax rate was high. Reform of the tax system was not feasible, politically, at the time the credit market was regulated.

With a fixed-exchange rate, the possibilities of employing monetary policy in areas other than managing the exchange rate are severely limited. The few opportunities that did exist were utilized, however. Sterilized interventions in the spot and forward market, as well as the scope available within the exchange-rate band, were used to maintain interest rates at a level higher than required to keep currency flows in balance.

Amortization of the State's foreign debt also helped to tighten monetary policy. However, low sensitivity to interest rates due to the tax system, notably in the household sector, substantially reduced the effectiveness of monetary policy. It thereby became the task of fiscal policy to offset the strong inflationary pressures created by the supply problems and the expansion of credit. This assignment failed. Despite many years of strong growth in tax bases, and a progressive tax system without indexation, the government budget showed only limited surpluses. In fact, the fiscal policy was expansionary and the underlying budget, adjusted for cyclical factors, had a large structural deficit (see Figure 21.1).

Despite substantial decreases in competitiveness, unemployment in Sweden continued to be very low for a long period. The strong growth in sectors that were not exposed to competition — the service sector and construction sector expanded explosively — were important factors (see Figure 21.2).

Nor did the growth of employment in the public sector provide scope for growth in other sectors. As a result, the labour market did not signal the negative consequences of rising inflation.

The downturn in the international economy in the beginning of 1990, and the reform of the tax system, made the need for cost adjustments clear. After the government, at the end of 1990, had announced its intention to apply for membership of the European Community and the krona had been linked to the Ecu in May 1991, confidence in the fixed-exchange rate strengthened, and awareness increased that the cost adjustments had to be effected through reductions in wage and salary costs. Despite this, there was underlying uncertainty with respect to the long-term viability of exchange rate policy. This uncertainty was expressed in recurring foreign exchange crises, crises that were overcome through foreign exchange interventions and sharp increases in interest rates. By letting the krona weaken within the framework of the foreign exchange-rate band, the Riksbank also took advantage of opportunities to create expectations of a stronger krona and thereby generate capital inflows. For such a strategy to succeed, however, confidence in the fixed-exchange rate had to be strong. But the effectiveness of monetary policy decreased with each crisis, and successively higher interest-rate differentials were required in order to reverse currency flows.

The 1992 foreign exchange crisis

High interest rates in Sweden caused the private sector to increase its liabilities in foreign currency over a period of several years. These liabilities were largely offset by assets in foreign currency in form of direct investments. In many cases, however, the corporate sector borrowed to finance

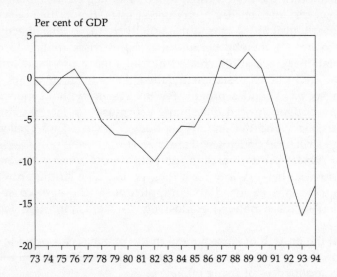

Figure 21.1   Government financial savings, percentage of gross national product
1993-4 forecast: Ministry of Finance, April 1993

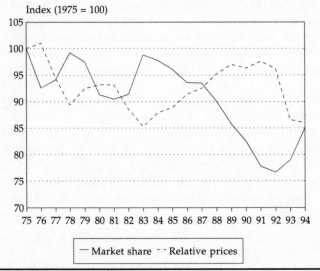

Figure 21.2   Relative prices and market shares
1994 forecast: Ministry of Finance, April 1993

financial or tangible assets in Swedish krona. As a result, large unsecured currency positions were built up.

During the latter part of the 1980s, international investors' placements of funds increased, both in terms of volume and opportunities to select a country in which to invest. Technical developments, deregulation and private savings that were increasingly being channelled to institutional investors other than banks provided the background for this trend. The Swedish government's application for membership in the European Community and the krona's linkage to the Ecu spurred the interest of international investors in Swedish securities. The G10 Report[1] of the autumn of 1992 noted, for example, that many American investors invested in securities in high-interest-rate countries within the European exchange rate mechanism (ERM), while guarding against risks in low-interest-rate currencies within the ERM. Prior to the Danish referendum on the Maastricht Treaty in June 1992, confidence in exchange-rate co-operation within the ERM appears to have been so strong that investors ignored exchange-rate risks associated with this type of strategy. With hindsight, considering the imbalances between the economies in Europe that had built up over a period of years in the absence of exchange rate adjustments, the confidence in the ERM system was excessive. However, the existence of deregulated financial markets and well-developed derivative markets led investors to believe that they had good possibilities to close their positions if a currency should come under pressure. Despite the fact that the Swedish krona's link to the Ecu was unilateral, it is likely that it was regarded as a substitute for the currencies of other high-interest-rate countries. This induced international investors to purchase Swedish securities.

Capital controls in Sweden were abolished by degrees during the latter half of the 1980s. The final step was taken in 1989 when the prohibition against foreign investors' purchases of Swedish securities denominated in Swedish kronor was lifted. However, technical innovations and the growth in financial markets had diminished the effectiveness of currency controls for some time. As a result, the volume of capital flows did not increase significantly after deregulation.

While changes in capital controls are not considered to have contributed substantially to net exposure in kronor, many other factors resulted in such exposure during the latter part of the 1980s and the early-1990s. For example, technical innovations and the fact that Sweden has a large number of

[1] 'International Capital Movements and Foreign Exchange Markets', A Report to the Ministers and Governors of the Group of Ten by the Group of Deputies, April 1993. Lamberto Dini of the Banco d'Italia is the chairman of the Group of Deputies.

multinational companies increased currency exposure. Many of the players who were exposed in kronor also acted as professional investors, in the sense that they immediately took corrective measures when concerned about exchange rates.

During the spring of 1992, the currency market in Sweden was relatively calm, except for a period in April when instability in the Finnish market spread to Sweden. However, investors' greater propensity to control more carefully currency risk during the recurring currency crises clearly showed that uncertainty about the fixed-exchange rate had increased, since it was no longer possible to stimulate inflows by allowing the exchange rate to weaken within the fluctuation band. On the contrary, the weaker krona resulted in larger outflows. The Riksbank accordingly decided that it was no longer possible to utilize the full width of the formal band. The exchange rate was thus stabilized at a level just above the central rate.

Following the Danish rejection of the Maastricht proposal in June 1992, the imbalances that had developed between the economies in Europe could no longer be obscured by expectations that the move toward a common currency would create convergence. When it then became clear that the outcome of the French referendum, to be held in September, was highly uncertain, the high-interest-rate currencies in Europe came under heavy pressure. In addition, the Swedish krona was hit especially hard by concern about the Finnish markka and, later, the decision to let the markka float.

Rapidly accelerating unemployment and sharply rising budget deficits clearly showed the seriousness and size of the imbalances that had built up in the Swedish economy during the latter part of the 1980s. Although cost-adjustments had begun, and many structural faults in the economy that had caused the imbalances were being corrected, the dramatic increase in the budget deficit overshadowed these actions. The market became increasingly concerned about the ability to maintain the fixed-exchange rate, and the krona was subjected to severe pressure. To some extent, the crisis in the financial sector may also have contributed to reduced confidence in the possibility of defending the fixed-exchange rate.

During the September crisis, the government, the Parliament and the Riksbank showed great determination in their efforts to defend the fixed-exchange rate and to correct the underlying imbalances in the economy. The marginal interest rate was raised successively to 500 per cent, while massive interventions were made in both the currency and the money markets. Two crisis packages were introduced in Parliament, both of them the result of collaboration between the governing coalition and the opposition parties. The uneasiness in the currency market subsided, but resurfaced with renewed force in November when it became clear that the measures taken in September had not significantly remedied the deficit in the government's budget. In a situation where the professional agents in the market were prepared to terminate their exposure in kronor at the least sign of instability, the Riksbank initially elected not to raise marginal interest rates when currency outflows resumed. These outflows occurred when Swedish companies, wanting to reduce their exposure at year-end, accelerated the realignment of currency positions due to concern for interest-rate hikes and consequent high costs of financing. On 19 November, after an increase in the interest rate and following massive interventions in the spot and forward markets, the Riksbank was forced to abandon the fixed-exchange rate.

Interventions by the Riksbank during 1992 totalled nearly SKr 250bn, including SKr 115bn in the spot market and SKr 133bn in the forward market. State borrowing in foreign currency, which amounted to the equivalent of approximately SKr 180bn, had replenished the foreign exchange reserve. Approximately SKr 60bn was used for loans to commercial banks, which had experienced problems in rolling over their foreign loans in September, due in part to large credit losses. After abandoning the fixed-exchange rate, the Riksbank had forward liabilities exceeding on-balance sheet assets in its foreign exchange reserve.

It is difficult to identify with any certainty the players and the motives behind the massive outflows of currency. In a situation where many players have large open exposures, there is always a risk of substantial outflows once the market shows sign of instability. Efficient financial and derivative markets make it possible to close out quickly currency positions. Although some problems related to the markets' operation (liquidity, for example) arose during the foreign exchange crises, the markets continued to function. As a result it was possible to reduce exposure in kronor even during the worst turbulence.

Much of the currency outflows were generated when many players reduced their exposure in kronor in the forward market. These transactions took place to a large extent via foreign banks. Developments in the forward market may have been caused by many different decisions. First, Swedish companies with liabilities in foreign currency may have turned to foreign banks to hedge those liabilities. Second, international investors may have hedged their holdings of securities denominated in kronor through foreign banks. During a period of currency instability, American investors who held Swedish securities, and who earlier, based on their confidence in the so-called convergence theory, had hedged their currency exposures in the German forward market, probably hedged their kronor assets in the Swedish market instead. Third, developments in the forward market could be explained by foreign players' forward sale of kronor for speculative purposes. The G10 Report showed, however, that a very large percentage of the portfolio changes in Europe during the autumn were caused by a desire to reduce currency exposure, and were due only to a small degree to pure speculation. A Riksbank survey of important players in the Swedish market indicates that this was also true in Sweden.

The lesson that can be learned from last autumn's turbulence is that it is impossible for a central bank to defend a fixed-exchange rate if there are major unsolved imbalances in a country's economy. A fixed rate can be defended for a brief period. However, if market participants believe that the fundamental problems responsible for loss of confidence in the fixed-exchange rate are not in the process of being solved, instability in the market will increase.

Floating-exchange rate

Shaping monetary policy

When the Riksbank was forced to abandon its fixed-exchange rate policy, the simple, intermediate objective that this represented also disappeared. The long-term objective of stable prices remained, but other intermediate objectives or models had to be designed to control monetary policy. On 15 January 1993, the Riksbank set an inflation target of 2 per cent, plus or minus one percentage point, in Sweden in 1995 and onwards.

With a floating-exchange rate, several indicators are used in order to pursue a monetary policy in accordance with the objective. The aim is to predict, in time, if inflation is heading in the wrong direction. It is also important to understand the manner in which monetary policy affects inflation, as well as the time-lag involved. The optimal situation occurs when it is possible to establish an intermediate objective that is directly controllable and which shows a stable link with inflation. In countries that have established an intermediate objective, various measures of money supply are most commonly used. But money supply has, in most cases, either been difficult to control or has shown instability relative to the rate of inflation. Studies of Swedish data show, for example, that there is a connection between M3 and inflation, but that M3 is not suitable as an intermediate target due to problems in controlling the money supply directly by means of interest rates.

Instead of establishing an intermediate objective, Swedish monetary policy is designed with the aid of a broad spectrum of indicators of inflationary pressure in the economy. It has been demonstrated that the exchange rate, the long-term interest rate, yield curves, as well as various monetary aggregates, can serve as indicators of inflationary trends. Econometric estimates designed to illustrate the connection between monetary policy instruments and inflation have also been made. Since the data used in the estimates are derived from a period with a fixed-exchange rate and other structural differences — a different tax system and a different situation in the financial markets, for example — interpretation of the results is complicated. A report showing how the development of indicators is proceeding has been published[1]. It shows that an increase of one percentage point in the nominal interest rate appears to reduce real aggregate demand by approximately 0.5 per cent within one year. A one-per cent increase in the real exchange rate seems to result in a decrease in real aggregate demand by some 0.1 to 0.2 percentage points within a year.

The change to a floating-exchange rate has not involved a need to change monetary policy instruments. The marginal interest-rate scale, used to control the overnight interest rate, is functioning efficiently, but has been adjusted so that it is easier to adjust this rate in small steps.

The so-called 'foreign borrowing norm' was lifted in connection with the change to a floating-exchange rate. An important purpose of the rule was that to restrain fiscal policy and to support the fixed-exchange rate policy. With a floating-exchange rate, the need for this type of norm decreased. Because the amount of borrowing must still be co-ordinated with monetary policy, decisions of the National Debt Office with respect to borrowing in foreign currency are made in consultation with the Riksbank.

Developments in 1993

When the fixed-exchange rate was abandoned, the necessary process of adapting to 'permanently' lower wages, salaries and prices had begun. The Riksbank thus continued to face the task of pursuing a monetary policy that did not interrupt this trend, in the new environment with a floating-exchange rate. However, the recession in Sweden — which is deeper than that in most other industrialized countries — and the example set by Great Britain in dealing with interest-rate policy after sterling was allowed to float, created expectations of a substantial and rapid easing of monetary policy. The recession in Sweden is largely attributable to necessary adjustments following the imbalances built up during the 1980s.

The deep recession points to the need to reduce interest rates on a long-term basis. It is the Riksbank's view, however, that premature reductions in short (policy-controlled) rates would have little chance of becoming permanent due to the negative effects such reductions can have on inflationary expectations and long-term interest rates.

Against this background, the Riksbank has elected to reduce interest rates cautiously. With a floating-exchange rate, the evaluation of monetary

---

[1] 'Monetary indicators', Sveriges Riksbank, June 1993.

policy must be based on the overall impact that changes in interest rates have on the economy. However, experience gained during the past half-year with a floating-exchange rate shows that — in a situation with an accelerating budget deficit, rising unemployment and great uncertainty with respect to the parliamentary situation — exchange rates and long-term interest rates can easily move strongly. The exchange rate has shown high sensitivity to uncertainty about economic policy. As a result, it has been difficult to anticipate and control the total impact of monetary policy.

Since the krona began to float, on 19 November 1992, and up to July of the current year, the Riksbank has reduced the marginal interest rate from 12.5 to 8.50 per cent, reductions that have been made in nine stages (see Figure 21.3). Short-term rates in July were slightly more than 3 percentage points lower than during the spring of 1992, before the crisis started. Rates in Sweden have been lowered somewhat faster than in Germany, with the result that the interest differential in short-term rates has declined by approximately half of one percentage point during the past year. Long-term rates were more than one percentage point lower in July, compared with the spring of 1992 (see Figure 21.4).

The Riksbank's primary concern is the inflationary stimuli generated during the first six months after the sharp depreciation of the krona. These inflationary stimuli derive, in the first place, directly from rising prices of imports. Since imports account for 30 per cent of consumption, these price increases have a strong impact on consumer prices. The depreciation of the krona is also substantially strengthening the competitiveness of Swedish companies. They can choose between exploiting the improved relative prices of their products or increasing their profit margins. If companies do not believe that the improvement in their competitiveness will be lasting, there is a substantial risk that much of the gains attributable to depreciation will be used to boost margins. This in turn can lead to demands for higher wages and salaries. At the same time that the sector of the economy that is exposed to competition is being stimulated sharply, higher prices of imports directed to the protected sector results in lower demand.

Domestic demand is weak. Private consumption is being restrained by consolidation of household debt and the increased propensity to save — both caused by high unemployment and the structural reforms that have been implemented or announced. As a result of over-production in the construction sector during the latter part of the 1980s, it will also take some time before demand in this sector again increases. There is thus a clear risk that the Swedish economy may be divided into an over-stimulated export sector and an excessively-weak domestic sector. Pursuing an aggressive interest rate policy, leading to an excessive weakening of the krona, will therefore not contribute to lifting the economy out of the existing problems.

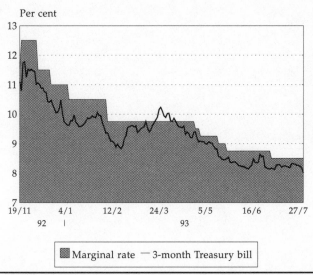

Figure 21.3   Marginal interest rate and short-term market rate

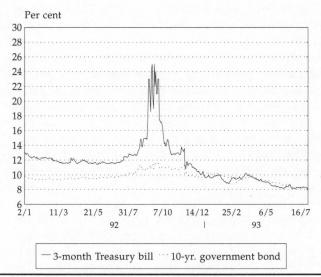

Figure 21.4   Short- and long-term interest rates in Sweden

Figure 21.5   Trend of exchange rates, 1 January 1992 - 31 May 1993

The combination of the depreciated krona and declining interest rates is providing a strong stimulus to aggregate demand. Accordingly, Sweden's monetary conditions have eased and contributed to an expansionary effect on the economy during the period since the krona was allowed to float. As of 1 July, the krona was 17 per cent weaker (against the Ecu index) than at the beginning of November last year. At its lowest level at the end of March, the krona had depreciated 20 per cent (see Figure 21.5).

What has happened to inflationary expectations? The long-term interest rate and information that can be derived from the yield curve constitute key indicators of the trend of inflationary expectations. The shift in the implicit forward interest rate curve (a more sophisticated method of interpreting yields over varying periods) shows that inflationary expectations have not increased since the krona was allowed to float. Long-term interest rates have also followed the downward trend of short-term rates, but not as much. The earlier distinctly negative slope of the yield curve has thus tended to flatten. The collective wage and salary agreements concluded during the spring also indicate that inflationary expectations will be dampened. Despite the strong increases in earnings forecast for industrial companies, it appears that wage and salary demands are kept down. Other indicators of inflationary pressure in the economy confirm that such pressure is very low over the short-term, but they send mixed signals as regards the somewhat longer-term trend.

Experience during the floating-rate period shows the sensitivity of the currency market to changed expectations. In retrospect, it may be noted that the 5 February reduction in the marginal interest rate by three quarters of one per cent was too large. The market's reaction showed that this was interpreted as indicating that the Riksbank had reduced its emphasis on the inflation objective and had started on a path toward rapid reductions in interest rates. Money market interest rates declined, accompanied by a substantial weakening of the exchange rate. To stem the market's unwarranted expectations, the Riksbank intervened in both the money market and the currency market. This produced the desired results in the form of a stronger krona and lower long-term interest rates.

Another incident illustrates how strongly the market is influenced by uncertainty with respect to policy. This involved the period of political unrest in March when there was concern over the government's ability to obtain parliamentary approval of its budget consolidation measures. The exchange rates weakened noticeably, while long-term interest rates rose. The Riksbank decided that there were no prospects of influencing expectations through currency interventions. The interventions that had been made for some time to support the strengthening of the krona therefore ceased. It was not until the political unrest had subsided that long-term interest rates declined and the exchange rate again strengthened.

The currency interventions by the Riksbank were made because the government was borrowing in foreign currency. During the coming half-year the government will borrow a net amount of approximately SKr 50bn from outside Sweden's borders. The Riksbank believes that this level of foreign borrowing is well in line with the objectives of monetary policy at the present time. If it is deemed desirable to do so, the government's borrowing in foreign currency can be siphoned into the market, a move equivalent to a sterilized intervention in the currency market. Another alternative would be for the Riksbank to replenish the currency reserve. To prevent such a move from causing increased liquidity in the economy and lower interest rates, the Riksbank will have to drain the liquidity in some manner.

As has been publicly announced, large parts of the government's borrowing in foreign currency during 1993 will be siphoned into the market. The reason for this is that the Riksbank believes that the weakening of the krona has gone too far. This weakening has probably been caused by players who were left with unsecured liabilities in foreign currency when the fixed-exchange rate was abandoned, and who are now liquidating them at a rapid rate. The incentive for portfolio adjustment lies partly in the reduced interest-rate differential — which offers opportunities for interest arbitrage — and partly in the fact that the shift to a floating-exchange rate has increased uncertainty about the future trend of exchange rates. Balance sheet reconstructions in the corporate sector are also contributing to the reduction in foreign loans.

The Riksbank is therefore electing to siphon currency derived from government borrowing into the market when conditions for exerting a positive impact on the trend of exchange rates are deemed to be favourable. Up to and including July this year, the Riksbank had intervened for a total of approximately SKr 54bn.

Future exchange rate regime

For a small, open, economy with a large volume of foreign trade, a fixed-exchange rate regime is very likely the preferable one. The fixed-exchange rate must be credible, however. This requires that the country's own economy be in balance and that the country or countries to whose currencies the economy is tied exhibit stability and parallel developments. The events of last year show that these requirements become more imperative in a world with large, well-developed deregulated financial markets. Co-ordination of economic policies increases the credibility of exchange rates. This experience also shows not only the interdependence between different economies in respect of formal links, but also the fact that a unilateral link to a currency or basket of currencies is not as likely to be successful as a bilateral connection or participation in a co-operative exchange rate program. As Sweden moves closer to association with the European Community, it is natural to link the krona to one or more EC currencies.

As a member of the Community, Swedish participation in the EC's system for exchange rate co-operation will be an equally natural step. This is true even after the recent severe strains on the ERM and the resulting changes to the rules of the system, announced in early August. Exchange rate stability is an important part of the European integration process and efforts to find ways of re-establishing stable exchange rates within the EC must be made.

How and when this goal will be achieved is, as yet, too early to tell, but it will undoubtedly take time. The absence of a stable institutional framework to which the krona can be linked implies, in combination with the imbalances still characterizing the Swedish economy, that the krona is likely to remain floating for quite some time.

Chapter 22

A UK perspective

Robin Leigh-Pemberton
Former Governor, Bank of England[1]

On Wednesday 16 September 1992, in chaotic market conditions, the UK
was obliged to suspend its commitment to maintain the value of sterling
within the European exchange rate mechanism, which had been a key element in our monetary policy framework. It is my view that the decision to
join the ERM in October 1990 was right in the circumstances; that having
joined, we were right to endeavour to stick with it; and that, in the circumstances which evolved, we were also right to withdraw. In this chapter, I
hope to persuade you that that view is correct, before going on to discuss
briefly the prospects which we now face.

The decision to join the ERM

The protracted debate about UK membership of the ERM aroused great
passions on either side. It was not solely a debate about monetary management. In a fundamental sense it was about this country's role in Europe.
Were we — in the context not just of monetary, but also of wider political,
evolution in Europe — going to remain on the outside with minimal influence on the course of the debate or were we going to join in arrangements
even if some might have misgivings about them, in order to be able to
influence their evolution from the inside? For a long time we temporized —
we would join 'when the time was ripe'. But there came a point at which
we could no longer duck that issue. It is an issue that will not easily go
away.

[1] *This chapter is based on the governor's speech to the CBI Eastern Region Annual Dinner on 8
October 1992.*

The monetary arguments for and against ERM entry were difficult to disentangle from that political context. At one extreme, Euro-enthusiasts argued as if tying ourselves to the D-mark was the only way of securing internal and external stability. At the other, Euro-sceptics argued that joining the ERM was inevitably a recipe for disaster. At this level, both statements were too sweeping in their generality.

It would frankly be humiliating — and I mean nationally rather than institutionally or personally — if we had to accept that we could only manage our affairs effectively and responsibly if we were subject to external constraint. It could only mean that we lack either the wit or the determination to manage our own affairs. In fact, we came very close in the mid-1980s, outside the ERM, to achieving a stable basis for sustainable longer-term growth, until the excessive expansion of some five years ago sparked off the inflation, the consequences of which we are still suffering. Belonging to the ERM is not, therefore, a necessary condition for a successful monetary policy.

But that does not mean that tying our currency to those of a group of countries with a common commitment to stability may not be helpful in achieving our domestic goals, as a support to self-discipline — or indeed that it may not be the best means in certain circumstances; and exchange rate stability against our major trading partners, while it cannot simply be decreed, is — if it can be maintained — in itself a benefit to industry. For eighteen months or more after we had joined, the ERM was in my view indeed helpful. It provided badly needed reassurance that we would persist with the policy of stabilization notwithstanding the pain that this was bound to cause in the short-term. This helped to maintain financial market confidence, notably — because it was a bipartisan approach — through the sensitive election period; and, as domestic inflation subsided, ERM membership allowed interest rates to be steadily reduced from 15 per cent to 10 per cent — that is, to around the levels of our major Community partners, which is more than might have been achieved had we been outside the ERM during that period. During that period, therefore, membership did not seriously conflict with our domestic monetary policy needs.

But over the summer a conflict began to emerge and it became increasingly severe. There was, it has to be said, always a risk that such a conflict would develop. In any pegged-exchange rate system where there is confidence that parities will be maintained, nominal interest rates tend to converge. As a result member countries lose some of their independent ability to direct monetary policy to domestic stabilization. In fact, it need not matter if all member countries are at a similar point in the economic cycle. But it becomes a source of tension if their cyclical positions diverge, with the single interest rate becoming both inappropriately low for the country seeking to moderate inflation and inappropriately high for the country trying to combat recession.

In practice the ERM, which provides for margins of fluctuation around central rates, can accommodate a significant degree of what one might regard as normal cyclical divergence. It operated after all satisfactorily for five years without any parity adjustments until the recent upheaval. And in opting for 6 per cent margins the UK had significant protection against this potential problem of cyclical divergence, in either direction.

Our problem arose because the degree of divergence between the domestic policy needs of Germany on the one hand and those of much of the rest of Europe on the other became wholly abnormal, and it was this quite abnormal tension that tested the margin of tolerance built into the ERM to destruction.

Chiefly, this degree of divergence resulted from the very severe difficulty which Germany is having in coping with the consequences of reunification. This has in the event required public sector transfers to the East, largely financed by borrowing, on a scale which has contributed to inflationary pressure which the Bundesbank has had to combat through severe monetary restraint. Meanwhile, in this country, inflationary pressure has substantially eased under the impact of recession which has been unusually protracted by the debt overhang. There was as a result a growing domestic justification for easing monetary policy which, under the ERM constraint, was becoming unnecessarily tight in relation to our objective of medium and longer-term price stability. In each case the domestic circumstances were quite out of the normal run.

This imbalance in the mix of German fiscal and monetary policy was transmitted, through the mechanism of the ERM, to policies being applied elsewhere in the Community and was by no means unique to the UK. For other countries too, the German position was a source of strain. But it was this quite exceptional tension between domestic policy requirements in Germany and the UK, that was the root cause of the pressures that ultimately forced our withdrawal.

I freely admit that, although we recognized the possibility of strains of this sort, we did not foresee the degree to which they would develop when the decision was taken to enter the ERM two years ago. I can only say that in this we were in good company! Indeed, the German government itself underestimated the costs of unification. The monetary case for joining was, still in my judgment, not only a very reasonable course but also a desirable one in the light of our knowledge at the time. And the broader political case for being involved in the European debate rather than watching from the sidelines, was a powerful factor in its favour. I would remind you that at the time the decision was very widely welcomed by both finance and industry and across the political spectrum.

Sticking it out

Many, even among those who had doubts about ERM entry, argued that once we had joined, we had to stick with it — toughing out periods of tension as necessary and accepting the external constraint on domestic policy in the short-term, in order to establish the government's commitment to stability in the longer term. An important monetary reason for joining in the first place was, as I have said, to provide reassurance that prudent policies would be persisted in; and leaving the battlefield at the first whiff of grapeshot (whether by floating or realigning) would have been more damaging — to long-term confidence and inflationary expectations, and hence to the economic costs of stabilization — than not joining the battle at all.

I am not persuaded by the view — expressed more frequently with the benefit of hindsight — that we should have seen the writing on the wall much earlier and drawn the appropriate conclusion at that time. Until quite soon before the UK withdrew from the ERM it was not unrealistic to think that the strains of reunification in Germany could be sufficiently controlled to allow interest rates to begin to fall in the second half of 1992; nor was it unrealistic to think that activity in the UK would be showing clearer signs of recovery by that time. In that case, the ERM constraint on our domestic policy — and the accompanying tension affecting sterling in the ERM itself — could have been expected to ease not far ahead, which in itself provided a justification for hanging on. In the event, far from converging in this way, the domestic situations in Germany, and in the UK and elsewhere, continued to diverge; and the tensions within the ERM intensified.

We knew through the summer that we were sitting on a grumbling volcano. The Danish rejection of Maastricht caused a detectable tremor by putting in doubt progress towards Emu, and thereby seemingly weakening confidence in the commitment to existing ERM parities; and the uncertainty surrounding the French referendum provided further impetus to the build up of pressure and a precise focal point for predictions of an eruption. Fissures developed as first the Nordic currencies that had been linked to the Ecu, and then the Italian lira, came under intensive attack. And the explosion came — as far as sterling was concerned — in response to press allegations that our German partners were looking for a wider realignment that would include the devaluation of sterling.

These latter factors were, however, essentially symptoms of the underlying problem, which was — as I have said — the exceptional and increasing tension between the domestic needs of re-unified Germany on the one hand and much of the rest of Europe, including this country, on the other. In principle it is true that this tension might have been relieved by a real appreciation (through revaluation) of the D-mark, enabling Germany to draw in from abroad resources necessary for the reconstruction of the East (with a subsequent real depreciation as reconstruction progressed). A number of other countries were not prepared to contemplate a realignment of the Deutschemark alone, so that in practice this possible solution was not on the agenda and may in effect have been rejected before sterling joined the system.

It was possible that this situation would change if the French voted to reject Maastricht; or that the immediate pressures in the exchange market would ease if the treaty were enthusiastically endorsed. Even in the later stages of the crisis, therefore, there were powerful reasons for seeking to hold on until that outcome was clear. To have thrown in the towel unilaterally sooner than we had to would have seriously undermined confidence in the government's commitment to its long-term counter-inflationary strategy; and, if it had triggered wider upheaval within the ERM, it could have influenced both the outcome of the French vote and the future evolution of Europe. But when the explosion came, quite suddenly, just a few days before the French vote, its force was quite irresistible.

If general realignment was ruled out, would it have been sensible to devalue on our own? The case for unilateral realignment by the UK (or even in conjunction with Italy, which was in a quite different condition) was, in fact, never very strong in terms of the usual analysis of competitiveness. I recognize, of course, that judgments about competitiveness, and 'appropriate' exchange rate levels, always have a large subjective element in them. But such evidence as has been advanced in support of the assertion that sterling entered the ERM at too high an exchange rate is far from conclusive.

You have to remember that we had already seen a huge sterling depreciation. Against the Deutschemark, sterling fell from around Dm 4.00 in 1985 to around Dm 2.75 in early 1987. Indeed, the attempt to cap sterling's recovery at Dm 3 in 1987 and early 1988 contributed to the subsequent inflationary boom. Some of the competitive advantage we gained at that time was then eroded by our relatively rapid inflation — but much less in terms of, for example, relative labour costs than in terms of relative retail prices. The degree of competitiveness of the Dm 2.95 parity does, of course, depend critically upon the benchmark for comparison. But against the standards of the 1980s as a whole — a period in which the UK was unusually successful in holding its share of export markets — that parity was not uncompetitive. This is clear from the fact that our trade performance vis-à-vis the rest of the EC has actually been rather strong over the past year or so. And businessmen themselves — not least the CBI, which is not well known for its reticence made few representations that, at Dm 2.95, they were uncompetitive against our major European partners.

What does absolutely stand out is that we have been suffering from increasingly weak competitiveness against other parts of the world, notably against the dollar. And this has been true of other ERM currencies which have been collectively driven upwards by the tightness of German monetary policy. In these circumstances the case for unilateral devaluation within the ERM — as opposed to a D-mark revaluation — was unpersuasive, especially since its effect on confidence in the UK was likely to make more remote the lower interest rates which the domestic economy needed, and could instead actually have led to higher interest rates.

Perhaps I might at this point digress for a moment to challenge two suggestions that I have heard made by a number of commentators. The first is that the turmoil in the ERM was all the result of 'the wicked speculator'.

I well understand the widespread distaste at images of dealers gloating over the quick profits they had made at the expense of the nation. But don't be misled into thinking that this is the whole picture. It is in fact a caricature. Much of the selling — almost certainly most of the selling although it is difficult to demonstrate — originates with corporate treasurers or fund managers who are seeking to protect the value of their assets, or those of their employers, clients and customers — including depositors and investors — against devaluation, often in relation to foreign currency liabilities. When there is a clear risk that a currency will lose 5 or 10 per cent of its value overnight there is inevitably a rush for the exit, some of it by the banks but much more through the banks, which anyway have prudential limits on the open position (i.e. the speculative position) they can take against sterling. There are, of course, those who are simply taking a gamble, some on a very large scale. But while they can accelerate or accentuate a problem — acting as a catalyst, if you like — it is implausible to see straight market speculators as the arbitrary origin of a problem in the markets; you have to remember that, if they get it wrong, they can easily lose as much as they hope to gain.

In the emotionally-charged aftermath of sterling's withdrawal from the ERM, I have seen various suggestions for measures to penalize the speculators. I hope that we will think long and hard about any such suggestions. What you cannot do is to target just the supposedly guilty. Any restrictions on the free movement of capital designed to prevent speculation against sterling will equally hit those who are simply attempting to preserve the value of the assets they own, or manage on behalf of others — the funds that will pay for all our pensions, for example. The trouble with freedom is that it comes as a package. It would be nice to think that freedom — in any sphere — could be confined to the freedom of people to do only those things we happen to approve of. But that's not the real world.

The second suggestion is that what happened in September 1992 could have been avoided if only we — the Bank of England and the Treasury — had employed different market tactics or used better operational techniques. You wouldn't expect me to agree with that — and I don't. But it's the easiest thing in the world to say that things would have been different when there is no possibility that you will be called upon to prove it!

The root cause of the pressure against sterling was, as I have explained, the unexpected emergence of the extreme tension between Germany's domestic monetary needs and our own. It was clearly much more fundamental than technicalities. Because of that fundamental tension, trying to defend our ERM parity was forcing us into actions which were, by the end, becoming increasingly perverse.

Take, for example, intervention in the foreign exchange market. We did, of course, deploy the whole range of techniques at our disposal, running from covert, tactical, intervention on an increasing scale, both in London and in other markets, through innovative foreign currency borrowing, to overt intra-marginal intervention both on our own and in conjunction with our partners, before being forced back to intervention at the margin. But for much of the time what we were having to try to do was to force sterling up through $2=£1. Now you didn't have to be a genius to know that sterling at $2 was unsustainable. Certainly, the whole market knew it in their bones. In those circumstances we knew very well that if we got into an overt pitched battle with the market the chances were that we would be seen to lose and that was likely to pull the house down on top of us. As it was, we almost made it to the French referendum, and I am wholly convinced that had we moved to large scale, overt, intervention sooner than we did, we would have hastened rather than postponed the collapse.

Or take interest rates. All would have been well, say the critics, if only we had moved interest rates up sooner than we did. The problem again, was that raising UK interest rates, when the economy was so weak and inflationary pressure so subdued — especially in the context of the debt overhang — would have been regarded not just by the financial markets, but by the world as a whole, as transparently perverse. Ministers rightly were prepared to do whatever was necessary to preserve the parity, but the real question increasingly became whether raising rates would actually help. Frankly, given the persistence of our recession, it would have been regarded as quixotic; far from adding to credibility, it was always likely to bring — indeed in the event it did bring — the latent pressure to a dramatic climax.

Right to withdraw?

When that climax came, and with the imminence of the French referendum, we had no realistic option but to seek the suspension of our obligations. There was no prospect of realignment in that week; the lira had just realigned and failed to hold onto its new parity, and since the outcome of the

French referendum could not be predicted, it would have been impossible to know what set of parities would have been sustainable.

Not surprisingly, given our long struggle to avoid that outcome, the immediate sense of defeat was depressing. But it was, it has to be said, mixed with a sense of relief that we were free from the distortions to policy that the ERM had imposed over the previous six months or so because of the particular pressures arising from German reunification. Sterling's exchange rate fell to a more rational level against the dollar. It was possible, again, to argue with conviction that the government should stick to its plans to control public expenditure rather than contemplate the indulgence of further fiscal relaxation to compensate for an excessively tight monetary policy. And, in the context of the government's public assurances on both its continuing commitment to counter-inflation and on the fiscal position, we were able to recommend an urgently needed 1 per cent easing of monetary policy.

Let me be absolutely clear, I am not suggesting that leaving the ERM frees us from all constraints. Nothing could be further from the truth. Inside or outside the ERM, the crucial need — in the interests of the UK national economy — is to achieve and maintain price stability as the basis on which to achieve sustainable growth in activity and employment. And that will take every bit as much wit and determination outside the ERM as inside. But we are now free to avoid what was threatening to become excessive deflation, going beyond what is necessary to achieve internal stability or convergence; and we are now free to adopt a mix of fiscal and monetary policy which is more appropriate to our domestic needs, and to the longer term.

As I say, in the end, we had no choice but to suspend our membership of the ERM — and the manner of our leaving was of course embarrassing. But it is now clear that the French referendum result was not decisive enough to remove, once and for all, uncertainty about progress towards Emu; and there is still no immediate prospect of an end to the pressures associated with German reunification. In these circumstances, had the mechanism survived intact until 20 September, I suspect that the tensions would have persisted.

Where now?

Our ERM membership once having been suspended, the timing and the exchange rate at which we re-enter — and eventual re-entry should be our objective — will need to be very carefully considered. As Germany succeeds in bringing under control the consequences of reunification, it must be supposed that German interest rates will eventually fall and that the present abnormal strength of the Deutschemark against other currencies generally will decline. Sterling, on the other hand, although immediately weaker than before, following our departure from the ERM and the rebalancing of domestic policy, is likely to recover against the D-mark as activity improves. Once a greater degree of convergence has been re-established, our re-entry into the ERM would help to promote and sustain stability in both a domestic and a European context. But it would not be helpful either to ourselves or to our partners for sterling to rejoin the mechanism until the divergent conditions that led to our suspension had begun to subside.

In the meantime, there have been demands that we should not be afloat without a policy anchor. This is a legitimate concern, but we must be careful not to exaggerate it. Anchors can certainly be useful in the right conditions — as I said earlier on in discussing our decision on ERM entry in 1990. But they cannot always be relied upon, and can indeed provide false security if you have the wrong anchor for the conditions — or the chain is too short.

The chancellor addressed these when he announced his new framework for policy on 8 October 1992. The crucial thing, as he has made clear, is that we should be clear in our policy objective and in that respect nothing has changed. Inside or outside the ERM — and I make no apology for repeating this — the objective of policy is to achieve and maintain long-term price stability, not simply for its own sake, but as a necessary condition for achieving our wider economic and social goals through sustainable growth. After the dispiriting experience of boom and bust in the 1960s and 1970s, sadly repeated over the last five years, there is a broader consensus now on the objective of monetary policy than at any time I can remember; and it is a consensus that we unreservedly share with our partners in Europe. That is what we have to hold on to. It is embodied in the Maastricht convergence conditions which in any case remain appropriate aims for the UK in the interest of the national economy, treaty or not.

Of course, it is unrealistic to pretend that there is a precise range for any given measure of inflation that would correspond to price stability irrespective of economic conditions. Inflation is defined as a 'rise in the general price level' — yet all the available price indices measure particular, and arbitrary, baskets of goods and services. Furthermore, like any statistics, price indices are subject to measurement error. The most notable problem is their inability to adjust adequately for quality improvements, but in addition they exhibit marked seasonal patterns, which makes interpretation of short-run movements extremely hazardous.

Nevertheless, it is essential that we — and by 'we' I mean not just policymakers, but everyone with a vested interest in economic stability and non-inflationary growth — have a firm idea of where we are headed and how we intend to get there. Our destination has to be defined by giving substance to our ultimate objective, as the chancellor did in his letter of 8 October 1992 to the chairman of the Treasury and Civil Service Committee. We must head towards an economy in which, in the long-run, in the absence of external shocks (such as changes in oil or commodity prices — in either direction), prices — perhaps best measured by the retail prices index excluding mortgage interest payments — grow by 2 per cent a year or less.

It would be convenient — for policy-makers as much as for commentators and operators in both financial markets and the wider economy — if the road to our final destination could be encapsulated in simple policy rules. It cannot. Of course, we must continue to search for the Holy Grail, but I have to say that our experience over the past decade and a half is discouraging. The conduct of monetary policy is an inherently difficult, judgmental process. There is no reason why we should limit our assessment to any single variable or set of variables. Rather, we should utilize all of the information available from the monetary/financial economy and the real economy.

That includes the whole range of broad and narrow measures of money and of credit, not just in aggregate terms but in terms of their components and sectoral composition. It includes asset prices. It includes the whole range of factors bearing directly and indirectly on prices and costs, from the pressure of demand in relation to the supply capacity of the economy, to international influences such as world commodity prices and global demand conditions. And it includes, importantly, the exchange rate, which is far too important a price to ignore, whatever the exchange rate regime.

Over recent months our assessment of all these indicators has convinced us that we are making good progress towards stabilization. And there is strong evidence — in slow monetary growth, in depressed asset prices, especially in the housing market, and in the increasing unused capacity within the economy at large — to suggest that inflationary pressures will remain subdued in the period ahead. It was this context that justified some easing of monetary policy through both the weakening of the exchange rate and the cut in the interest rates a fortnight ago.

What is important now is that this progress towards stabilization in the medium-term is not put in jeopardy and to demonstrate beyond a peradventure — that risks really will not be taken with inflation. If this is accompanied by a willingness to be open in explaining, to Parliament and to the public at large, the influences on inflation and our response to them, that will, in my judgment, be the best way to restore confidence in the intentions of policy while we remain outside the ERM. Persistence in that policy is what is absolutely necessary to re-establish the basis for sustainable growth.

APPENDIX 1

Official responses to the ERM crisis

Appendix 1

Official responses to the ERM crisis

Reports from the Committee of Central Bank Governors and the EC Monetary Committee[1]

The implications and lessons to be drawn from the recent exchange rate crisis — **A Report by the Committee of Governors of the Central Banks of the member states of the EEC**

In response to the invitation of the European Council's special meeting in Birmingham in October 1992, this report summarizes the views of the Committee of Governors on the implications of, and the lessons from, the recent exchange rate crisis. The report is divided into four sections, dealing firstly, with the causes of the crisis; secondly, the assessment of the sustainability of central parities; thirdly, policy responses to stabilize exchange rates; and fourthly, institutional and technical arrangements in the EMS. The main conclusions are presented at the end of the report.

1. The causes of the recent exchange rate crisis

A turnaround occurred in the summer of 1992 when a prolonged period without severe tensions in the ERM, giving at times the impression of a quasi monetary union, gave way to a new situation. There was a growing awareness that divergences in national economic trends had been building up for some time, as well as a growing awareness of differences in prospects and policy requirements, and, as a result, markets exerted massive destabilizing pressures. There is broad consensus in the Committee that the exchange market crisis was brought about by a number of concurrent factors:

---

[1] *These reports were released to the general public by decision of the finance ministers and central bank governors of the EC at their meeting in Kolding, Denmark on 22 May 1993. For the sake of consistency in this publication, some minor typographical changes have been made to the original text.*

- for a number of years price and cost developments diverged and in the face of stable nominal exchange rates, gave rise to changes in real exchange rates and in international competitive positions within the Community; this was due to excessive wage claims and to the insufficient correction of fiscal imbalances in several Community countries, resulting in an unbalanced policy-mix and an over-burdening of monetary policy in its fight against inflation;

- the economic environment in the Community became more complex in the wake of German unification. Given the challenges of the process, the fiscal policy that was adopted, demand pressures and the behaviour of wages, a tight monetary stance was the necessary response for Germany to counter price increases, leaving little scope for interest rate reductions. In those Community countries where lower rates of inflation had been achieved, the prolonged weakness of economic activity and deteriorating labour market conditions were felt to warrant a lowering of interest rates. The conflict between domestic policy needs and the maintenance of ERM parities complicated monetary policy co-ordination in the Community. These policy dilemmas became more severe after the rejection of the Maastricht Treaty in the Danish referendum when exchange market tensions began to mount and required interest rate increases in defence of the weaker currencies' position in the band. The room for interest rate increases was seen by markets to be particularly limited in those countries where higher official and money market rates threatened to be quickly transmitted to sensitive lending rates, particularly mortgage rates, or to have an immediate adverse impact on the debts of non-banks as well as on governments' budgetary position;

- markets seem to have been attentive to what they perceived as insufficiently co-ordinated responses of the authorities to the crisis. Public statements, in general, did little to alter this market sentiment. Policy actions, in particular regarding central rates, were taken on a piecemeal basis and after market pressure, with insufficient attention devoted to the restoration of the credibility of the parity grid as a whole;

- although the major causes of the recent exchange rate crisis were domestic, developments outside the Community also played a role. The very significant easing of US monetary policy, leading to an unprecedented widening of interest rate differentials with Germany, resulted in strong downward pressure on the US dollar *vis-à-vis* the ERM currencies, especially the Deutschemark, with implications for the parity grid. The turmoil in the Nordic countries' exchange markets added to the climate of market nervousness.

The impact which economic imbalances and/or policy dilemmas could normally be expected to have on exchange rate relationships was offset, prior to June 1992, by market expectations that the process towards Emu would reduce the likelihood of changes in central parities. These market expectations motivated large capital inflows into higher yielding EMS currencies since the late-1980s until the summer of 1992. Furthermore, at first the dominant impact of German unification on its partners was felt mainly through an increase in exports and a strengthening of their current-account positions, masking to a certain extent the importance of the imbalances accumulated since the last realignment. Serious attempts to correct imbalances were postponed and those domestic adjustment measures that were taken turned out to be insufficient. A break in market sentiment occurred after the outcome of the Danish referendum (on 2 June 1992) and the French referendum (on 20 September 1992) was seen as a reference date for an expected realignment and hence a focus for hedging against currency risks or for outright currency speculation.

As the crisis developed, it became evident that the liberalization and deregulation of financial markets and their growing integration — which had greatly facilitated the flow of private capital to Community countries with financing needs — had also provided scope for capital movements of an unprecedented size. Within these capital movements, speculative operations proved at times to be a notable destabilizing force giving rise to serious problems also for currencies of countries with sound economic fundamentals, thereby imposing sizeable costs on the countries concerned. Speculative operations also imposed a disproportionate burden on currencies of small countries.

Three broad conclusions can be drawn from this diagnosis.

Firstly, without sufficient progress in convergence central parities cannot be kept stable in the longer run and it would be premature to manage the EMS as a *de facto* monetary union as long as the necessary degree of convergence has not yet been achieved. Exchange rate adjustments remain a crucial feature of the EMS which, however, should not develop into a crawling-peg system which would weaken convergence. Instead, the EMS should remain a system of fixed-but-adjustable central parities and be operated within the rules of the Basle-Nyborg agreement. In accordance with this Agreement there is a need for early recognition of fundamental disequilibria and when these are identified a realignment should be decided soon and before markets come to regard it as inevitable. The difficulties in reaching such judgements and implementing them before the markets reach their own conclusions should not be underestimated but it is vital that they should be addressed. This leads to the issue of the assessment of the sustainability of existing parities, which is examined in Section II.

Secondly, a successful management of the system depends on an appropriate policy mix. Monetary policy alone cannot bear the burden of ensuring both price stability and exchange rate stability in the ERM. It needs adequate support from the fiscal policy and other policies. This consideration is particularly important in the anchor country because it exerts a dominant influence on the monetary conditions in the countries participating in the ERM. But it also applies to the other countries because without adequate support from fiscal and other policies they will not be able to maintain central rates.

Thirdly, in a situation where financial markets have become closely integrated and full freedom of capital movement has been realized, massive speculative pressure may take the management of desirable realignments more difficult. Moreover, such pressure may arise even *vis-à-vis* currencies whose central parities are in line with economic fundamentals; this raises the issue of policy responses to stabilize exchange rates, which is examined in Section III.

II. The assessment of the sustainability of central parities

All central banks share the view that the assessment of the sustainability of existing central parities should be based on two major components: macroeconomic performance and the credibility of policies in maintaining price stability.

1. Macroeconomic performance

There is a broad agreement that the assessment of macro-economic performances in ERM countries should be based on a set of economic and financial indicators. However, there is little doubt that the exercise of assessing whether parities are in line with performances cannot be mechanistic but will have to be to a large extent judgmental.

The assessment would begin on the external side, with particular attention to international competitiveness. However, changes in real exchange rates will not necessarily call always for a realignment, and unchanged real exchange rates will not necessarily rule out the need for a realignment. Therefore the assessment will also have to be based on an analysis of underlying macro-economic developments in each ERM country, with due regard to external accounts, private saving and investment, domestic growth, budgetary balances and the stance of monetary policy with respect to the objective of price stability. In addition, account should be taken of indicators which describe the economic situation at the Community level.

2. Credibility of policies

The sustainability of central parities does not only rest on macro-economic performance but also depends decisively on the credibility of national policies. The assessment of the credibility of policies thus constitutes an indispensable element of the authorities' surveillance of exchange rates.

The assessment of the credibility of the ERM countries' economic and financial policies while taking into account the past record should focus mainly on current and future policies. An important additional aspect should be the extent to which national policies, at the level of each country but also in combination and interaction, are conducive to maintaining the credibility of the system as a whole.

Particular attention should be paid to the track record of individual governments and central banks, respectively, in formulating realistic targets and in meeting them, the political consensus on the commitment to stability-orientated policies and on the exchange rate objective and the institutional status of the central bank.

The crucial element for the short-run credibility of a given central parity comes from the commitment of monetary policy in its defence. It is therefore important that there are no inhibitions to the use of interest rates preventing an effective defence of the currency against speculative attacks. The existence of constraints on nominal interest rates seems to be related to a number of factors; the size of public debt (in particular the share of floating-rate debt) and deficits, the size of private debt, the extent to which GDP deviates from potential, the level of unemployment, the degree of fragility of the financial sector, the speed of transmission of official and money market interest rates to sensitive lending rates and the institutional status of the central bank.

3. Surveillance of exchange rate relationships

The Committee of Governors is fully aware that the assessment of ERM parities is an extremely difficult task. For this reason there is broad agreement that the primary purpose of the surveillance of exchange rate relationships is to function as an early warning system and to bring views closer as regards the sustainability of central rates or the desirability of a timely realignment. The Committee stands ready to play its role in this surveillance exercise and to devise procedures for communicating its views to the ministers.

III. Policy responses to stabilize exchange rates

There might be situations in which macro-economic performances and current and future policies would not warrant a change in parities in the judgement of the authorities, but where nonetheless market pressures arise. This raises two issues. The first is whether and to what extent concerted action of strong and weak currency countries should be employed in the defence of the parities, and the second, how to use, in particular, the various instruments provided by the 1987 Basle-Nyborg agreement.

1. Concerted action in the defence of central rates

The Governors emphasize that all Community countries benefit significantly from the EMS. While there is agreement that the defence of a currency's exchange rate remains primarily the responsibility of the country concerned, it is also recognized that central banks have a collective responsibility for the system and that there is thus a need for close co-operation.

The form of such co-operation in a situation where unwarranted market pressures arise cannot be easily defined in advance. On the one hand, the management of the system calls for a high degree of flexibility with due account to the prevailing circumstances and the objective of promoting price stability in the Community. For this reason, there cannot be an automatic and mechanistic response to market tensions, involving symmetrical action on the part of the authorities of countries with weak and strong currencies. On the other hand, there were situations in the recent past where concerted action in the field of $intra-marginal intervention;Basle-Nyborg agreementintra-marginal intervention took place and proved helpful in countering market pressure. The Governors do not rule out the possibility of such action taking place on an ad hoc basis, provided that it does not jeopardize the control over domestic monetary conditions in the country issuing the intervention currency and that it is consistent with the primary objective of achieving price stability in the Community. The appropriateness of such action would have to be judged also in the light of the prevailing market situations and the accompanying measures to defend the currency in the country concerned.

2. The desirable mix of the Basle-Nyborg instruments

The recent ERM crisis has confirmed that interventions alone — whether intra-marginal or at the margin — have a limited effectiveness in containing tensions and may even exacerbate them, if market operators perceive that they are large and continue over a prolonged period. Letting a currency depreciate within the band and reach the lower limit may also encourage speculation although in the recent past this has on some occasion proved to be an efficient way of handling market pressure. Timely increases in interest rates remain the most promising course to counter market pressure, although if interest rates have to be kept at very high levels over a prolonged period of time, they may not be sustainable in the light of domestic economic and financial conditions.

The Governors feel that it would not be advisable to lay down precise rules on how to employ the Basle-Nyborg instruments in a situation of market pressure. Rather, the use of the instruments should be decided in line with the objective of achieving price stability, taking into account the prevailing market circumstances and previous experiences with defending the exchange rate.

There is full agreement among the Governors that making market operators aware of the risks of, and possible losses from, speculation is a critical element in the successful management of the system. To this end, in certain cases it may be advisable to allow a currency to strengthen within the band when market pressures ease and to make less predictable the conditions at which central banks will offset the liquidity impact of exchange market intervention on the money market.

3. The usefulness of public statements

The Committee of Governors has strong doubts about the usefulness of collective public statements in support of the existing central parities if not backed by immediate action. Experience has shown that such statements may fail to have a positive impact on market expectations and could also be damaging to the credibility of the authorities. However, where combined with decisive and visible action, demonstrating the authorities' determination to defend central rates, statements may play a useful, complementary role.

IV. Institutional and technical arrangements governing central bank cooperation in the framework of the EMS

There is no evidence that the institutional and technical features of the EMS have as such been instrumental in bringing about the recent exchange crisis. Current arrangements remain on the whole appropriate. The Committee, however, examined two particular issues: the first related to decisions on the width of the fluctuation bands, and the second, to the denomination of Very Short-Term Financing (VSTF) balances.

1. Fluctuation bands

While under the EMS Agreement the establishment of, and changes in, central rates are subject to mutual agreement, decisions regarding the fluctuation bands are left to the respective national authorities. These rules have been in effect since 1979. Experience with operating the EMS has shown that the width of the fluctuation band must be regarded as a matter of common concern. The Committee is in full agreement that decisions pertaining to the size of the band should continue to be made in accordance with the rules in effect since 1979 and should be preceded by close consultation taking due account of the same factors as those considered when sustainability of the parity grid is examined.

2. Denomination of VSTF balances

In the context of the recent large-scale interventions financed through the VSTF, the Ecu-denomination of VSTF balances had resulted in substantial exchange losses for participating countries. All Governors agreed that this matter deserved further consideration and the Committee intends to study various possibilities of changing the present arrangements, taking due account of the need to preserve an Ecu-based system, the requirements of the multilateralization within the EMCF, the fairness and predictability of the results and the simplicity of the arrangement.

V. Main conclusions

Three main conclusions can be drawn from this report. Firstly, the examination of the causes underlying the recent crisis in the ERM suggests that the emergence of unprecedented turbulence must be essentially ascribed to insufficient progress in economic convergence, the effects of which were compounded by a deteriorating cyclical situation and growing policy conflicts. Moreover, structural changes in financial markets have greatly increased the scope for capital movements and speculative operations proved at times to be a notable destabilizing force. There is full agreement among Governors that, for central parities to remain credible, they must be supported by sound underlying economic conditions and credible national policies. Realignments of central rates remain and important feature of the system and provision must be made for timely realignments when parities have become unsustainable in the light of a country's macro-economic performance and its current and future policies. It is therefore of crucial importance to assess on a regular basis and in a candid and frank manner the sustainability of the existing ERM parities.

Secondly, the existing general rules governing the management of the system remain appropriate. When a currency comes under unwarranted market pressure, the country concerned should use all instruments provided by the 1987 Basle-Nyborg agreement in defending the exchange rate. Particular attention should be given to making market operators aware of the risks of, and possible losses from, speculation. However, it would not be desirable to lay down precise rules on the desirable mix of the instruments which should be decided in the light of the prevailing market circumstances and individual country experiences.

The defence of the exchange rate remains primarily a national responsibility but it is recognized that the authorities have also a collective responsibility for the system and there is thus a need for close co-operation. In the recent past, on some occasions concerted action was undertaken and proved helpful in countering market pressure. However, the circumstances in which such a course should be followed cannot be defined in advance. Concerted action can therefore take place only on an ad hoc basis and provided that it does not conflict with the primary objective of achieving price stability in the participating countries.

Thirdly, while current institutional and technical arrangements in the EMS remain on the whole appropriate, the Committee of Governors intends to study possible changes in the present arrangement with respect to the denomination of VSTF balances with a view to adapting the sharing of exchange rate risks among central banks.

The lessons to be drawn from the disturbances on the foreign exchange markets - **A report by the Monetary Committee of the European Community**

Following the mandate given by the European Council in Birmingham, this report presents the position of the Monetary Committee on the issues raised in this context in the European Council's conclusion.

1. The external environment

1.1. The international environment has changes since the EMS was designed, and even since the Basle-Nyborg agreements. Exchange controls have been abolished and there has been an enormous increase in the funds which can be mobilized on the markets on short notice. New instruments and channels have arisen through which market pressure can build up. National authorities have increasingly to take their stance in a multi-currency system, that is, a system in which all Community currencies are traded in several centres, while several currencies are held, used and traded in each national centre in the EC. The expansion of the markets was, to some extent, encouraged by the growing readiness of governments to borrow in foreign currencies.

1.2. The phenomenon of a weak US dollar provoking disproportionate flows into some EC currencies has long been familiar. The flows last year

were, however, particularly strong because of the very large short-term interest-rate differentials which opened up between the USA and Japan on
one side and Europe on the other. These differentials corresponded to some
extent to cyclical differences among these three economies.

1.3. Monetary systems have become much less subject to administrative
regulation in the last decade or so. The Monetary Committee welcomes —
and has played its part in facilitating — this development, which has
greatly increased the efficiency of our economies. The Committee has no
desire to go back on the liberalization which has been achieved. The question arises, however, as to whether the deregulation of financial markets
has impeded the efficiency of monetary instruments. The Committee of
Governors might also find it useful to devote some attention to the role of
some very specific financial instruments like short-term swap lending and
borrowing.

   Closer integration of financial markets requires faster progress in achieving convergence in order to avoid turbulence in foreign-exchange markets.

1.4. A useful degree of co-operation with the USA and Japan has been
achieved in recent years. Notwithstanding the need to improve on this co-
operation, it is the Community countries' prior responsibility to develop
economic polices and to make better use of existing co-operation to cope
with turbulence when it arises.

2. The domestic context in the Community

2.1. Monetary and exchange-rate policies have been conducted against a
background of important changes, some of them of historic significance. After the 1987 realignment, the system was supported by improved convergence of prices and costs, particularly in the countries which have respected
margins of +-2.25 per cent since the start of the system. Nevertheless, with
the passage of the years since 1987, deteriorations in competitive positions
and cumulative inflation differentials began to build up, particularly in
countries initially respecting the wider margins, leading to tension on the
exchange markets.

2.2. In particular cases, the tension reflected other factors in addition to the
foregoing. In the specific case of the United Kingdom, besides other factors,
the sustainability of the sterling central rate was brought into question by
the perceived incompatibility of the high interest rates ruling throughout
the ERM with the cyclical need of the UK economy. In the case of Italy,
slow progress in reducing inflation was accompanied by weaknesses in the
area of public finance; in particular, the government deficit had been at an

excessive level for many years; its persistence in spite of the announcement of corrective measures (and not least of a convergence programme) appeared to indicate that the Italian government was finding it progressively more difficult to bring about a turn-around. In Spain, the significant and cumulative deterioration in the competitive position became increasingly apparent to markets when the parity grid was seen to be unstable. This undermined the credibility of the peseta central rate, unchanged since its entry into the ERM in June 1989.

2.3. The system also had to cope with the consequence of German reunification. This had two aspects: firstly, an increase in public expenditure, which was seen as an unavoidable or even desirable response to events of historic significance; and, secondly (given the uncertainties of such a situation), the necessity to finance that extra expenditure partially through increased borrowing. It was the extent of financing through borrowing which was of greater significance for the EMS. There was a large increase in demand in the German economy; much of this was met by a turn-around in the external account, but there was nevertheless felt to be a severe inflationary danger. It was associated with excessive growth of credit and money supply. Moreover, wage developments deteriorated and, in order to fight inflation, monetary policy had to be tightened. In short, the policy mix in Germany became unbalanced and the effects of this became apparent when the initial expansionary impulse to the European economy subsided.

2.4. From mid-1992 onwards, the level of interest rates in Germany and the newly perceived risk of exchange-rate adjustment in the ERM provoked a flow of speculative funds into the Deutschemark. Even countries having low inflation and sound fundamentals found their currencies under pressure, in spite of the use of the interest-rate instrument to curb capital outflows. The markets had the impression that governments in low-inflation countries faced a dilemma, in which the adoption of the same nominal interest rates as Germany (or even higher ones) implied very high real interest rates in a context of significantly slowing economic growth and increasing unemployment.

2.5. One reason why imbalances were able to accumulate lies in the momentum towards Emu which culminated in the Maastricht Treaty. This had the side effect, for a time, of leading the markets to regard the system as a quasi-monetary union. Deteriorations in competitiveness were thus able to accumulate without provoking pressure on parities. Realignments of central rates did not take place, although convergence was clearly insufficient.

2.6. The time at which the markets recognized the problems, which had been accumulated, was partly determined by political factors. The delays and temporary set-backs encountered in the process of ratifying the Maastricht Treaty led markets to assume that the apparently receding prospect of convergence and economic and monetary union would imply a weakening of commitment to the current EMS parity-grid and possibly even to the system itself.

3. The vigour of the EMS policy consensus

3.1. The EEC Treaty commits the Community to the promotion of "...a continuous and balanced expansion, an increase in stability...". The conclusions of the European Council of 4 and 5 December 1978, which led to the creation of the EMS, laid down that "the purpose of the European monetary system is to establish a greater measure of monetary stability in the Community. It should be seen as a fundamental component of a more comprehensive strategy aimed at lasting growth with stability, a progressive return to full employment, the harmonization of living standards and the lessening of regional disparities in the Community". In the pursuit of these general objectives, the specific task of monetary policy and monetary institutions and arrangements, such as the EMS, is to bring about price stability. The EMS is a system of fixed-but-adjustable exchange rates, which requires timely adjustments in response to trend divergences; but the system must not be allowed to develop into a 'crawling-peg system'. For the system to be credible in the eyes of the market, it is evident that price stability must underlie exchange rate stability, that appropriate policies must be followed to that end, and that divergent price developments must not be allowed to accumulate.

3.2 The recent turmoil has shown, once again, that the stability of the EMS over time depends on the adoption of stability-orientated economic policies in all participating countries and on the determined adaptation of the policy stance and the policy mix to the dictates of those policies as and when macro-economic difficulties or unexpected shocks emerge. It was widely accepted that recent difficulties were pre-eminently that result of economic policies and policy-mixes, insufficiently attuned or not attuned sufficiently promptly to the basic objective, which is price stability. However, a major lesson to be drawn is that even countries with sound fundamentals may face difficulties in defending their parities as a consequence of external economic developments. This indicates that strengthening the convergence process, although essential for the stability of the EMS, may not be enough unless accompanied by an improved coordination of economic policies and a continued commitment to defend the system as a common good.

3.3. It is, therefore, essential to restate the consensus concerning the conduct of economic policy, which is presupposed by participation in the EMS. This consensus covers the following points:

i) The commitments of all members to price stability is the foundation-stone of the system and the achievement of this objective is a matter of common concern.

ii) Monetary policy, in particular, must be used to reach this objective; a firm stability-orientation of all economic policies is necessary in order to increase credibility.

iii) The sound management of public finance is an essential element in the policy mix; the over-burdening of monetary policy in any country can have grave consequences for the system and all of its participants.

iv) Respect for the above principles is of systemic importance. Therefore, they should be respected by all countries.

v) The obligations on members are symmetric in the sense that all countries are obliged to pursue stability-orientated policies. This means that asymmetric actions have to be taken in those countries where inflation rates are higher and where policy mixes are unbalanced.

vi) Any situation of persisting inflationary divergence of cost prices must lead to an appropriate response. If policies have not been corrected in good time and inflation persists, exchange-rate changes will have to be considered in order to offset, at least partly, the effect on competitiveness; any realignment decisions must be accompanied by adjustment measures in order to be effective beyond the short-time. The hard-currency option has a disciplinary role to play but cannot be a substitute for adjustment of other policies when that is necessary, or for an appropriate development of domestic costs and incomes.

4. Putting the policy consensus into practice

4.1. Putting the policy consensus fully into practice in future will require action at three levels: the frank discussion, at Community level, of the design and implementation of economic policy by the member states; the use of instruments, which are available to the Community; and the procedures followed at present.

4.2. The implementation of correct economic policies is the key issue and very important lessons have to be drawn at this level. The process of evaluating policy stances and policy mixes must not be marred by an unwillingness to face unpleasant facts or to make unequivocal judgements. The Community needs plain speaking, confrontation on policy issues and critical probing of forecast and policy intentions. The Monetary Committee considers that it is only in this way that it can be ensured that policy stances will be adapted promptly to changing situations, while remaining consistent with medium-term objectives.

4.3. Several instruments lie to hand. The Monetary Committee sees values in the convergence programmes. These have the potential to become a very effective instrument if it can be ensured that they build on intermediate targets, include the necessary specific measures, and cover a sufficient number of years. They must be examined frankly at Community level and member states must be ready to make changes accordingly. It is equally important that their implementation be monitored year after year and that supplementary measures are taken, as necessary, to meet the objectives. If these programmes are to realize their potential, the Community must be extremely anxious to exert peer pressure in order to reach a programme's objectives, once they have been adopted.

The twice-yearly surveillance exercises are concerned with the whole range of goals of economic policy. They also enable the objectives of monetary and exchange-rate policy to be seen, and defended, in a wider context. They further permit an evaluation of the performance and prospects of member countries, which have not needed to present a convergence programme. The Monetary Committee is also aware of the great potential value of the provisions of Article 103 as given by the Treaty of European Union and will, in particular, take an active role in the development of broad guidelines for the economic policies of the member states and of the Community. The Maastricht Treaty provides the Community with new developments, from the beginning of next year, which is the start of the second stage of Emu, notably the excessive-deficit procedure and the establishment of the European Monetary Institute.

4.4. The need for frankness on such issues of great importance certainly means that all deliberations must be conducted in confidence, where appropriate.

5. Reviewing the sustainability of the parity grid

5.1. Recent events in the markets have demonstrated the necessity to increase vigilance as regards to sustainability of the parity grid. There is always a danger divergences will accumulate and there is evidently a need to become more alert to such developments. The Community must, therefore, continuously ask itself whether and to what extent the parity grid is sustainable and corresponds to the underlying economic situation; and, thus, whether the necessary policies are being applied and are having the desired effects. This investigation must be sufficiently routine to ensure that appropriate policy-mixes and any misalignments of exchange rates are detected as soon as possible.

5.2. A confidential set of indicators would be of value to the Monetary Committee in conducting this investigation; they would not be thought of as 'warning lights' and they would certainly not dictate the outcome of the investigation. They should include, primarily, measures of external competitiveness. In addition, attention should be paid to indicators of domestic developments in each country and to the credibility of the commitment of the country to pursue a stability-orientated policy.

5.3. The question then arises as to how to give effect to the conclusions reached after consideration of the indicators. This question becomes particularly acute if the Monetary Committee considers that central rates are seriously out of line. One of the lessons to be drawn from the recent turmoil is that the EMS should adapt its internal rules at this point and break new ground. Its procedures should lead to action, when necessary, well in advance of the development of expectations of change on the markets. Existing EMS procedures tend to be constructed on the assumption that generally the country, whose rates are out of line, takes the initiative. In future, they should also provide for the situation in which other member states consider that a central rate is out of line. In these cases, there is particular need for confidential procedures.

6. Crisis management

6.1. The Community and the member states must be in a position to continue to manage the ERM during periods of tension. The evolution of the financial system, since the Basle-Nyborg agreement, and recent international conditions have had consequences for the effectiveness of the instruments used in the management of the ERM.

6.2. More effective pressure at Community level to put policy consensus into practice (as described in Section 4) and steps to ensure that central rates do not become seriously out of line would reduce the frequency, and probably the intensity, of such crises. Nevertheless, experience has shown that speculation can build up against the currency of a country in which economic fundamentals are sound and whose relative prices and costs are not out of line.

6.3. When a currency begins to come under speculative attack in spite of good fundamentals or in spite of strong adjustment measures judged appropriate, the member state affected must demonstrate its strong will to defend its parity through appropriate measures in accordance with the Basle-Nyborg agreement. The other member states will determine to which extent and how they can support these efforts through appropriate voluntary actions.

Interest rates

6.4. The Committee's report delivered at Nyborg stated: "Monetary authorities must stand ready to defend the stability of the parity grid by ensuring that interest-rate differentials between EMS countries are appropriate, and to this end there must be a willingness to make timely changes in national rates".

The Committee confirms that these understandings are even more important in the highly developed markets of the 1990s. It emphasizes that interest-rate changes must be made in good time and that co-ordinated operations between member states could prove all the more efficient, provided that the primary objective of ensuring price stability is respected. It is also important to demonstrate that the full use of this instrument is available. Delayed interest-rate changes, grudgingly made, can have a perverse effect on the markets to the extent that the resulting very high short-term rates can lead markets to doubt whether the authorities will be able to maintain them for long because of the impact on the domestic economy.

A situation that is not easy to handle arises if a country with sound fundamentals has allowed doubts to arise as to its willingness to raise its interest rate in time if its exchange-rate comes under pressure. The only way to demonstrate to the market that the country regards the pressure as unjustified is precisely by such an increase. Other courses increase the risk of untenable speculative attacks.

Intervention

6.5. The Monetary Committee is conscious that questions relating to intervention are receiving particularly close attention in the Governors' Committee and that the techniques of intervention are primarily a matter for that Committee. At this stage the Monetary Committee will confine itself to the following remarks.

6.6. The intervention instrument is an important element in the management of the ERM. The commitment to unlimited intervention, financed in Ecus by the Very Short-term Financing facility (VSTF) when exchange rates are at their EMS limits, is part of the system. Intra-marginal interventions, as a signal to the market, can be effective in situations where market perceptions can be easily influenced.

Nevertheless, the recent ERM crises have confirmed the Basle-Nyborg conclusions that interventions alone have but a limited effectiveness in containing tensions. Large and prolonged interventions alone may even have a destabilizing effect and they can thwart monetary policy in creditor countries.

The most effective and efficient choice and/or mix of interest rate changes and interventions, at or within the margin, cannot be laid down in advance since it will crucially depend on the particular reasons, which led market operators to shift their portfolio positions.

Statements

6.7. The Committee feels some reserve about the use of public statements to calm a crisis. They can only be effective if they are backed up by economic fundamentals and convincing policy action. In a crisis, of course, it becomes particularly important to avoid conflicting statements. Public statements should not be used too often. Otherwise, they would lose much of their impact.

Exchange control

6.8. The Committee does not see much value in even the limited use of exchange controls as an instrument of crisis management. However, the Treaty provides for exceptional measures.

Post-crisis management

6.9. Action after a crisis must be determined case by case. Nevertheless, given the desirability of ensuring that speculation is costly and risky, consideration should be given, when reflows begin, to keeping the exchange rate high within the band. Appropriate attention should be given to stimulating reflows by maintaining a sufficiently high level of interest rates for some time. This would also permit a timely repayment of intervention debt.

7. EC currencies which are floating

7.1. The countries with floating currencies are members of the EMS and are bound by their obligations under the Treaty of Rome to "treat their policy with regard to rates of exchange as a matter of common concern" (Article 107 of the EEC Treaty). They should keep other member states fully informed about policies which may have a significant effect on the exchange rate. Non-participation in the ERM must not mean the abandonment of policy coordination. Their most important obligation is the continuation and the reinforcement of the anti-inflationary orientation of their economic policy. Firm commitment to price stability is the foundation of their membership of the EMS.

7.2. The re-entry of a currency which has previously been in the ERM will be a new phenomenon in the system. Re-entry will need careful preparation on both sides; it can only be undertaken in circumstances in which it does not endanger the stability either of the currency to be brought back in or of the system as a whole. It can only take place by mutual agreement, with regard to the time and the conditions and, in particular, the central rate, in a common procedure. The member states should have regard to the stability of the currency on the foreign exchanges, the sustainability of its exchange rate and, above all, the economic policy in force. There should be an explicit understanding that a country may ask to re-enter the ERM either with the normal or the wider margin.

8. The European non-member currencies

Recent monetary turmoil shows that destabilizing movements can start in non-member currencies and spill over into the EMS. European non-member countries have, in recent years, seen attractions in relating their currencies in some way or other to the zone of monetary stability. It would be helpful to find some order of monetary relations with these countries which would both set qualitative standards for their involvement and allow the Community to have some impact on their intervention and economic policy orientation.

APPENDIX 2

The impact of German reunification on other European countries in an IS-LM framework

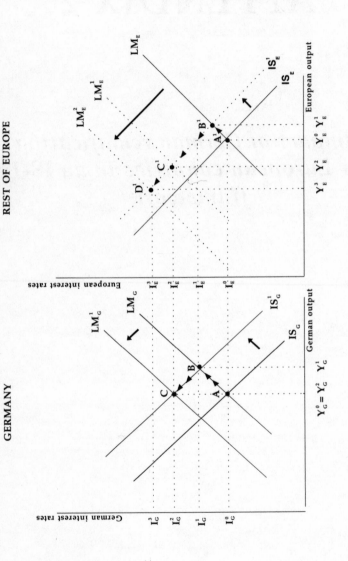

Figure 24.1   Impact of German reunification on other European countries in an IS-LM framework

Appendix 2

The impact of German reunification on other European countries in an IS-LM framework

The increase in the German budget deficit as a result of reunification leads to a rightward shift in the IS curve from IS_G to IS_G^1 in Figure 24.1. This raises the level of German output from Y_G^0 to Y_G^1 and the level of German real interest rates from I_G^0 to I_G^1. The Bundesbank tightens German monetary policy to compensate, pushing output back down to Y_2, the same level as Y_0, and the level of real interest rates up even further from I_G^1 to I_G^2.

Some of the German fiscal stimulus spills over into the rest of Europe, pushing the IS curve in the rest of Europe from IS_E to IS_E^1. As the Bundesbank tightens, the rest of Europe is forced to do so as well in order to maintain exchange rate parities in the ERM, shifting the LM curve to the left from LM_E to LM_E^1. In the diagram the rise in European interest rates is shown to be the same as the rise in German rates (i.e. I_E^2 minus I_E^0 equals I_G^2 minus I_G^0). Although the German fiscal/monetary policy mix results in a level of output unchanged from the original level, there is an overall fall in output in the rest of Europe from Y_E^0 to Y_E^2. The extent to which the level of output drops depends on the extent to which the German fiscal boost spills over into the rest of Europe as well as the extent to which interest rates in the rest of Europe have to rise. In 1991 and 1992 interest rate differentials between other European countries and Germany tended to narrow, hence reducing the extent to which rates had to rise.

During the ERM crisis, however, the 'riskiness' of other European countries increased, necessitating wider interest rate differentials with Germany. A risk premium — shown as I_E^3 minus I_E^2 in the diagram had to be paid, resulting in an even further contraction of output to Y_E^3.

Index